P9-BXX-560

DISCARD

Nurture
the Nature

JB JOSSEY-BASS

Nurture the Nature

UNDERSTANDING AND SUPPORTING YOUR
CHILD'S UNIQUE CORE PERSONALITY

Michael Gurian

BICENTENNIAL
1807
WILEY
2007
BICENTENNIAL

John Wiley & Sons, Inc.

Published by Jossey-Bass
A Wiley Imprint
989 Market Street, San Francisco, CA 94103-1741   www.josseybass.com

Jossey-Bass books and products are available through most bookstores. To contact Jossey-Bass directly call our Customer Care Department within the U.S. at 800-956-7739, outside the U.S. at 317-572-3986, or fax 317-572-4002.

Jossey-Bass also publishes its books in a variety of electronic formats. Some content that appears in print may not be available in electronic books.

In nearly every case, the names appearing in case histories, family stories, and anecdotes have been changed to protect privacy. Certain details have also been changed for this purpose. In some cases, composites have been used. Whenever possible, however, parents and other caregivers have been quoted verbatim.

The information in this book does not constitute medical advice. Please consult your family physician or other local resources for medical advice regarding *your* child.

Library of Congress Cataloging-in-Publication Data
Gurian, Michael.
 Nurture the nature : understanding and supporting your child's unique core personality / Michael Gurian.
     p. cm.
 Includes bibliographical references and index.
 ISBN-13: 978-0-7879-8633-9 (cloth)
 1. Child psychology. 2. Child development. 3. Individual differences in children.
 4. Child rearing. 5. Parenting. I. Title.
 HQ772.G87 2007
 649'.1—dc22   2006038696

Printed in the United States of America
FIRST EDITION
HB Printing   10 9 8 7 6 5 4 3 2 1

CONTENTS

To Gail, Gabrielle, and Davita
and
To the parents and children I've met and worked with over the years.
You are my inspiration.

ACKNOWLEDGMENTS

A book such as this one is the work of not just one author but a team of contributors—the many people whose dreams and hopes for children the author's words serve. As you read this book, you'll meet families and professionals who have shared their experiences with me and provided wisdom. I thank all of them. Without them, this book would have been inadequate. Although some of their names and details of their lives have been changed in order to protect confidentiality and children's privacy, all their stories are representative, I believe, of a growing social movement, one that is beginning to focus clearly now on protecting the inherent and inborn nature of each of our children.

A major part of the team responsible for this book is the publishing group who gave it their most professional care. Alan Rinzler, my editor at Jossey-Bass, has helped me for over fifteen years to make words out of the human life experience. He brings a strong and clear editorial vision to all his work, and I thank him deeply. He is surrounded by true professionals on the Jossey-Bass and John Wiley teams. My profound thanks to Jennifer Wenzel, Carol Hartland, Michele Jones, Susan Geraghty, and Seth Schwartz for your many efforts, and to Debra Hunter and Paul Foster for your confidence in my work.

A special thanks also to Candice Fuhrman, my advocate and agent. Candice is one of the parents and professionals I have met in publishing to whom what we write regarding children is important not only as professional documentation but also as service to society.

Perhaps the pivot point for all the team efforts I've been involved in as I wrote this book has been the Gurian Institute staff, powerfully led by executive director Kathy Stevens and assisted so ably by Pat Crum, Don Stevens, Mittie Pedraza, Marcia Watson-Hilton, and our certified trainers. If you go onto the Internet to www.gurianinstitute.com, you'll see a group of professionals committed to helping families, schools, workplaces, and communities thrive. Because of the outreach of this staff and its certified trainers, this book has been able to reflect a very diverse group of families and communities. Kathy Stevens is a valued friend not only to this work but also specifically to this book. Thank you for everything, Kathy!

This book has also been able to reflect a number of scientific views—something that would not have been possible without the openness of collegial scientists, academic researchers, and journalists who have provided specific advice, scientific information, and personal wisdom. My deep thanks to Daniel G. Amen, M.D.; Judith Kleinfeld, Ph.D.; Scott Haltzman, M.D.; Harold Koplewicz, M.D.; Howard Schubiner, M.D.; and many others, including our Gurian Institute advisory board, and Mary Jacobs. Without your scientific information, direction, and critique, the nurture-the-nature philosophy would have inadequate practical implications for people's everyday lives.

Finally, among the teams that have come together to form the research team for this book, my family deserves gratitude and praise. Gail, Gabrielle, and Davita, as well as Phil, Pam, and our extended family and community friends, have made possible the philosophy and practical strategies in this book. They are patient with me, they critique me and support me as I hope to put into words our shared love of children.

As you read this book, I hope you will find yourself inspired to join a very human team of researchers, family members, and friends in the human journey of raising children toward success and happiness.

"If we are to achieve the richest culture possible, we must recognize the whole range of human potentialities, weaving not an arbitrary social fabric, but one in which each diverse human gift can find its place."

—Margaret Mead

"Follow the child."

—Maria Montessori

INTRODUCTION:
REDISCOVERING OUR CHILDREN

Our own nature hides from us, but wants to be found.

—HERACLITUS

MY WIFE, GAIL, GAVE BIRTH TO OUR FIRST DAUGHTER, GABRIELLE, during a snowstorm in the winter of 1990, after forty-four hours of labor. There were times of abject terror for both Gail and me during Gabrielle's birth process. Doctors, nurses, and specialists rushed around. (At one point, there were nine crowded into the hospital room, deciding what to do.) First, an emergency C-section was planned, then an epidural brought Gail's blood pressure down enough to return to a plan for a vaginal birth, but then, after eight hours of Gail's cervix remaining insufficiently dilated, a C-section again became a necessity.

When I cut the umbilical cord and the nurse held this infant girl to Gail's cheek, when Gabrielle cried out her first command, my wife and I, two young parents, thirty-two years old, gave ourselves over completely to the most natural expression of love imaginable: caring for a child. And not just "a child," but *this* child.

From the moment of Gabrielle's birth, her core nature, her unique self, came through. A naturally quiet baby, she was an observer of the world, except for what we quickly came to call the evening "fussies."

The day's events would ultimately overwhelm her, making her cry inconsolably and squirm and "complain." A number of things that Gail and I tried to do didn't calm her down until we finally learned to carry her on one of our chests and walk with her around the neighborhood.

As she grew, Gabrielle was an agreeable, loving child, who tried to fit within her environment at first, then gradually altered parts of it to fit her. When she was three, four, and five years old, Gabrielle wore only dresses to preschool and kindergarten because she saw her friends dressed that way, and she wanted to do so as well. Never once did she wear the very warm pants Gail bought for her. Even on cold and snowy days, she would choose to wear dresses—but she very practically innovated among her peers by wearing colorful leggings under the dresses.

As Gail and I think back on the first months and years of Gabrielle's life, we can see her nature coming through strongly—and we see it continuing to come through now, even in her later teens. She is loving. She is an observer. She takes time before engaging—watching first, taking a while to decide how she wants to be involved. Once she does engage, she looks for ways to take whatever her peers do and mold it to "Gabrielle's way." She no longer has fits of complaints every evening, of course, but she still gets irritated when she's overstimulated by too many tasks or people. We joke with her that she does still have the "fussies." Of course she rolls her eyes.

When Gabrielle was three and a half, her sister, Davita, was born. Hers was a less complex birth—a planned C-section—yet we felt no less adoration and no less natural pull toward her as she came free, offered her umbilical cord, cried out, lay on Gail's chest, and asserted herself.

Davita was in many ways quite different from her sister, from the very beginning. She was physically active, and she would let the world know her needs with a very loud voice! Our next-door neighbor joked that she always knew when Davita woke up from her nap.

Davita also demanded more prolonged physical contact than Gabrielle. Gabrielle was content to sit in a chair or swing and observe the world. Davita was not. She seemed to bounce and sometimes barge her way into situations in order to get attention. Each day at preschool, she was politely asked to stop bouncing before entering the classroom. Her teacher called her Tigger, from the Winnie-the-Pooh stories.

Unlike the quieter Gabrielle, Davita was so demonstrative and affectionate that she would overwhelm other children. We and others who cared for her had to teach her about respecting boundaries and space.

One way Davita's unique natural personality came through was in her sleep pattern. As a small child, she took very short naps if she was just put down in her crib; she would sleep for only ten to thirty minutes. But when someone slept in close physical contact with her—at least while she fell asleep—she would sleep for two to three hours. Conventional parenting advice might say, "You're spoiling that child with all that attention . . . lying down with her for hours!" But we did it, and gladly. Gail and I knew in our bones that Davita's innate temperament and brain chemistry needed this physical contact in order for her to build her sense of security in the world. In both Davita's and Gabrielle's childhood, we stayed as close as we could to trusting our intuitions about what I will call in this book our children's *core natures*.

As Gabrielle and Davita thrived, grew, and developed over the days, months, and years of their childhood, both Gail and I committed ever more to nurturing each of these children's unique, inborn natures every day. Our kids are teenagers now, yet we find ourselves increasing, not decreasing, our attention to their natures. Both Gail and I, family therapists, have been involved in scientific research on child development that bolsters our innate sense that these children had unique natures that needed our specific nurture.

As Gail and I push forward with this focus, we are living the same lives you are living. Every day in this culture is an opportunity to gain insight into the many outside influences our kids and yours are under from their friends, school, community, and culture. Our two girls have been under immense social pressures as they've grown up—pressures your children have certainly also experienced—and over the years, we and others who help us raise our kids have developed a number of ways of understanding, countering, and combating these pressures. Some of these pressures come from the media, some come from peers, some from teachers and other parents. Many are well meaning, and each one needs careful attention. Focusing on our children's core nature, we must focus on the positive and negative pressures that try to mold, change, even destroy that nature.

I'll never forget a time when Davita was seven. Many people pressured her to go to a three-week summer camp. Other kids and even their parents said she "must" go, that it would help her succeed, make her more popular. The social pressure was so intense, we finally closed off discussions about it.

Sleep-away camp was not a natural fit for our particular seven-year-old's nature, not only in its academic emphasis on certain areas in which she was not naturally developing at this stage of her life, but also in its hyperemphasis on peer-group interaction and its lack of parental influence. As Gail and I look back on this incident now, we remember some parents even "dissing" us for not "talking Davita into going to camp." Davita is now very strong academically and socially. The camp that year was not needed in her life—perhaps even just the opposite: if we had gone against her nature and sent her, she may well have suffered unnecessarily.

Whether or not Davita went to camp was a "small moment" in her life, but as you know, our lives today are filled with so many small moments of pressure—and many of these involve people, media, even social trends trying to get us to act counter to our own children's nature. Gail and I felt in this particular family moment something we've felt throughout the raising of our children: that our culture pressures families to make children into minicelebrities, that this pressure overstresses kids at the wrong moments of life, and that few parents are immune to it. You yourself may well be a parent who is trying right now to decide which stressful experience to talk your child into.

Like many parents, Gail and I didn't have any immediate family living in the area to help us understand our children's needs when they were young. In lieu of blood family, we relied on close friends and our child-care team, which comprised an in-home day-care owner, Marianne; her assistant, Sadarah; and our dear friend Pam, our children's godmother, who helped us stay attuned with and fulfill the practical needs of each child.

This "second family" often saw aspects of our children's nature and needs that we didn't see. Later, when both my and Gail's parents moved to Spokane to be near the grandkids, we relied on them, too, for insight into each particular child's nature, and relief from social pressure. To this day, Gail and I believe that the single most fundamental thing we've done to raise happy and successful children is to use every asset available in our immediate "family" to nurture the nature of each of our children.

Your Child's Nature

Have you felt the deep inner sense that each of your children came into this world with his or her own nature, from day one asking, needing, demanding a particular kind of tailored care, from the inside out? Have you noticed particular strengths and vulnerabilities in your particular child—similar, perhaps, to many of other kids' qualities and tendencies, but nevertheless unique to *this* child? Have you felt that each of your children is unique in personality, temperament, ways of caring for himself or herself, and ways of asking for care? Have you felt that your child is called to become someone in particular—not necessarily a celebrity, but still a very important person of unique character?

I believe every parent has. I believe (and now, fortunately, can share with you the science to prove my belief) that our children come into this world with assets (and liabilities) that are "hardwired" and unique to them as individuals. Those unique selves gradually emerge, taking months, years, decades to express themselves and grow. As they do so we often think, "I've finally got a lock on this kid," only to see the child go in a completely different direction; then, as more years pass, we see how even in the "changing child," that same core nature we sensed early in life shines through.

Gail and I noticed that Gabrielle, who was quiet and observant as a young child, became a confident young woman who speaks her mind and stands her ground without fear of other people's opinion. When she was so quiet as a youngster, we would not have imagined this assertive girl. We might even be tempted right now to say, "That little girl wasn't real; this assertive woman is real." But then again, when we look closely at this seventeen-year-old, we see that for every assertion Gabrielle makes, she has still quietly observed first. She has both changed and remained exactly who she was when she was born.

Have you noticed this growth, and yet this continuity, in your child?

And Davita, who was so energetic and demonstrative toward friends, has become a much more reserved young woman. She has both a vivacious outer self and a very sensitive core, easily hurt by a sharp word or tone. When she was young, we could not have imagined she would hold back with friends; yet when we look closely at her, we see no loss of that Tigger, that bouncing self, but rather the maturing of the high-energy girl into a young woman who is quite engaged in the world, in her "Davita's way."

Have you seen this kind of development as your children grow?

If your children are still quite young, do you remember from your own childhood how your own unique core personality and temperament shined through, altering, changing, flowing with new life circumstances, but still, remaining "you"?

Throughout the raising of our two daughters, Gail and I have fought to use both science and intuition about the children's nature as our theoretical and practical reference points. We are so convinced of our children's natural assets that we try to look constantly into our children's eyes and actions in order to discern what these children need. Gail and I have worked to protect our children and other children from social systems that often seem as if united against them.

When social trends around us in the media or elsewhere say, "Your child needs this kind of education, this kind of food, this kind of computer, this kind of cell phone and clothing, this kind of time with peers . . . ," we instinctually say, "Wait a minute. Is this right for Gabrielle? Davita? What is their nature, and is this a fit?" When our children face obstacles, and when our clients' or community's children face hardships, we ask ourselves and others to return as quickly as possible to "Who is *this* child?" Within the child's natural assets are generally the wisdom and tools to deal with life's great and small challenges.

This is the philosophy and practice we bring to *Nurture the Nature*. This is the hope and clarity I believe we must all fight for today. We must begin by asking, Who is *my* child? Margaret Mead called each child's (and family's) answer to that question "the diverse human gift." Maria Montessori called it "following the child." Heraclitus called it "the nature hiding within," Whitman "the child going forth," Piaget "the nature of the child." The nature of *your* child is far more powerful than you might realize, and it provides a parenting plan and a direction for your everyday life as a parent that is like no other.

Nurture the Nature of Your Child

In this book, I will share with you a vision of child raising that will, I hope, take your questions and answers about what your child needs very far into a journey of love and success. Answers will come not only for babies but for all stages of childhood, all the way through late adolescence. We can always discover our natural and unique children again, always discover new things about who they are, even after they are grown.

My vision will suggest a kind of parenting that takes into full account all the social and cultural assets around us, but begins with asking what the guiding nature of an individual child might be. We can answer this essential question in new, scientific ways that help our generation raise its children safely. In *Nurture the Nature*, I'll provide you with conclusive proof that a *specific temperament, personality, talent set, and way of being is inborn in each of your children,* a specific *nature* that is your child's base of operations—the deep beginning place of his or her path of success. This is something you have probably known intuitively since your child was born, but now we have the scientific proof. In just the eighteen years since Gail got pregnant, amazing things have happened to make this book possible. The human genome has been mapped; PET and other brain scans are prevalent. The sciences that began receiving attention two decades ago now constitute a scientific revolution that is sweeping many aspects of life, business, and family.

Indeed, as you read this book, I hope you'll join a revolution in parenting—a refocusing of your energy as parent, grandparent, teacher, community member on *nurturing your individual child's inborn nature*. Not only is the science able to help you, but there is also a community of parents, teachers, practitioners, and other professionals emerging all around us. You'll meet many others who are already involved in this big change in raising kids. They have provided tried-and-true advice in this book, advice based on their understanding of human nature—and especially their own children's nature.

In this book, I'll try to help you tailor their specific advice to your particular child. Many of these wise people are motivated toward a revolutionary new way of parenting because they think, like I do, that there is something wrong with the way our society has been parenting over the last four decades. That "something wrong"—what I will call the excessive influence of a social trends parenting system—will get looked at closely in this book so that we can fully make a revolution in parenting.

The Social Trends Parenting System

In Chapter One, I will provide you with conclusive and at times disturbing evidence of families and children in distress—distress that shows how far away our society and culture have come from understanding the nature of the individual child. Many of our children are losing themselves in our chaotic social system—a high-pressure, overscheduled, undernurturing system from which Gail and I have remained vigilant to protect our children. The social pressures today constitute, I believe, a *social trends parenting system* that has too much control over parents and children today. Fortunately, there is a way of focusing on individual children and their individual natures that can make this social trends system unnecessary (see the following box).

TEN MYTHS OF SOCIAL TRENDS PARENTING

1. Experts from society and in the media know more than you or I do about what's best for our kids.

2. Children are born as a tabula rasa, or blank slate, without a core nature to guide their own development, and their parents and cultures take care of them.

3. Our job as parents is to engrave on the slate, to input the necessary training and information, to create a child with the necessary characteristics we hope will contribute to success in life.

4. In order to fulfill the parent's expectations, children's daily experiences must be constantly packed with lessons and activities that will prepare them to excel in a scarcity-based view of a highly competitive world.

5. Children will not reach their success potential as adults unless they become alpha high achievers in all or most groups they get involved with.

6. Children should all learn to read (and do various other cognitive tasks) as soon as possible, it is hoped by the age of four, or they will have problems later in life.

7. The most successful adults are people who were, as children, extroverted and assertive.

8. Criticizing a child will most often damage her self-esteem.

9. Talking about feelings with your child (and getting the child to talk about his) is the most important thing you can do as a parent.

10. Don't breastfeed, it's bad for your baby; do breastfeed, it's good for your baby; never sleep with your baby, always sleep with your baby. . . .

What do we mean by the term *social trends parenting?* Social trends parenting is a media- and society-driven system of raising kids that takes the locus of control for child raising away from the parents' instincts about their own children's nature and puts it in the middle of constantly changing social fads, experts, and infotainments. We can see this social trends parenting system as we observe parents following the latest expert opinion, newspaper or magazine article, or TV advice segment. The content and players in this system are like the proverbial pendulum that swings, for instance, from "Don't do anything; be your kid's best friend" to "Jump in and make a big difference by playing tapes for your child every night—or else your child won't learn or succeed in life." Right now, social trends parenting is advocating a manic and frenetic lifestyle that encourages parents to prod, poke, and hyperstress children in order to make them fit into preconceived or hypersocial molds. This system conditions parents to raise children in ways that conform mainly to conventional expectations; it forces a child (and his or her family) to compete academically for "the best schools," to achieve perfectly in sports and classes, to always deliver a "performance" that compares favorably with prescribed social criteria—including how the child should look, behave, work, play, set goals, achieve milestones, win prizes, and build a great-looking résumé. Some of the trends pushed into our homes by this system have worth, but unfortunately, social trends parenting often entails pounding a square peg into a round hole. Quite often, the social trends system actually works against who your child really is—*against the nature of your individual child.* In fact, our social trends–oriented parenting system is not really focused on who our children are; thus, it often becomes an unnatural and dangerous system that leads children and families into anxiety and chronic stress. In Chapter One, we'll look at how this chronic stress has become a major health issue for children and parents nationwide. We'll suggest a very practical solution to this stress immediately in Chapter Two and apply it in the rest of the book. That solution is nature based.

Chapter Two provides a number of scientifically oriented assessment tools and exercises that any parent can enjoy over the course of a few weeks or months of active use. You can modify them for your family to help you understand the core nature of *your* child.

For the twenty-five years I have been researching and working in child and adult development, I have worked with this nature-based theoretical framework and striven to make it ever more practical. As a therapist and science-based philosopher, I have checked all intuitions, insights, and even all social trends advice against information from actual brain and other biological sciences. The Gurian Institute team—a group of associates you'll meet in this book—have helped me immeasurably.

Over the last ten years, the Gurian Institute staff has asked parents what they consider essential information for nurturing the nature of their individual children. We've asked parents of older or grown children, "What information do you wish you had access to as you were trying to understand your children when they were younger?" These parents have helped us select and sift information that is most useful.

That information is presented to you in the final seven chapters of this book. In them, you'll find information and insight divided into seven stages of child development, from birth through the teen years and then into young adulthood. All the essential information follows your understanding of your child's core nature and thus can be easily altered and customized to fit *your* child, *your* adolescent.

You'll read about successes in child and adolescent development that many individuals have experienced through what we call *wisdom of practice* in homes and communities across the country: testing in homes, schools, and communities by people like *you*, of biological and other sciences. The "lab" for this parenting science is not some isolated, white-coated place, but rather is your family, your world.

This new approach to science does not negate the importance of the academic or private laboratory; it doesn't discard age-old wisdom, nor any of the good theory and practice that parents, educators, and clinicians have developed over the years. Rather, it brings all the primary sources—PET scans, genetics research, modern neuroscience, and other areas of the new science—into the parenting arena.

I hope that as you read of the science, insights, and wisdom-of-practice research presented throughout this book, you will say, "Aha! I knew that about my child!" Even though you will probably never have your child undergo a genome test or a PET scan, understanding the new sciences can lead you to amazing insights into your child. That's the beauty of wisdom-of-practice research. My team and I hope that as you read the many anecdotes in this book that support the new sciences, and put into practice the parent-friendly tools, you'll forge your "Ahas!" into a self-developed plan for what to make *essential* in your home for nurturing the nature of *your* child.

Essential Parenting

Your child's core nature is thrilling to observe and appreciate as it unfolds before your eyes. It's wonderful to feel confident as a parent, to tailor parenting techniques to fit the unique needs of your child's nature. Gail and I have felt it, even as we've made mistakes, and even as our children move into areas where they don't compete well or where they seem to fail, but then pick themselves up again.

Gail and I both remember how anxious it made us that Gabrielle, when very young, did not adapt well to sudden changes in her daily life. She had difficulty transitioning from being at a friend's house to getting into the car, then going from the car into our house. Sometimes she would be rude and inappropriate. We tried various kinds of discipline, and she learned our expectations from those; at the same time, we took a deep breath and looked into Gabrielle's eyes. We asked, "Who is this child?" It was her nature, we realized, to have this difficulty. She came about this genetically. I was this way as a child. Gabrielle needed more time to transition! From another parent who had already understood the similar nature of her own child, we learned the practical strategy of "rehearsing." We learned how to rehearse the upcoming events and transitions, including arriving and leaving a friend's house. Those arrivals and departures became much easier as we adapted our day to help Gabrielle adapt to life—to understand ahead of time the events and changes to come during a day and to learn some mastery of her own difficulties.

In her own way, Davita too required adaptation from us—and herself. She had difficulty learning to read the alphabet initially; later, she had difficulty reading. This was painful for her (and us), especially when friends in her class made fun of her. In early elementary school, she was diagnosed with mild dyslexia. At first we couldn't believe it—not *our* child! But when we saw the scientific evidence that this was indeed a part of Davita's nature, we knew that nurturing her meant changing our lives around: practicing reading to improve her skills and to help her increase her confidence, spending more time with her teachers and other tutors. Once we went beyond feeling only the pain of "failure" and instead understood and *appreciated* her unique and natural gifts—for instance, her immense inner perseverance against obstacles—dealing with her dyslexia became a bonding opportunity in our family and a source of increased closeness and joy. To better meet the needs of Davita's core nature, she completed her elementary school years in a Montessori school, which allowed her to learn at her own pace. By the time she got to middle school, she was able to get an A in language arts. As you can imagine, this was a very big deal in our family!

These are small stories of using science to nurture the nature, but of course, in a given family, they are very thrilling, powerful stories. They represent the bonding of a family by expanding that family's deep sense of love. They tell of letting go of desires for perfection and overcoming social pressures. They show how what seems at first to be a problem can become, once its nature is understood, a way that strength of purpose can come through even more fully. The thrill in parenting comes from looking so deeply into the eyes of your child that you can see what is there, what you are really working with, and work specifically with that.

Throughout every stage of our children's development, we have nurtured the nature by developing an action plan by which to support our children's strengths and accommodate their weaknesses. We have constantly asked, "What is essential for this child's nature, and what is excess, unnecessary, even dangerous?" As you proceed in this book, I hope you will develop a deep certainty regarding what your children need, enabling you to create your own *essential parenting plan*. I will help you do this in every page. Indeed, this book is a tool by which you can discover the parenting activities and vision that are essential for *your* child—and waste little time with everything else. I hope to help you develop a feeling of essentiality and solidity in parenting that cuts out distractions but is not a formula passed down by an expert; instead, I hope to help you design an essential parenting plan in tandem with a team of other family members, friends, and professionals who help you nurture the nature of your children.

You are the parent. You know your kids from the gut, instinctively, intuitively in your heart and bones. As you read this book, I hope you'll come to enjoy very deeply *your own* vision and design of essential and true parenting. If as the book begins you find the nature-based approach to be a pretty different way of doing things, I hope that within a few pages you'll see its power, so that you'll be able to say, "Sure I make mistakes as a parent, but my eyes are fully on my children's real needs. I know who my children are now, so the future is open and bright for them."

A Special Feature for
Moms and Dads with Newborns

TEN TIPS FOR NURTURING THE NATURE OF YOUR BABY

From the day your baby is born (even before!), you'll be able to see his or her core nature peeking through. Some babies are more calm than others, others more fussy. Some like to stare at Mom or Dad a lot; others like to move their eyes around a room. All have subtle differences in their eating or sleeping patterns.

Following are some examples of a baby's core nature coming through. Here too are some things you can immediately do to tailor your care of your child to fit his or her inborn nature.

1. If your baby seems by nature quite fussy (squirms a lot, can't be satisfied), try calming music, and enjoy singing to the child (no matter if you can keep a tune!). Try setting the baby down safely on a towel on the floor for a brief period.

2. If your baby seems quite calm (and this personality type can sometimes worry parents, for the baby can be almost listless), stimulate the child with two or three voices (Mom, Dad, Grandma, care provider), and turn the baby outward to look at the world as much as he or she is turned "inward" (in the cuddling posture in the crook of your arm). If your baby is hearing other voices, being carried, and seeing the world, his or her "quietness" is nothing to worry about.

3. If your baby is hypersensitive or cries a great deal (or both), swaddle him or her tightly (with baby's arms inside the swaddling), so that the womblike feeling of safety calms the neural system. Some babies are by nature more sensitive than others, and some are colicky by nature (no one is sure why); tight swaddling can help this child gain some self-control and drift out of crying into sleep or a respite from tears.

4. If your baby won't take the breast or has difficulty breast-feeding, make sure to pump breast milk for around two months (consult with your doctor) so that the baby gets the natural colostrum that build his or her immune system. For natural or environmental reasons, some babies don't take to the mom's breast as well as others, but they need the protection of colostrum at a minimum.

5. If your baby is one of those who by nature does not seem to sleep well (sleeps restlessly or is colicky), you can put into practice the carry-rock-vibrate strategy. Try carrying the baby, rocking the baby, and placing the baby on washing machines (while in cycle) or in cars (while you're driving) so that his or her neural system can find the vibrational feeling of being in the womb again.

6. If you have a baby who doesn't hold eye contact with you as long as another baby might, this is generally not something to worry about. This natural inclination of some kids' brain and retinas is to move from eye contact to observing objects moving in space (mobiles, other people, any physical movement). This baby might like refracted light. It is not recommended, however, that you put this baby in front of a TV; the visual movement of the "virtual world" is not what his or her brain needs.

7. If you have a child who seems only to want contact with one person for one task (like feeding) and another person for another task (like being rocked to sleep), you may be seeing the child's core nature—his or her inborn self—already shining through. Already the child is discerning through action what and who is needed when. As you follow this child's guidance, you'll see roles change and shift over the years, but you'll also enjoy (rather than feel rejected by) the ever growing, internal wisdom of your child.

8. If you have a baby who seems "difficult to attach with," who is resistant or who even cries in seeming anger when you are around, you will most likely need to "wait out" this phase. At the same time, there may be something subtle going on to watch for. An example might be that your infant is uncomfortable with a smell on you (if, for instance, you are a smoker or you work near chemicals). If you can identify no habit or any stimulant on your body that could be affecting this child—and if the baby's behavior goes on for a month or more—it is best to consult a pediatrician or other specialist.

9. If you have a baby who by nature is quite easy on all fronts, enjoy the peace while you can! This baby may well end up being an easy child all through life—or adolescence may be a time of sudden "difficulty" for this child. The baby you have is going to become the child and then the adolescent and then the adult you have—but not everything about core nature is obvious at birth because the brain is so young.

10. If you have a difficult child, it is essential to get the help you need but also not to worry that this child will therefore become a violent kid, a bad kid, a rebellious and dangerous kid, or a kid who fails. Some of the most difficult infants become some of the most successful women and men. What made them difficult, overstimulated, fussy, or overwhelming as infants can make them creatively aggressive, visionary, and successful as adults. From day one, they are already trying to conquer the world and mold it to fit *their* expectations; they may not be compliant, but they may be very strong. If you have one of these kids, worry just enough to get three or four other good people to help you care for this infant (don't try to take on the baby by yourself) and then enjoy the journey.

Protecting the Nature of *Your* Child

"If we as a generation neglect to nurture the nature of each of our children, we'll be remembered as parents who were so stressed we inadvertently failed to support the unique and special way each of our kids dream. If we aren't careful, our children may look back on childhood with regret. Making sure that does not happen is the reason for a parenting revolution."

—KATHY STEVENS

"We cannot just 'construct' a perfect human being. Young people must also 'sprout.' We must plant and wait, and we must have faith."

—LAWRENCE KELEMEN, *TO KINDLE A SOUL*

Escaping the Social Trends
Parenting System

My stress level and that of my husband is so high, and it's the same for our kids. What we really want is to find the love and healthy direction a family is supposed to be.

—CARLA JAMES, MOTHER OF THREE CHILDREN

CARLA CAME TO SEE ME WITH TEARS IN HER EYES. HER FIFTEEN-year-old daughter, Katie, would not speak to her, she said, and her twelve-year-old son, Andy, was obsessed with video games. Carla felt overwhelmed, unsure of how to be a parent, and unable to get the help from family, school, and friends that she needed. She worried that Katie would become promiscuous.

"The way she dresses, the way she acts, it's becoming out of control," Carla said. "And no matter what my husband or I do, our son Andy just lives in his own world, his own little box. And I know it's not just me and my kids. It seems like a lot of my kids' friends are having the same kind of problems. They're good kids—deep down these are all good kids—and we're a good family, but there's something wrong. We're just too stressed out!"

Another couple, Angie and Bert Stohl, brought their daughter, Susan, to see me. When I met this young woman of sixteen, I saw dark circles under her eyes. Susan was so busy she only got five hours of sleep per night (she needed nine), and some of that was fitful. She was losing herself to the stress of everyday life, compounded by lack of sleep. For Susan it was like a badge of honor that she could survive with so little sleep. At the same time, she was acting in ways that did not fit her natural needs as a teenager: she was not healthy.

In another case, the Royce family came to me with their son, Devin, who was failing first grade. Well liked by other kids, he did not perform in the way either his parents or school wanted him to. His parents had done all the right things for producing a high-performing son: reading to him early, playing Baby Einstein tapes, putting him in the best school. They had even started him on the computer at three years old. But his teacher said, "Devin simply refuses to concentrate and learn." At the age of six, Devin was wetting the bed again and beginning to withdraw from school.

These are all good families, good people, trying their best. But they are struggling, and they are not alone. I constantly receive e-mails and letters from parents and other caregivers who notice significant stress and anxiety in their families and the families around them. Some of the stress they notice shows up as disorders in the young children, some as listlessness in the young adults, who just aren't finding success or a place in the world. Everywhere I travel in my community work, I'm seeing families struggling with stressed-out children. These parents love their kids, and these kids want to grow and develop successfully. But something is wrong.

In this chapter, let's all take a collective pause for breath. Let's figure out what's wrong. In the busyness of contemporary life, let's ask the right questions in our own homes and schools. If you feel as though everything has sped up and is going too fast and there isn't enough time in the day to do it all, pause a moment and ask yourself some questions:

- Is my child's life overscheduled? Am I spending all day taking children from one class, rehearsal, workout, team practice, and social event to another? If so, why?

- Is the frantic struggle to keep up with other kids and their parents doing my child damage? If so, do I sense it but feel powerless against it?
- Do I have a child who just "doesn't fit" the conventional expectations of well-intentioned teachers, doctors, and other experts who complain about him or her? Is my child just plain "different"?
- Is my five-, six-, or seven-year-old on behavioral medication, unable to calm down or function properly without a chemical stimulant? Or has this medication been recently suggested for my young child, though I don't believe deep down that he needs it?
- Has my teenage daughter gotten into trouble recently in ways that seem "not who she is"?
- Has my teenage son begun turning away from my home and authority in dangerous ways?
- Do I worry constantly about my child getting into the best college—and does that stress push me to create an overwhelming daily life for my kid?
- Is my child obsessed with the computer, video games, television, cell phones, text messaging, blogging, or other "electronic addictions"?
- Does my child have a materialistic sense of entitlement that cripples his or her ability to fully mature and find purpose and meaning?
- Do I live in a constant anxiety that I as a parent am failing one or more of my children?

Many families and children today are not necessarily sick, ill, or destroyed, but nevertheless suffer from one or more of these issues. Some children play three sports, have team and personal coaches, and are rushing from one grueling athletic practice to another. Some are constantly taking test-prep workshops, dance classes, and music classes, and are rehearsing daily for one academic or artistic performance after another. Others develop social or emotional skills but little character.

Still others act out in uncivil, angry ways, while at the same time struggling to keep up with the latest competitive trends.

I believe these children and their parents are suffering from *chronic stress*. After two decades of research and practice, I now believe that far too many families suffer from this dangerous condition. Let's pause for a moment to look at it carefully so that we can protect our families from it, then let's look at a major social force that might be causing it—one we can battle very well if we decide to become revolutionary and nurture the nature of our children.

What Is Chronic Stress in the American Family?

Stress—whether the daily stress of life or a major trauma, such as a car accident or death in the family—is a constant in our lives and in the lives of our children. It's normal for our kids' brains and bodies to experience surroundings of great complexity, all the while trying to maintain stability. Much of this is what neurologists call "positive stress." Our bodies and minds work to understand and integrate the stressor—put out the daily fire; learn a new, difficult skill; recover from an accident; or allow grief into our lives—and we notice that we've gained strength, understanding, new power, new purpose. Thus we can say that the stress has been helpful and meaningful, and our brains have not strayed into danger.

Negative stress, in contrast, is something we need to be very careful about, especially with our children. In the most general terms, as experts at the University of Maryland Medical School wrote recently, "When these symptoms persist, you are at risk for serious health problems. This kind of stress can exhaust your immune system. Recent research demonstrates that 90 percent of illness is stress-related." When stress goes beyond the stimulating (positive stress) and becomes debilitating (negative stress), symptoms fall into three categories: physical, emotional, and relational.

- Physical symptoms include sleep disturbance; weight gain or weight loss; fatigue; asthma or shortness of breath; and increases in viral and bacterial infections, migraines, or other tension headaches.

- Emotional and psychological symptoms include anxiety, depression, moodiness, lack of concentration or motivation, feeling out of control, substance abuse, and overreaction to daily situations. Oppositional Defiant Disorder (ODD), Obsessive Compulsive Disorder (OCD), Attention Deficit Disorder (ADD), and Attention Deficit Hyperactivity Disorder (ADHD) are all exacerbated by negative stress.

- Relational symptoms include antisocial behavior; increased arguments, nastiness, conflicts, and isolation from others; and increased aggression and violence.

When does negative stress become *chronic* stress? When the stress continues for years at a time. The question I began asking ten years ago, when I started identifying negative stress patterns in families like the Jameses, Stohls, and Royces, was this one: "Could our families and large numbers of our children be experiencing not just negative stress for a given day or week, but a socially sanctioned chronic stress?" And continuing along those lines, "Could it be that we don't realize the extent of this condition in our own homes, schools, and communities?"

Having conducted some clinical "detective work," I believe I can now answer these questions.

Research on Chronic Stress

Present scientific research on chronic stress appears mainly in two fields of scientific inquiry:

- Study of children traumatized in their early relationships by inadequate or violent care at the hands of parents and caregivers (this includes abuse). Such trauma raises cortisol levels (stress hormone levels) and thus "rewires" normal brain chemistry and circuitry.

- Study of families caring for severely disabled or chronically ill individuals. Both the ill individual and the constantly vigilant caregiver can experience raised cortisol that can lead to depression and other brain chemistry issues.

When these people are acutely stressed, they exhibit and report these experiences:

- Feeling as though they are always rushing, always late, always on the run
- Taking on too much, keeping too many irons in the fire
- Feeling overaroused
- Becoming short tempered
- Feeling constantly anxious
- Being overreactive and tense
- Worrying a great deal about a lot of little things
- Focusing on negatives, especially negative self-judgments and negative judgments of others close to them
- Thinking a lot about failure, possible disaster, lack of success
- Constantly feeling inadequate

Looking at these symptoms, as well as those listed earlier as symptoms of chronic stress, I came to realize that they applied all too well to what Carla James and so many others faced in their families. . . . In each case, parents and children had felt this panoply of symptoms for long periods of time, but without quite being able to figure out what was going on.

Our Survey

As I tried to understand the connection between chronic stress research and the families I was seeing, I asked the Gurian Institute research team to help me reach out to parents and find out what they thought.

In 2005, the Gurian Institute staff decided to measure the level of parental stress in families. We conducted an e-mail survey in which we asked 1,859 parents and caregivers to rank

- How supported they felt as parents in this culture
- How protected their children were in their social circles
- What they most feared as parents and caregivers

The results were powerful. Two-thirds of the survey participants considered themselves "unsupported as parents in the United States," felt "inadequate," and felt "constantly worried that their children would be harmed." Worry for children's safety is natural to any generation of parents, but the greatest fear among parents in our survey came not from physical violence or even from terrorism or sexual predators. More than two-thirds of participants believed that their children were in more danger from "subtle harms" than they were from "overt harms." As one respondent put it, "Our society has taken care of a lot of the obvious harms to children—like lack of food or shelter—but now the subtle harms are far worse." Subtle harms for surveyed parents included media stereotypes (thin girls, buff boys) as well as media exploitation of violence and inappropriate sexuality, loss of family bonding in everyday life, and high social pressure on kids. A number of participants reported variations on this theme: "There are inordinately high social and family expectations on my kids to perform in ways that just don't fit who my kids are. This is really stressing them out."

Also interesting in the survey was this finding: three-quarters of the respondents felt that their children were in more danger than they themselves had been as children. Many of these respondents were brought up during the Cold War—a time when Americans thought they could lose their lives in a nuclear catastrophe at any time—yet they felt that their children's exposure to subtle harms in contemporary society was worse.

Previous Work on Chronic Stress in Families

These survey results inspired our Gurian Institute team to look deeply at what these parents might be hinting at—especially the sense of stress and anxiety linked to social expectations and pressures. We reviewed other literature and surveys on parental stress. Although our survey was perhaps one of the first of its kind to try to determine an exact link between chronic stress and family life, there have been other surveys that measure general parental anxiety and child health. These others supported our survey results.

The Michigan Healthy Start survey of 2003, for instance, found that 66 percent of parents measured at "significant stress" on their Parental Stress Index. According to the Michigan researchers, this result showed a significant generational increase when they compared the baby boomers to their children. The Carnegie-Mellon corporation conducted a long-term study in the 1990s on child and family health, and discovered significant parental and family stress. They called this "a quiet crisis in child rearing."

These surveys followed the calls and hints of other researchers to look closely at family stressors. David Elkind, professor of psychology at Tufts University and the author of *The Hurried Child*, first wrote about stressed children in his clinical observations in the 1980s. In the 1990s, a number of fields began to report on children's deteriorating mental health due to such severe family stressors as abuse, neglect, and dangerous media stimulation. Robin Karr-Morse and Meredith S. Wiley reviewed the literature in *Ghosts from the Nursery*, showing the roots of violence in chronic stressors in early childhood. Jane Healy also reviewed the literature in *Failure to Connect*, showing correlation between excessive media exposure and children's stress.

In the late 1990s, the field of physical therapy began to discuss the possibility of a condition therapist T. W. Myers called "kinesthetic dystonia," a neurophysical state in which the child's body is constantly under neural stress because it is living out of sync with its own natural needs. The exponential increase in child obesity in the last decade falls into this category.

In the last few years, our nation's colleges have also been noticing a situation that supports the chronic stress theory. In November 2004, college health service workers from a wide variety of schools noted the severity and incidence of student mental health referrals in university health services. Steven Hyman, provost of Harvard University and former director of the National Institute of Mental Health, recently pointed out that students' mental states are now so precarious that they "interfere with the core mission of the university."

According to Hara Estroff Marano in *Psychology Today,* by 1996, "anxiety overtook relationship concerns and has remained the major student problem" in student health services. Eating disorders of some kind or severity now afflict 40 percent of women at some time in their college career. Psychologist Paul E. Joffe, head of the suicide prevention team at the University of Illinois at Urbana-Champaign, tracks the increase of dangerous drinking among young people. He finds among our late adolescents "an inverted world in which drinking to oblivion is the way to feel connected and alive."

Something Is Wrong

As I mentioned earlier, I began my clinical detective work because families seemed to be saying, "Something is wrong." I believe we can now see what is wrong. Families are struggling with chronic stress of children and parents. There is no question that statistics and individual stories can be manipulated, that there can be many various causes behind a particular statistic or outcome, and that claims that our children are utterly worse off than they were even a generation ago must be taken with a grain of salt. There are many ways in which our children are flourishing. Nevertheless, surveys, expert analyses, and anecdotal information do show a profound sense of anxiety in families and in social systems that are set up to care for children. Taking all this information into consideration, the Gurian Institute team decided to collect quantitative data on stress-related illness among children to see to what extent it had increased in the last two generations. Kathy Stevens, our training director, Mittie Pedraza, our parent programs coordinator, and our attachment specialist, Pat Crum, were especially helpful in compiling these rather frightening but also, I hope, revolution-inspiring statistics described in the Did You Know? box—statistics indicating not only that our children are showing the same symptomatology chronically stressed adults show but also that, in general, the basic mental health of our children is in significant decline.

Did You Know?

- Child depression rates in the United States have jumped exponentially in the last decade. Between 1995 and 2002, the number of hospital visits for depression among seven- to seventeen-year-olds jumped from 1.44 million to 3.22 million. The majority of these children are girls. The number of girls under six who are taking antidepressants and similar drugs has jumped to over a million.

- Over four million U.S. boys are on Ritalin or other mind- and mood-altering drugs. They are being medicated at ever younger ages, even though the FDA has not approved these drugs for these age groups. In general, the use of antipsychotic drugs for both girls and boys has jumped fivefold in the seven years between 1995 and 2002.

- Increasingly, the minds of our children are growing up to be antisocial. Children diagnosed with Antisocial Personality Disorder now number in the millions. As the Carnegie-Mellon survey notes, our primary social response to the new antisocial nature of children has not been to rethink how we raise them, but rather to expand punishment and incarceration systems. A Department of Justice study reports that at our present rates of incarceration, one in twenty babies born in the United States today will spend some part of life incarcerated. As of 2004, 1 in every 138 U.S. residents was in prison.

- More than seven million U.S. girls struggle now with eating disorders—quite often their brains' serotonin levels are so askew in their high-pressure lives that they must excessively diet, vomit food, and impede their own physical maturation just to rebalance themselves.

- Just under two million girls each year cut themselves with knives and other sharp objects in response to desperation and need for emotional contact.
- Millions of adolescent children abuse substances and binge drink. (Boys especially fit in the latter category.) These children seek emotional relief and escape from pressure through means other than healthy human contact and healthy personal growth.
- Boys and girls are sleeping one to two hours less per night than their brains need for healthy growth. This lack of sleep is an underreported epidemic with profound consequences, including antisocial behavior, substance abuse, and school failure.
- In the last twenty years, our children's physical weight rates have risen to nearly one in two children overweight and one in five obese. Obesity is the number one health problem among American children and is tied to many other problems: alcohol abuse, drugs, self-cutting, depression, media addiction, and listlessness. Dr. Philip Thomas, a pediatric obesity specialist, fears "This is going to be the first generation that's going to have a lower life expectancy than its parents."

In total, even after accounting for overlap in a number of these statistics, about one-third of our children are now diagnosed with some significant mental or physical disorder.

Present-day children's health statistics must give us pause. And we need to listen to the voices of parents. Between scientists studying children's health and parents trying to protect it, we have some of the smartest people around. When notes of discomfort in children's lives are reported from all quarters, we need to listen—one family at a time—

so that we can best protect our children. Regardless of the age of your child, his or her chances of experiencing chronic stress are increasing constantly. Where is this stress coming from? What is a first step in protecting our children from it?

The first step is to become aware—not only of the chronic stress itself but also of its source. Aside from the obvious stressors like abuse or neglect, there are very powerful forces of social conditioning that we must confront in order to become revolutionary on our children's behalf.

The Social Trends Parenting System

A grandmother in Texas wrote, "The ten-year-old son of one of my fellow volunteers at church is whisked from home to school, then school to basketball practice, then to a snack at a Taco Bell drive-through, then our 90-minute church program. This doesn't include homework and tutoring. What this kid needs is time to chill out in the backyard. Just because all these school and other programs exist, doesn't mean the family needs to sign up for all of them!"

Another mother wrote, "When my children were young (they are now in college), I realized they were overstressed. So we decided to make a big transition as a family. We saw that for years we had pushed them into a lot of activities we thought would help them in future society, but the kids didn't seem to enjoy them as much as we did. We decided to give them support for a few activities they wanted to engage in, and we supported them when they decided not to participate in an activity that became too demanding on their schedule."

These moms, and many other parents I hear from, are wise. Parents, other family members, and professionals are "taking back" their kids—removing them from a social trends parenting system that has subtly told these parents they are bad if their kids are not stressed. These parents recognize that our society has developed an unnatural and artificial approach to the needs of the child.

Social Trends Parenting

What do I mean by the *social trends parenting system?* It is an entrenched social system that conditions us to basically obey unscientific and untested ideas about how to help our kids succeed—ideas based on assumptions that all kids should be a certain way and be tested to prove it. This emphasis on social trends and pressures often leads us to raise children in ways *contradictory to their nature.* That is a pivot point of the chronic stress our kids (and we) get into. Living within this system, our families move farther away from feeling safe, whole, protective, and successful on a daily basis.

To see if this system is operating in your life and the life of your child, please take a moment to ask yourself a few questions. I constantly revisit these in my own life and family.

- Do I neglect my natural instincts as a parent, believing that everyone else—experts writing in books and magazines, family, friends, or neighbors—knows more than I do?
- Am I looking for answers to my parenting questions from ever-changing theories about how a mother, father, grandparent, teacher, or child should treat my children—rather than seeing both the question and the answer within my own child?
- Do I tend to apply negative, deficit-based approaches to my children's development? For instance, do I find myself saying or thinking things like "You won't make it in the world unless you get up to speed right now!"
- Do I try to compensate for not having enough time with my children by constantly trying to keep them stimulated and appeased with material goods, competitive activities, and technological "friends"?
- Do I focus on the latest fad in "emotion talk" and "feelings talk"—often neglecting the equal importance of universal moral and ethical values in family life?

- Do I put a lot of pressure on teachers, coaches, schools, physicians, other professionals, and children to produce only the highest levels of competition and perfect success, when realistic expectations of excellence—tailored to my child—would be more of a blessing to his or her development?
- Am I isolated and alienated, feeling immense pressure to solve all parenting problems on my own?

I confess to having experienced each of these with my own daughters at one time or another. We're all part of this vast social system, and we're all beholden to a social trends–oriented parenting and family system. We all look outward, listen to trends, hope to hear "the perfect plan" for child raising. We all want to get ahead, have children who get to the top, and experience for ourselves the social perfection "everyone is talking about." We are loaded up with constant information about children, and that information can come to run our lives.

Social trends parenting is a systemic response, I think, to the complexities of ever-changing family systems largely rooted in the increased mobility and major social changes instigated by the Industrial Revolution—which is one of the reasons I am calling for a "revolution" now, to take our children back. The Industrial Revolution created a cookie-cutter kind of existence, at least in many aspects of life. Our whole society tried to meet the new demands of factories. Our families became economically tuned, highly mobile, out of touch with natural roots. As a society, we grew a system of caring for children that focused on the so-called social and technological perfection of the human child.

As our society moved gradually into the information age, we carried the industrial values forward into an outward-looking, information-based social trends parenting system. This system creates serious stress in our children's lives.

The Anxiety of External Success Goals

We're conditioned to create families whose standard of success is how *a child will function as a competitor at the* highest level *of the competitive hier-*

archy. In the shadow of this stressor, we hyperprepare children from prebirth for entrance into "the best" college or highest-paying job even though we know that (1) most children will not achieve this top-end acquisition, nor need to in order to be successful and happy; and (2) that we and all other adults end up most successful and happy by living and growing in sync with who we really are, not by making huge amounts of money or fitting a rigid mold.

The disconnect between our individual natures as growing human beings and the monolithic expectations of society causes both children and parents to become anxious. Parents become anxious not only to make sure their kids are recognized as super-smart achievers who conform to "perfect" standards of financial success, interpersonal relationships, and self-esteem but also to define the "perfect" child by whatever latest definition has come down the pike.

When we feel we have failed as parents in our society, it is often because our children don't do well on a kindergarten entrance exam, or get what they think is enough ice time on the Pee Wee youth hockey team. These "small slights" come to hurt immeasurably; further, the information that creates the sense of failure is impossible to keep up with.

A prime example is the issue of breast-feeding. It was "out" for over a decade. Now it's back. Another example: sleeping with your child is out now, but once was encouraged. Lately the huge growth of the Baby Einstein–type tapes has swept the country, creating new anxiety among parents who want to buy more and more of them to make sure their kid grows up smart. But stay tuned, because recent studies show that some of the claims for these tapes are unrealistic; perhaps next year this fad will become obsolete also. High-stress consumerism has also infiltrated every aspect of our society. The constant push to buy, buy, buy the next best thing for your baby/toddler/child fuels and feeds on the social trends parenting system.

Aren't we constantly deluged with the latest trends in parenting and relational development? One day we read that parents don't matter—it's only friends who influence our impressionistic young kids; the next day we hear that constant emotion talk or giving kids their space or tough-love intervention is the only and best way to parent, or that if we don't

the nursery, our kids will fall behind. We see the morn-
 d every year dozens of new books are published, add-
 nd stress, piling on more pressure and anxiety. Many
 s contain wonderful insights, but they add up to a kind of
 ous wreck" atmosphere and to off-center parenting. We are constantly being told how to be perfect parents and have perfect winner
kids, and meanwhile we are exhausted.

How do we parents keep up? We can't. So we constantly fail. And in
raising kids through the following of social trends, we tend to listen
less to wise ancestors or our own instincts and instead take our cues
from test makers, psychological theorists, personality-based gurus,
morning show sound bites, and magazine advice columns regarding *all
children in general.* Our children thus get pulled in many directions,
often far away from their own core nature.

One clear example of the symptoms of social trends anxiety has
been the school system. Filled as it is with wonderful teachers and
many other excellent resources, our educational system—primary and
secondary—is so swamped with children (even in crowded preschools)
that it must socialize boys and girls with differing learning styles as
though they were all of one single type in terms of their social capabili-
ties, socioeconomic status, and psychological makeup. Many of the
children educated through this approach are often unable to achieve
basic levels of reading, writing, math, and science learning; even worse,
many with naturally diverse learning styles are pathologized, labeled,
medicated, and ultimately lost. They are captives of a monolithic system that many of them simply come to hate.

Losing the Nature of the Child

By participating in the social trends parenting system, we are taking
our eyes off of what our children, our family, our schools *really* need.
The outside-in model of society-as-guide for parenting cannot do otherwise than take our eyes off the deep and complex nature of *our* child.
Although setting high goals for our kids is crucial for their thriving,
what is problematic is the lack of attention to understanding and nur-

turing who our specific children really are—so that we can help them set the *right* high goals for themselves!

Certainly, many social trends are wonderfully helpful. Many parenting experts are immensely helpful. Some surveys are very helpful, as I found in providing surveys and results in this chapter: we need to listen when parents talk. But in overrelying on social trends to help us raise kids—and in neglecting the individual and inborn nature of each child—we are overstressing millions of children toward anxiety and other disorders, toward painful labels and misdiagnosis, toward antisocial behavior and unhappiness. It's time for parents to act on behalf of the human child in revolutionary ways.

Nurturing Your Child's Nature

Perhaps in the last week, month, or year you've heard a whisper from your child: "Look, here is the person I am. Look into my eyes! Pay attention to *me*. All the other stuff you are throwing at me? I'm trying to do it, but what I really need, what is essential to me, is for you who love me to help me become who I am already trying to be."

My experience, research, and theoretical analysis tells me that this whisper is not some fantasy—it is the voice of nature in the child. This chapter has asked you to look at some profound issues you might be facing as a parent in this society. I hope you'll take awareness and vigilance of the issues—of chronic stress and social trends—into the rest of this book. I hope you'll join me now in discovering the fruition of your needs, hopes, and dreams in a parenting revolution: a refocus of parenting away from ephemeral social trends and on to the *core nature of the individual child.*

Focusing on that *unique* temperament, personality, and genetic disposition leads to your trusting your instincts about what is *essential* for your child and family. Focusing on that core nature will help you raise your child to adapt to anything. A child whose parents nurture the nature grows strong and learns how to flourish in any future circumstance, wherever the child may find himself or herself as an adult.

The remainder of this book proposes a new model of parenting that includes not only old wisdom but new science—science that focuses specifically on the nature of children. The psychologist Kurt Lewin taught that there is nothing so radical as a good theory. I hope you'll find in the remaining eight chapters of this book a nature-based theory that you can apply in your home. By the time you end this book, I hope you will have in hand an essential parenting blueprint.

What is an essential parenting blueprint? *Nurture the Nature* provides not only theory and insight but also practical tools by which you will develop a clear sense of your child's nature and, in that context, a *blueprint* of what is essential if you are to nurture the nature of your child. This blueprint is a plan of action that will grow from your understanding of your child's innate talents and skills, temperament and personality. It will allow you to understand the strengths of *your* child and to waste no more time on focusing on social, educational, or media trends that aren't right for his or her unique nature. This blueprint will develop organically in your relationship with your child and also in the many wisdom-of-practice strategies of other parents, shared with you in this book.

Your blueprint will make it a lot easier to make good choices. For example, if the Baby Einstein approach to parenting is right for your child, you'll be able to make that decision from within the truth your child is living. If it's not right for your child, you won't need to feel guilty that he or she is no genius at science.

So it is with all potential activities, missions, ideas, media—the hard work of the essential parenting blueprint really pans out once you look back after a month or so of developing it and a month or so of applying it and are able to say, "Now I understand *this* child. Now I see how to do right by him, by her. Now I have in place the safe life, the right teachers, the successful pathway for the person I love more than myself."

Here's an example. Karen, a mother of two in North Carolina, wrote, "When I started focusing on the actual strengths and real vulnerabilities of my two children—their core personalities, their genetics, their real abilities, strengths and weaknesses, warts and all—I discovered a deep sense of peace in my family and myself. My husband and I even changed my son's school. This had to be done. We developed rituals and relationships that make it possible to really love our kids. These wisdom-of-practice strategies, as you call them, really work."

Allan, a father of four in San Jose, wrote, "The key for me was understanding who my daughters were. I discovered your nature-based theory when I started coaching girls' soccer. My first three kids were boys, and I understood how to help them. With my daughter, there's a whole other world. When I saw who she and these other young girls are from the 'inside out,' I started knowing how to encourage them and help them succeed. It's a real good feeling, I can tell you."

As you develop your essential parenting blueprint, don't be surprised if you have times when you feel reluctant to step away from social trends parenting. There is a lot of pressure in this society to be a social trends parent! We all can feel afraid sometimes that our children will not succeed in school, relationships, future work, and life. I hope you'll stick with this book. As its research will show you, *when we pay attention to the nature of children, the children succeed!*

The Gurian Institute has trained tens of thousands of parents, teachers, and other caregivers in nature-based theory and its wisdom-of-practice strategies. Kids do better in school, act out less at home, and feel better when we nurture their nature rather than try to superimpose trendy expectations on them. Many parents' stories of success and innovation appear as Wisdom of Practice sections between the remaining chapters of this book. My team and I want to extend our gratitude to the parents and caregivers who have sent their stories to us so that we can show you the revolutionary steps others are taking toward real child-rearing success.

Getting Started

Let's move forward now into the positive, hopeful, and practical work of this book. Each chapter will provide you with essential steps you can take immediately to incorporate nature-based theory into your present parenting work. As you use this book in its entirety, I hope you will find wisdom and practice that inspires you to base your family's life in loving attention toward the sometimes hidden and always beautiful assets of your child whether he or she is newborn, school-age, or adolescent.

Let us now begin in Chapter Two by looking through both a loving and a scientific lens into exactly who your child is, from the inside out—this amazing asset, your child, whom you as a parent have only borrowed for the few years of childhood and adolescence from the natural and social world in which he or she will ultimately flourish.

Wisdom of Practice

AS FAR BACK AS I CAN REMEMBER, MY SON, DAN, HAS HAD A PASSION for cars. As a toddler he went from playing with small cars to fire trucks and then to construction trucks. When he was four we would take him to the local fire station and sit and look at the different trucks, where he would entertain the firemen with all his knowledge of the equipment. In the summer, we would take him to the local fair, and he would check out the farm equipment and impress us all with his knowledge of what the machinery was called and how it was used. Every time we traveled in our car, he would find construction trucks working and identify them as well.

As Dan continued to grow, so did his passion and love of cars. Lucky for Dan, both his father and I enjoy seeing his eyes light up when he follows his passion. Many nights at the dinner table we have discussed carburetors, new models, car production. As the years went by, we helped Dan look at a career in engineering. He saw that this career would mean he had to get good grades. This helped him stay motivated in school.

One year for Christmas I purchased a car designer art kit made by a company called Career Builders. It was the best gift he received that year. He spent several hours that day drawing different designs of cars. It was amazing to see, for a child who doesn't like to sit still. Years later I found another car drawing book that came with special stencils that you can use to draft and design your own car. It is still his favorite pastime to draw and design cars. Dan now wants to study aerodynamics and solar energy. He talks about developing alternate fuel sources to reduce our dependence on oil and help the environment.

Dan has taught me many things, but maybe one of the biggest is that if I just focus on what he wants to focus on, he'll show me what he needs in order to succeed.

2

Understanding the Core
Nature of Your Child

From the mother and the father comes a child who is asking every
day, "Who am I?" Boy or girl, toddler or teenager, that child wants
those of us who care to open up the world as the answering ground,
but not without a map in hand.

—TERRY TRUEMAN, FAMILY THERAPIST
AND AUTHOR OF *STUCK IN NEUTRAL*

WHEN SAM AND SHOSHANA WALKED INTO MY OFFICE, THEY WERE
clearly worried about their two children. Brandon, the child of their
marriage, was six, and Alicia, Shoshana's child from her first marriage,
was twelve. Sam, thirty-seven, and Shoshana, thirty-eight, were both
lawyers. They had moved to Spokane from the East Coast, one to work
for the government, the other to join a major corporate firm. They
entered my office dressed for work—our appointment was set for the
lunch hour—and got right to the point.

Shoshana said, "I think Brandon has ADD."

Sam said, "Alicia was diagnosed with depression by a psychologist
in Syracuse."

These parents described Brandon as a boy who didn't read well, was
unable to sit still during story time at school, and spent too much time,
in Shoshana's opinion, on the computer.

Sam and Shoshana described Alicia as a very driven soccer player who was depressed, both back in Syracuse and here in Spokane. The psychologist in Syracuse had suggested Prozac.

"We've heard that you take a different approach to parenting than some professionals do," Shoshana said. "Can you meet with our kids and let us know what you think?"

Sam said, "We know we've got to change something. We can't believe both our kids are sick."

There were tears in their eyes. These two wonderful people felt like failures as parents. They felt very alone. I talked to them, asked questions, helped them fill out my intake questionnaire, and asked them to bring Alicia next time, then Brandon the next. We created a plan for family counseling.

When I met Alicia, I was faced with a twelve-year-old girl who, though short in stature, weighed 150 pounds. My sensors for nature-based and biological components to her depression went on high alert. She had dark circles around her eyes; her fingernails were bitten to bloody skin. She admitted to having "no self-esteem" and being sad a great deal of the time.

"Before doing anything else, let's look at her biological nature," I said to this family. This was indeed a different approach than had been taken by the Syracuse psychologist, who had not brought up hormonal biology with the family, but instead had focused only on potential psychodynamic or family systems origins for Alicia's issues. Although I agreed to look at those issues with the family as well, I also asked them to get a biological and biochemical analysis as the "nature base" and science base to our work. I referred them to a psychiatrist who specialized in adolescent female biology.

When I met Brandon, I asked him to read a book with me. I wanted to ascertain as much as I could about how his brain worked in the areas where his parents sensed his vulnerability in life and learning. We chose *Good Night, Moon,* which Brandon indeed did not read well. He stumbled, became anxious and even ashamed.

I asked him to do sand painting. Now he came to life. He could "paint" nearly anything he wanted. As he worked, I talked with him about what he enjoyed. I also slipped in a question about why he thought he couldn't sit still. He concentrated for a moment and then told the truth of his nature, as he knew it: "I just like to move around."

When I met with Shoshana and Sam again, I gave them a referral to have Brandon checked for a possible learning or reading disability, and a referral to a clinic that could do a brain scan, should they wish it. Again, I wanted to marshal as much hard science into the therapeutic process as I could. I also predicted, "I don't think you'll find Brandon has a disability. I think he's a normal boy whose nature is not well understood by his teachers and even, perhaps, by you guys. Science should be able to help with this."

Shoshana and Sam were open to acknowledging their own misunderstanding of the natural development of their son. As they got involved in the tools you'll find in this book, they came to understand the natural range of "normal" for brain development of a six-year-old boy, especially development of his brain's verbal centers (the reading, writing, and talking parts of the brain). I showed Shoshana and Sam results of brain scans and neuropsychological studies that indicate how unnatural it is for some six-year-old boys to sit still for long periods.

These caring parents spent a good part of the next month discovering much of what you'll find in this book: they learned what was the core nature of a little boy and, more important, the core nature of *their* little boy. They engaged in processes to develop both a picture of the core nature of Brandon and of Alicia and a blueprint for appropriate expectations for each child.

When Brandon's diagnosis for a learning disability came back, it was indeed negative—that is, normal. There was nothing wrong with the child. His behavior, which had worried the home and the school, was in fact natural for him. The institutions of school and family had applied to him a social trends way of thinking about "how boys *should* learn" that was somewhat misleading. After learning who her child really was, Shoshana said, "It's such a relief to know my son is okay."

In Alicia's case, the medical diagnostic report showed that her menstrual cycle was abnormal, especially in its progesterone and estrogen balance. This was causing substantial difficulty for Alicia in mood and was one cause of her depression. Like so many professionals, the psychologist in Syracuse was not trained in female hormonal biology—a crucial aspect of female *nature*. Although the Prozac the Syracuse therapist had suggested did indeed help regulate some of the hormonal issues, the new psychiatrist prescribed hormone patches to help balance hormone flow more immediately. These worked within two weeks. Alicia's depression lifted, and she also began to move toward a healthier weight.

As time passed and therapy continued, the lives of everyone in this family improved. Family relationships benefited from the focus on each of these children's core natures: *who they were, from the inside out*. Alicia was able to get off the Prozac. Brandon entered a first-grade classroom that understood boy nature—it fit him very well. Sam and Shoshana "reacquainted themselves" with the two children they were raising, coming to understand the *natural needs* of each child.

Using Nature-Based Theory in *Your* Family

Science has to be tried out in the laboratory of the home and the community before we can know it works. If we use science wisely, it becomes a great ally for parents. Sam and Shoshana added nature-based theory, new science, and new insight into their lives, adding to other powerful aids—religion, intuition, family life, community.

One of the first things I ask parents to do to start incorporating new science and nature-based theory is this: keep a record of your growing knowledge of your child's core nature. I suggest that you begin documenting your child's development, identifying the issues most important to your family, and planning the actions you are going to take.

I keep a parenting record for each of my children—one that reveals my fits and starts as a parent, and my sense of their core nature. My children are teenagers now, and I've shown them pieces of my journal about each of them already. We've enjoyed noticing together how their core nature has been developing. Later in their lives, I'll give them their whole journal. I'm hoping it will help them understand their own children's core nature because it will help them understand themselves.

As you proceed in this book, I hope you too will keep some kind of record. A journal would be ideal, but please don't feel that it's mandatory or that you can't go on with this book unless you keep one. Not at all. Perhaps you could write out your thoughts on your computer or even record an oral journal on digital tape or other new technology. I'll refer to "your journal" throughout this book, but if you just read the book and only write in the margins, you will still fulfill a great deal of this book's promise.

In keeping a journal (whatever its form), you may find, as have many of my clients, that your days and nights are often moved with "Aha" and "Wow!" You will feel validated for the ways in which you already sense that some things seem immutable about your children ("He just came out of the womb that way"; "She was always a very practical kid") and for the ways in which your children are constantly developing, changing, growing.

I think that as parents we are doing best when we can say with some certainty: "My child came out of the womb in this, this, and this way . . ." *and* be able to say: "I will nurture and support all the inherent strengths, talents, and skills my child has had from birth, and also work diligently to help my child in the areas where he or she might need extra help, because in those areas, my child is not inherently very strong."

Keeping the journal helps you see what is core nature—in all its strengths and weaknesses—and what is illusion, conditioned by the social trends society and its crucial assumption about bringing up a child to fit a mold: the myth of the blank slate child.

The Myth of the Blank Slate Child

The starting point of the nature-based theory my team and I have been demonstrating to parents in workshops is this: *Our children are not blank slates who need every possible color of pencil to draw in a self. If we can go beyond the blank slate idea, we'll best understand how to target our efforts for our particular child.* This is an important statement to make because many of us as parents are conditioned by our society to carry a kind of myth that our children are blank slates. This myth is a hinge of the social trends parenting system, so deeply embedded in our thinking that we don't even recognize it. For instance, a parent may say, "Oh, I know Tim isn't a blank slate" or, "Sure I can see how Carrie is real competitive," but then immediately say, "but that's because of socialization."

Inherent in this dialogue is the powerful belief that socialization factors are larger in personality development than genetic ones, and thus that social trends and external models should have greater power in molding kids than the nature of the child. Nature-versus-nurture arguments have been going on for some time in our society. At an instinctual level, we probably all understand that a child develops through both nature *and* nurture, but in the last decades especially, our social trends parenting advisers have moved us far toward focusing mainly on socialization as the most powerful cause of how our children are—and should be. We've moved so far this way in four decades that we neglect, at times, to look deeply into each child's eyes.

Join me a moment in understanding how the blank slate myth works in your family and community, and how you can dismantle it. This is a crucial step in creating a nature-based, nurture-friendly parenting framework.

Becoming Aware of Blank Slate Parenting

According to the blank slate myth, the human child has no significant core nature. The child is like an empty vessel, a canvas with no picture, not a part of nature who came into this world with a foundational self, but rather a kind of vacant lot that exists mainly to be filled in as culture decides he or she ought to be filled in. Parents are socialized to believe their child has little internal and inherent self-confidence. The parent is supposed to grasp the blank child's hands firmly, pull him or her along in as many directions as possible ("provide every possible social opportunity") so that the child can "find his or her place." The parent's job is complete once he or she has fit the child into various social molds through which the child will gain confidence and success.

A Brief History of This Debilitating Myth

How did we get to a point in history where we stopped looking into our own children's core nature for their own confidence and purpose? I think the Industrial Revolution truly was the turning point. For most of human existence people were either hunter-gatherers or farmers in agrarian communities. They lived in small societies, in which family and tribe protected members' DNA, genetic development, natural inheritance, and social success. They had low crime, simple character development, clear gender roles, and a sense of purpose for each individual in a tribe—but they died young, lacked good medicine, and lived in emotionally and socially oppressive societies.

The advent of industrialization in the nineteenth century gave people a fresh start. Individual men (and, later, women) could "control their own destiny." They could "turn away from the past." Families could move away from oppressive systems and make fresh starts. A whole tribe was no longer needed for economic advantage—one entrepreneur or very hard worker in an assembly line could provide financially for his (and her) offspring. Women, who were long oppressed, could find the beginning of greater equality.

For about two hundred years, Western society has been engaged in the powerful and necessary industrial revolution. It is one of the most profound revolutions in humans' million-year history, a revolution that has brought us modern civilization. At the same time, because of this revolution's original need to create factory workers who would expand manufacturing productivity, people began to treat their children as blank slates. The blank slate model allowed us all to create cookie-cutter or square-peg-in-a-round-hole children who could best fit factory, assembly line, and corporate work. To this day, with what energy we have left after a very hard work week, we buy into standards of success that are external to the child, that compare him or her with others or with imagined industrial and celebrity idols. Even though it is now the new millennium, we say things like these:

"If she doesn't learn to play with trucks, she can't be an engineer."

"Can't he just sit still?! He'll never make it."

"He doesn't talk about his feelings; he's going to become a Columbine killer."

"There must be something wrong with him if he can't read yet— his friends can."

"She's too competitive—she won't be able to nurture her children."

"He doesn't talk about his feelings enough. He won't be a good husband."

"There's something wrong with her. No one likes her."

"There's something wrong with him. We've got to fix it right now."

If you think back to your own ancestors (regardless of their continent of origin), you'll note that for much of human history people assumed the genetic and biological nature of their children to be sacrosanct. They understood their own biology and nature to be "God given" or at least inherited. Industrialization questioned that assumption. Industrialization is not a villain, but it did harm child raising in that it imposed the idea of industrial utility—children's usefulness to economic structures—above all else: above family bonding, character development, emotional development, and spiritual joy. Families, without knowing it, have given up to the blank slate myth a great deal of their children's emotional, psychological, and ethical security during childhood in hope of bestowing national and economic survival to the society in their adulthood. The baby boomers—my generation—were raised, en masse, in this industrial and then postindustrial philosophy.

This is the history and the mythic atmosphere we must contend with now as parents. We must each wonder to what extent we have "industrialized" our individual children. And as we seek alternatives, we must keep listening to the voice inside us that says, "My children come into this world with a core nature—a personality, a temperament, an inner sense of purpose—not a blank slate." I think we can take a major step toward escaping the blank slate myth with our children if we think back to how vigorously we tried as youngsters to "live our own lives," "find our own individual place." We sensed ourselves that we were each much more than a blank slate. We were each a natural self trying constantly to emerge in family and social life. Our children are too. We can feel this in our bones. We experience it in little everyday comments and experiences.

When Grandma or Grandpa says about our child, "Don't worry; that's normal for boys [girls] in our family," we sense this is instinctual and true. Perhaps you yourself have said, "Wow, my kids have such distinct personalities—and they're each so different. . . . They were raised in the same house and society, but the first was a dream, the second so difficult, and now the youngest . . . a space cadet!" Many mothers tell me they could understand the personality and temperament of their children *before they were born,* just by the way they behaved in the womb during pregnancy.

Turning away from the blank slate myth means consciously deciding to listen to the experience you and most parents have of a child's core nature from the moment the child is born. It means, for example, paying attention to the signals that your child might be sending about shyness. It means not worrying that shyness will lead to failure "in this society." It means not pushing this child in five different directions and sometimes receiving back from the child a resigned effort or even a deep resentment that lasts a lifetime because you did not let this child be who he or she is.

Moving away from blank slate parenting means gradually gaining a new confidence about our children—one that acknowledges that we don't have to mold the child in order to have a successful child (as you'll see many times in this book). We will see that it's not true that a square-peg child must transform in order to become a success in life. Bill Gates did not, Charles Schwab did not, Maria Montessori did not, Oprah Winfrey did not. Countless successful people became so because they turned away from social trends and toward innovation and individuality. Why did they do this? Why were they successful?

Science is now joining our good instincts to show us the answer. Science confirms that *inherent from birth in our child is a core nature, a unique source of personal development and potential for success*. Genetics and a number of areas of neuroscience reveal the unique and infinitely variable hardwiring and genetic predispositions we and our children are born with. Practical application of this antidote to the blank slate myth is the subject of the rest of this chapter.

Eight New Sciences That Can Help You Understand Your Child's Core Nature

The next sections describe eight relatively new sciences that were not available while I was growing up—nor even when my own children were born—to the degree they are now. Later in this chapter, I will offer exercises that can help you apply these sciences and nature-based theory in your family's life. As I introduce these sciences to you, and as you make use of the tools in this book, you may want to keep referring to your journal or other record-keeping framework for note taking and personal focus. Always remember, however, that you should see the information from these sciences as secondary to your parental intuition about your child.

Genetics

Because the human genome has been mapped by scientists—2001 was the benchmark year—parents are even closer now than they were even ten years ago to understanding many of the inborn aspects of a child's personality.

The three billion bits of DNA in your child's genome are organized into sequence variations—haplotype blocks—that scientists can identify and that completely debunk the blank slate myth. Your child has a core nature of immense depth and complexity. Scientists can now isolate even specific traits of the child's core nature that come from the mother's and father's core natures. This process is called genomic imprinting. Chemical handles called methyl groups are attached to units of DNA and "turn off" and "turn on" aspects of the parents' DNA in the child.

These aspects of core nature "influence all sorts of social behaviors" later in life, according to Harvard biologist David Haig. Lawrence Wilkinson of Cambridge University recently summed up the research: "Imprinted genes and behavior are the new frontier."

Studies of twins and other children with the same genetic coding who are separated at birth show imprinted behavior patterns that amaze researchers. For instance, *no matter how or where the two children were raised, they share characteristics even down to how they flush the toilet or how much they smile or frown.* Similar studies now show that personality and temperament (including whether a child is extraverted or introverted, aggressive or shy); styles of walking, talking, and running; even physical and mental strengths and disorders are in large part inborn.

Yet another fascinating example of nature-based insights gained from new science regards emotional processing and social behavior. As a parent I certainly have found myself concerned about why my kids are popular or not popular, emotionally skilled or not skilled, in certain areas and groups. Studies funded by the prestigious National Institute of Mental Health (completed in 2005) have discovered genetically activated brain mechanisms that are responsible for children's social behavior. One of these mechanisms is found on "chromosome seven" of a child's genome. When, for instance, a child is missing twenty-one specific genes on this chromosome (which many children are), he or she is more highly social and empathic, even in situations that might cause another child, who is not missing these genes, to be fearful. At the same time, the lack of these genes also leads to more phobias (such as fear of spiders or heights).

Each of the inherited traits has its own degree of activation in your child's genetic structure. For instance, the development of ADHD in your particular child may have "low heritability" in later life—it might be carried on the genome of your child, yes, but would need a substantial environmental toxin or chronic stress to bring it out. In contrast, whether your child is an extravert or introvert has high heritability.

This means that generally, no matter the environment your child is raised in, he or she will develop one of these personality types.

Words like "extravert" and "introvert" are very helpful in putting useful language to genetics research. These two words come from the Myers-Briggs personality assessment. Katharine Briggs and Isabel Briggs Myers, an innovative mother-and-daughter team, were able to discover sixteen distinct and genetically imprinted personality types that have high heritability. Paul Tieger and Barbara Barron-Tieger, two practitioners of the Myers-Briggs system, summed up this research: "Children are born with a type and remain that type their entire lives; parents are the same type they were as children. Our personality type affects all aspects of our lives, from the way we play as toddlers to the subjects or activities in school that interest or bore us, to the occupations we find satisfying as adults."

These types, they note, pass through family lines genetically. Neurochemically, children who are more shy are inclined to have lower levels of blood flow and brain activity in a thinking center of the brain and more in an anxiety center of the brain when shown a face of a person experiencing emotion. These children feel more anxious around others, and may not read emotional signals as quickly as an extraverted child.

Having a shy or introverted personality is not a sign of "low self-esteem" (something we have been told by social trends parenting), nor is it a bad thing. It just *is:* inherited, genetic, and, even more—as we'll see throughout this book—it is actually a seat of your shy child's ultimate strength in life!

In 2007, as this book is being published, it is not generally possible to create a genome map for every child because of the costs involved. (There is also debate, to be discussed later, regarding eugenics.) Furthermore, most genome mapping concerns physiology rather than neurobiology (the blood-brain barrier makes mental health factors harder to work with than physical health factors). Although genome mapping may become more possible every year, it is important to keep in our minds that genome mapping is not necessary for getting to know the core personality of your child. Right now, before you go any farther into this book, you can begin your own "science" of getting to know your child's core nature.

Try This

Begin to get to know your child's genetic legacy through these exercises and resources. These activities will take time, so spread this out over a few months as needed:

- Talk to your child's other parent about what might be five key inheritable traits of the child's core nature. (These are "high heritability traits.") Perhaps you could say, "If we had a genome map—a way of reading our child's chromosomes—what do you think it would say are five traits he [she] has definitely inherited?"

- Send letters and e-mails to relatives and friends who know your child well. Ask them to list five core traits in your child. Some of these may appear in other family members as well.

- Make phone calls to trusted friends and family, your child's teachers, or others. Ask them what first comes to their mind when you say, "What is my child's personality to you? What does my child just keep doing or trying to do with her [his] time, energy?" And remember, even if your child is a teenager, these questions are still useful.

- Observe your child's behavior closely in many settings. Make notes and lists of repeated behaviors, traits, and interests. What activities especially engage your child, make him lean forward in rapt concentration? What are her passions? By answering these questions, you are beginning to ascertain what general traits appear the most in your child's "behavioral genetics." Your home and immediate environment are wonderful arenas for observing your child's genetic foundation.

- Ask your child what she sees as her self, who she is, what her most important interests are. Interview your child—if he is old enough; this especially works with adolescents—and can lead to wonderful bonding moments.

- Review all this information and match it to any you have about relatives and ancestors, what each of them were interested in, how their personalities operated, who they were.

These tasks are the beginning of a journey you will make in this book to meld insight and principles from science with your everyday life. We will delve more deeply into personality assessments later in this chapter.

Trauma Science

As crucial as it is to know the genetic base of your child's core nature and the personality traits your child was born with, it is also crucial to understand that if the child is placed in toxic environments—whether physical, social, psychological—the child's genetic template (his or her core nature and inborn personality and temperament) will be affected. In fact, new genetics research shows that your child's specific and particular ability to be resilient against trauma begins in his or her genetic predisposition. Scientists are now able to isolate an individual's inherent ability to be resilient to different stressors by studying that person's DNA. This is great for parents, because now, if you can determine your child's genetic personality assets (as, for instance, we discussed earlier), you can then also get a picture of how he or she will handle trauma.

We all try instinctively to protect our children from suffering. Have you ever wondered why? There are many reasons, of course—primary, I believe, is our instinct (now confirmed by science) that our child's core nature can become derailed by ongoing and prolonged trauma. With new brain scan research—PET, MRI, and SPECT—parents can understand the effects of both positive and negative childhood experiences on children's genetic structures, specifically the brain (even down to the specific part of the brain involved—the amygdala, the hippocampus, and the paralimbic-emotion system). Daniel G. Amen, M.D., a neuropsychiatrist whose Amen Clinics have performed thirty-five thousand brain scans, recently wrote, "The brain was once thought of as a black box too complex to understand, but neuroscientists are now uncovering the brain's function at a rapid pace. Within the brain there are systems that work together to produce our personality, cares, dreams, aspirations." Especially if you are raising a child who is having behavioral, mood, or learning difficulties (ADD/ADHD, behavioral disorders, Sensory Integration Disorder, eating disorders, depression), note in your journal the medical resources available in your community for conducting brain scans. To begin your exploration of this on a nationwide scale, you can go to www.amenclinics.com.

Often a brain scan professional can actually show parents a "blank spot" or "dark spot" on the brain. And although most of us may not be able to access these scans in our immediate community, the scientific research garnered from them has helped many people better understand the trauma their own children might be facing. It also helps parents separate "normal bad traumas" from "real and severe traumas."

I have discussed these scans in helping parents like Sam and Shoshana, who could not afford brain scans (and in their cases, scans were not needed) but who were able to move beyond the blank slate myth, the social trends parenting system, and their children's chronic stress by seeing scans of children in similar distress.

Gender Science

Because of new brain and biochemical research, parents can now understand how boys and girls are not only similar but also inherently different. Mothers and fathers can now parent according to the gender of the child—without stereotyping. Throughout this book, I'll help you get to know what brain scans are telling us about how boys and girls grow, learn, and interact differently, by nature. Right now, in your journal or elsewhere, you might note your "first instincts" about the nature of your sons and daughters, especially regarding how they're similar and different. "My boy is . . ."; "My girl is . . ." Start one sheet for each child, and add to them by asking your spouse, other relatives, and close friends for aspects of the child they think might have to do with his or her gender.

Noticing gender differences does not mean falling prey to social stereotyping or social trends regarding gender roles. The spectrum of gender identity and behavior is very broad and complex on our genome. Noticing gender differences is really about understanding an aspect of the core nature of each child. Knowing what part of the boy or girl is hardwired can help solve problems boys and girls have in school, in the neighborhood, and at home. It can also be a key element in their future success as human beings, leaders, spouses, and parents.

Throughout Part Two of this book, I'll provide you with results from studies in gender science related to your children's stages of childhood. In this research, you'll be able to discover aspects of *your* girl or boy from birth to twenty-five years old.

Attachment and Bonding Science

Thanks to new brain research on child attachment, parents can now understand the nature of bonding and how bonding helps a child's genetic template grow, flourish, and succeed in the world. We now know from neural imaging that certain parts of the child's brain don't activate as they are supposed to without certain kinds of bonding and attachment. Such scientists as Allan Schore use brain imaging technology to show how infants need secure attachment with their primary caregivers if the connections between the left and right hemisphere in their brain are to fully form. If such connections don't fully form, the child is less successful in life.

Human bonding is natural; it helps develop the child's core nature, and time spent bonding offers us opportunities to understand who our child is. In fact, *it is in your bonding time with your child that you will often glimpse his or her hidden core nature.* Now is a good time to write out what you know about your family bonding—it's bonding time, bonding rituals, and bonding opportunities.

Take a moment to think about the relationships in your family.

- How does your family work together, solve problems, have fun, help each other?

- How do family members sometimes line up with one side against another?
- Do you feel close to your children, really intimate?
- Do you feel closer to one child than to another?

Keep the list of these initial questions at the forefront of your mind as you proceed through this book. By the time you have finished, I hope you will have found ways of solving nearly every issue on your list of bonding questions and family bonding methods.

Hormonal Biology

Because of new research on the human endocrine system, parents are now able to understand more about the inherited, hardwired template of their children's moods and behavior, especially just before, during, and then long after puberty.

This new research on hormonal flow in both boys and girls can help you better handle the parenting of both easy and difficult adolescents. We will discuss this further throughout the chapters of this book, for it is a vast new field of science. You may well decide during your reading of this book that one of your children needs a test of his or her endocrine system. Your local physician and psychiatric resources will be able to help you get that test, if necessary. Just mention to them the words "endocrine system" and "mood." As professionals, they should be able to tell you if a hormonal assessment would help your child. And if they say no to such an assessment, but your instincts tell you something might be going on hormonally with your child, you should always feel free to get a second opinion.

Right now, you can begin utilizing research from this new science by noting excessive moodiness, up-and-down emotions, or aggressiveness in your child. These will be pieces of the "Who is my child?" puzzle that you'll take further into this book. The possible existence of a hormonal component is especially important if you are raising a child who is experiencing episodes of rage, severe behavioral issues, eating disorders, or depression.

If during the process of reading this book you decide to consult with medical professionals, consider seeing those who are actually trained in hormonal biology. Let these professionals see this part of your journal or whatever information about your child's genetic legacy and core nature that you have identified so far. Although therapy is about more than hormones, some children in my family practice would not have found their way out of adolescent self-destructiveness if not for a local professional who understood what part hormones played in the children's core nature and current behavior.

The Science of the Adolescent Brain

Because of new brain scan research on adolescent brains, parents can now understand how and when their teenager's brain is genetically hardwired to grow and develop in what particular ways. This new scientific research especially helps parents who are right now trying to guide their risk-taking adolescent children. We'll talk about this research in greater detail in Chapters Seven through Nine. Right now, however, you might enjoy taking a look at pictures of adolescent brain imaging on the Internet. If you Google "brain scans of adolescents," you will find Web sites that show you pictures of Paul Thompson's groundbreaking scans in this field. Through www.amenclinics.com, you can also access a DVD called "Which Brain Do You Want?" which shows scans of adolescent brains. These images can inspire you as a parent to gain general knowledge of what is normal for adolescent brains, to protect your adolescents from toxins, and also to think about whether a brain scan might be useful and feasible for your adolescent.

The Science of Human Stress

New stress research is showing us amazing things about children—from how boys and girls naturally handle stress differently to how much stress is healthy for a growing brain. Stress research intersects with the trauma research discussed earlier, but it is a broader category of research, as it also includes the study of positive stress.

Throughout this book, you'll see how to understand the stress your children may be experiencing. I'll help you to develop stress buffers for your child—and stress enhancers, when more positive stress might be needed in your child's life.

Spiritual and Religious Science

Brain scans and brain wave analyses show special and unique blood flow patterns in the brain when human beings are engaged in spiritual

---

Try This

To "get your feet wet" in the process of differentiating stressors, begin accessing the gifts of stress research by opening a blank page in your journal (or other tool). On it, write, "What are five areas of negative stress in my child's life?" Think about five (or less or more) ways in which your child is under the kind of stress that could lead to chronic stress symptoms in the future.

On a second blank page, note five other people besides Mom and Dad who have or can have a positive nurturing and bonding influence on your child—who can serve as a "de-stressing" influence. Can you get Grandma and Grandpa more involved with your child, even via the Internet? Can you find child-care providers or mentors who would want to be like a grandma or grandpa? Can you get your eldest child to do more to nurture the younger children? How can you bring more trusted adults into the care of your child? If, as this book progresses, you decide to approach these people to help you, they will benefit from being "briefed" in key aspects of your child's nature so that they can mentor or target specific ways of increasing your child's resilience to negative stress. In their discipline techniques, mentoring, and supervision of your child, these caregivers, whom I refer to as *parents-beyond-parents,* may well instinctively use their own abilities to "positively stress" your child and thereby combat negative stress in your child's life.

and religious processes, such as prayer and meditation. Because of the new sciences, we have learned that hidden in each of our children (and each of us) is a genetic potential for personal power and inner guidance. Study of such brain imaging as PET scans of the temporal lobe is showing us a seat of reverence, healthy group humility, and the search for God *deep within each person's core nature*. Not surprisingly, everyone's "map of the temporal lobe" is a little different, and thus so is every child's (and adult's) search for meaning and purpose in life.

You might think that the term *religious science* is an oxymoron, so perhaps you are surprised to see this area of brain science listed as one of the eight areas of very useful nature-based research. But even the renowned geneticist Francis S. Collins, an evangelical Christian, has shown in *The Language of God* that science and religion can work together. And even though in some areas our sciences and our religions will perhaps always be in some disagreement, information from neurochemical research on the role of religion and spirituality in a child's brain development is growing every day. From the University of San Diego to the University of London, researchers are using brain scan technology to help us better understand the power of religion and spirituality in our lives.

Information throughout Part Two will help you put on the neurological "glasses" neuropsychiatrists are now using to understand how children answer the question, "Who am I?" in their efforts to fulfill their spiritual yearnings. We have access now to research that aids in your discovery, with your child, of his or her possible purposes in life. Getting to know this material can be a great protector of your family as it inspires you to help your child choose productive spiritual pursuits, rites of passage, and, ultimately, paths of life success that have deep meaning for him or her.

For right now, lay a small foundation for later access of this material by asking your child to start a personal diary or journal (perhaps on MySpace) that talks about "big questions" and grapples with "Who am I?" Spend time with your child helping him or her begin expressing, writing, or even drawing answers to life questions. Begin a debate at the dinner table about the existence of God or other spiritual entity, about "what" or "who" you think God is.

Right now is a good moment to think about your own attitude toward religion and spirituality. Very interesting scientific-based research has shown that children who go through religious activities during childhood do better in life—less drug use, less early sex, fewer social and emotional problems. Religion is not a panacea, but spiritual development is a part of human nature. It is important right now that you ask yourself questions about how you want to be tuned into this area of your child's core nature.

Creating a Profile of Your Child's Core Nature

A mother of four wrote,

> I am a CEO of a biotech company. When I began looking at my children from the vantage point of the very science I work with, I saw different children than I had seen before. I saw how all four of my kids are individual personalities with individual talents. I saw how each of them needs different kinds of interventions. I let go of forcing my youngest daughter into my footsteps (something my father did with me). It took me about a year to really come to grips with who each of these kids were, but it has been the most liberating year of my life.

This mother is just one parent who changed her family life to suit her children's core natures. Let's work together now to do this with *your* child in mind. Having laid a scientific foundation for family life by getting to know how eight new sciences can show you your child's wonderful core nature, let's now move forward into more practical tools that can help you discover the core nature of your child without having brain scan or genome mapping technology in your own home. (Who does?!)

I've used these practical tools with families in my practice and workshops. I've also used them myself with my own children. I always remind participants (and myself) that the nurture-the-nature system is not just one technique or science: it is a worldview that utilizes science (and religion and social ideologies) but is not limited to any one field. Were it limited, it would risk becoming just another social trend. By putting science *into everyday practice* we constantly test it, and we get to know our children's core nature through means other than technological. There is nothing like paper-and-pencil tools.

First Tool: Genetic Personality Appraisal

Because a great deal of your child's personality is linked to his or her genes, one key question as you get to know your child's core personality is, "What parts of my child's genetic inheritance are most active in my growing child?" A Try This box earlier in this chapter got you started in answering this question. Now take it farther. As you use these tools, remember to adjust the appraisal tools for your child's age. (Some questions asked in these tools don't apply for babies, for instance.) You may well want to repeat the use of the tool every few years, as the expression of the child's genetic personality shifts in its emphases and shows new aspects you didn't see in earlier childhood.

Before you proceed any further, turn to Appendix B and look at the information about creating a genogram. If you do choose to begin one now, write in the names of ancestors as far back as you can go and that you have time for right now. Over the course of reading this book, keep filling in blanks in that family history. It will mean a great deal as you live the adventure of nurturing your child's core nature.

Looking through photographs is another way to explore your child's genetic legacy. As you notice that your child looks like Grandma or Great-Uncle Larry, you may recall also if he or she sings like her (or him) or chews with her mouth open or is very shy or is a good skier or has the same mood swings, the propensity to talk too much or too little. You are noticing here the influence of generation after generation of genes from the same pool, on each side of the family.

As you look through photographs from your child's photo book, note what personality traits you saw actively in the specific era of childhood itself. If, say, your child is ten, look back over her first ten years of life and make a note in your journal such as, "See how she's hiding behind my leg when we were at that party for her kindergarten." Near this note, write in your journal or just ponder what you remember her being like. Maybe she was very extraverted at that time, and her hiding behind your leg was an anomaly. Or maybe it was indicative of her shy personality. How did she tend to act with friends? Was she introverted or extraverted (or somewhere in between) in kindergarten? The idea here is not to label your child but rather to use pictures to help you take a deep look at your child's personality.

Perhaps answers to these sets of statements might help you corroborate in words what you recalled in pictures—a sense of your child's genetically inherited personality type. Select one element from each pair.

My child:

Seems comfortable around new people and in new places
Seems shy around new people and in new places

Eagerly joins into play with other children
Needs a lot of encouragement to join into play with other children

In the overall assessment of the years you've looked back on, what do you see? Ask your spouse, the child's grandparents, and others close to the child to tell you what they think about this. The Notes and References section of this book offers sources for the Myers-Briggs and Tieger work on this kind of personality assessment. The Myers-Briggs tool goes well beyond the "extravert-introvert question" into sensing, feeling, intuition, perceiving, and so on. You'll also find references to other tools and Web sites for understanding genetic personality markings.

Using the genogram, the references, and your journal, enjoy getting to know the inherent personality in your child! Take your time. Talk about the information, listen to your own instincts, and observe your child carefully; you are a "parent scientist." As you get to know your child, you will be able to care for his or her core nature, rather than imposing external and constantly shifting notions on this child. You'll be surprised at how well this works.

A mother of four told me at a workshop,

It has been such a joy for me as a parent to focus on each of my children's personalities from the genetic standpoint. Even my two adopted kids benefit from this focus. I don't have any records on the parentage of one of them, so I can't ask anyone about her exact grandparents, but the amazing thing for my husband and me has been that even with her, we can see her genetic personality coming through loud and clear. We just had to focus on it for a number of weeks of observation. We've taken her out of an activity we were forcing her into, dance—that didn't fit her core personality—and got her into rock climbing. It's a much better fit. It's like a passion for her, not something she hates going to.

A NOTE ON GENETICS RESEARCH   I've emphasized genetically inherited personality traits because the scientific mapping of the genome in the last few years is a profound moment in our civilization, and thus in family life. At the same time, we have to be careful. Although genetics research will figure in this book, I am not interested in, nor would I endorse, using genetics research to predetermine the kind of child I might want. As a Jew who lost most of his ancestry in the Holocaust, I have a healthy suspicion of eugenics or that kind of thinking. For me, the great benefit of innovation in genetics and all scientific research is that now we can bring this knowledge into the new science of child development to understand the human self from its individual, unique interior, rather than try to control it from the outside.

Second Tool: Trauma Assessment

If anything is going to derail your child's genetic personality development, it will be sustained trauma. Countless parents do not realize that their children have been traumatized—and have thus had the development of their core nature affected toward negative behaviors or dysfunction. In not being aware of childhood traumas—and the profound effect of these traumas on core personality development—we parents often spend difficult and relatively fruitless time in self-blame or blame of external factors that cannot help the child.

There are two major kinds of trauma that affect development of the core personality:

1. Brain injuries from accidents (for example, the head's hitting a hard surface)
2. Other environmental trauma, often sustained subtly over long periods (for example, bullying, physical or emotional abuse, the constant witnessing of violence, malnourishment, nutritional mismatch with the child's physical needs, media addictions, substance abuse, parent-child attachment difficulties, constant school or other social failure)

Trauma works on your child's brain to raise cortisol (stress hormone) to high levels for prolonged periods of time. This stress hormone washes through the brain, altering core-nature development of normal chemical flow (for example, adrenaline) and normal brain development (for example, links between emotion centers of the brain and thinking centers) in two ways:

1. Causing atrophy or truncated development of certain important areas of the brain—for instance, causing the prefrontal cortex, which helps with self-control, to work less than it should, thus losing in the brain some of the ability to decide against being impulsive or enraged or abusive.
2. Causing the full activation of genetic vulnerabilities inherent in the child's individual genome package. For instance, depression is carried genetically, but for many kids who now have the disorder, this genetic vulnerability would not have become such a powerful part of their brain functioning if they had not experienced a chemical trauma in utero; a toxin during the early years; a lack of attachment to necessary caregivers in the early developmental years; physical, emotional, or sexual abuse; a brain

injury; or another sustained social or family trauma. Without the trauma or traumas, the child might have exhibited some small traits, but not large ones.

A mother recently told me about her son who constantly had problems in school.

Until I got a brain scan, I thought I was doing something at home that was at fault for the problems he was having. When I got the scan, I saw right there what was going on in his brain. The doctor

---

Try This

To ascertain whether there has been significant trauma in your child's life, answer these questions:

- Was the pregnancy healthy and free of smoking, drinking, or substance abuse?
- Has my child hit his or her head in a significant way? Has he or she been hit in the head, or been hit many times by another person?
- Has my child experienced the loss of a parent, sibling, or close grandparent?
- Has my child ever been gravely ill or bedridden for a long period of time?
- Has my child been abused sexually?
- Did my child get enough holding, touch, caregiving, and talking to in the first three years of life?
- Has a divorce affected the developmental path of my child's personality?

If you have any questions about brain injuries or anomalies caused by trauma, you might look at the articles mentioned in the Notes and References section and decide if a brain scan is in order.

showed me a weird blank spot in the parietal lobe. He said this could have come from a brain injury during early childhood that we don't remember.

Seeing the actual problem in the brain really changed our lives, our expectations, how we helped him function, and how the school treated him. Our family and the school saw that he wasn't acting out because he was a bad kid, but because he couldn't learn in the way he was being taught. We got him tutoring at home, the school put him in an appropriate special education program, and we got the appropriate medication for him. We've also been exploring "brain development exercises" like brain gym. Our son is doing so much better now.

This boy may well have had a physical trauma whose residual effect is seen years later. Fetal Alcohol Syndrome, physical abuse, and other external and physiological stressors could similarly affect the brain; these traumas can show up on scans as areas of the brain that have atrophied or that are not working normally.

Third Tool: Gender Assessment

Your child's sex and gender really matter. Being a boy or a girl is a big part of what is hardwired into his or her brain. Although socialization certainly means a lot, and although there are exceptions to every gender trait we can look at in a few pages, you can ascertain many aspects of gender that are a part of your child's core nature. A man I was treating remembered playing dress-up with his sisters (he had five!) when he was between four and six, but he ended up a college football star and very "male" in his wife's (and his own) assessment. His being able to talk about this aspect of his childhood shows how these days we are more understanding and sympathetic toward a *wide spectrum* of gender identities and behaviors. Playing dress-up was a fun part of his imaginative life, but his core nature—in terms of gender—clearly came through in the very "male" guy I worked with.

Throughout the world, basic characteristics of male and female gender ultimately shine through to one degree or another, within a broad variety of possible expressions and within diverse cultural norms.

To help with a gender assessment of your child, here are some statements about your child that you might consider in your journal:

1. Seems to really care about winning
2. Likes to win, but seems to just enjoy playing

3. Reacts to the emotional moods of the children and adults in the environment
4. Doesn't seem to get caught up in the emotional environment around him or her

5. Seems most comfortable in an environment that provides consistent structure and limits
6. Seems comfortable with change and stays on track without lots of external structure

7. Reads, writes, and talks on the phone a lot in a given day
8. Does not read as much, write as much, or reach out to talk to others

If your child fits statements 1, 4, 5, and 8 (or two of those), and does so over the course of different ages of childhood, you probably are seeing some of the hardwired gender traits that lean toward the male end of the biological and brain spectrum (higher testosterone, fewer emotive centers in the brain, less access to words in the frontal lobe). Some girls can lean this way too, especially at certain times of life. And, of course, other personality factors can be involved here. But in general, many traits that can be characterized as "male" and "female" are wired into the brain.

In girls' brains, there is more wiring for what are called verbal-emotive responses to stimulation; boys' brains have more wiring for what are called spatial-mechanical responses. Thus girls tend to use more words and attach more emotions to words and objects around them (play more house, hospital, animal care clinic), and boys tend to treat things and even themselves as objects to move around, take apart and put together again, or compete over.

You'll also tend to notice that girls like to do a number of strands of tasks—multitasking—and boys tend toward one thing at a time. Girls tend to sit still longer than boys. Boys tend to be more physically aggressive than girls. Girls tend to run emotional slights in their mind longer than boys do.

Throughout Part Two of this book, you'll see boxes that describe developmental differences between boys and girls from birth to twenty-five years old. These differences affect not only the core-nature development of boys and girls but also marriage and parenting styles among adults. Spending a little time right now thinking about and looking at these hardwired gender differences in your children can add yet another tool to your parenting toolbox. If you haven't already, go to the Notes and References section and just check out one of the publications or Web sites listed. I promise you it will be an eye-opening experience, no matter what sex your child is.

Fourth Tool: Attachment and Emotional Style Assessment

Each child is genetically inclined to experience, process, and express emotional activity in his or her own way. All of us project onto our kids certain ways we'd like them to be emotionally, and there certainly can be benefit in doing this, for we help expand their emotional abilities—their emotional literacy—but we often know instinctively when our kids are resisting our projections or trying to please us and losing themselves.

To begin looking at your child's core emotional nature, take a moment to consider the following statements.

My child:

Tends to talk a lot about feelings
Tends to process feelings silently

Processes certain feelings with Mom, certain ones with Dad, certain ones with peers
Mainly processes feelings with one person

Needs exercise or quick physical bursts to process feelings, then the feeling is over

Stays with the feeling a long time, sometimes days, even when it's a "small" thing

Reads other people's feelings well and reflects them back accurately

Is confused by other people's feelings

Innately has a positive attitude

Is very self-critical and sees disasters and catastrophes where they may not be

None of these emotional states of experience, processing, and expression are good or bad, right or wrong—they are simply different ways in which a person's core emotional nature shows through. Studies of twins and other children, such as the work done by researcher J. Philippe Rushton at the University of Western Ontario, have shown how our children bring with them genetic and inherited emotional styles.

Twin studies show how twins—who carry the same genetic coding—can be separated at birth and sent to live with families that raise them in very different ways emotionally, yet turn out very similar in their ways of processing and expressing their emotions.

Rushton summarized how hardwired so much of our child's emotive style is by pointing out that children would remain the same despite the loss of many social or environmental factors (though they would certainly be affected by them).

Calling this unique emotional core nature the child's "social glue," he says, "Even if educational systems, families, and preaching all stopped tomorrow, children would still grow up with 'social glue.'" A child's emotional system is the glue that holds him or her to the world, and much of its emotive style is inborn.

Take time now to get to know your child's emotional nature even better by looking at your genogram (if you've created one) and noting which parts of your child's emotional and relational style are like those of which family members. This can take a few hours and will benefit from discussion in the family.

Perhaps Grandpa (or Grandma) was closemouthed when it came to talking about feelings. Does your son (or daughter) handle feelings somewhat like this relative?

Perhaps your daughter feels an amazing affinity for the person or life of Aunt Lily. Does that affinity come, in some part, because there is an "emotional comfort" between these family members—that is, does your daughter experience and "feel" things like Aunt Lily?

Perhaps your son has always been attracted to a certain time in Uncle Frank's life, wanting to hear stories about it—maybe Uncle Frank's time living in Japan and studying Eastern religions. Is your son's flight toward Uncle Frank's world in part a flight toward a kind of theology or personality that feels emotionally comfortable for him?

There are countless ways your ancestry is living emotionally in your children, and each of these helps you get to know your child's emotional nature.

As you go through the process of answering questions, looking at the genogram's emotional treasures, and intuitively assessing your child's emotional nature, you may find that you do not need to *mold* your child's emotional responses as much as you once thought, or as much as you were told to in the social trends parenting system. Much of your child's core nature will learn its lessons as needed, within the various safe emotional environments you help create for the child.

It is key to remember that as parents we were not given children in order to change them emotionally, but rather to experience the "Ahas" of realizing who the child is and then what is *essential* in helping the child's core nature develop its own emotional framework and possibility. We are our children's primary influences, but we are not them. In this light, you may look deeply into your child's eyes and see that perhaps she does not need to talk about feelings as much as you once thought. Or you may find that he needs to access feelings in more various ways than he is using now. Generally you will need to intervene in emotional core-nature development not in a hundred ways but only in one or two.

A magical thing happens once you get to know your child's core emotional nature: you immediately and intuitively know how to encourage his or her unique emotional life. Learning how *your child* "does emotions" and encouraging that natural way of emoting is natural to family life.

It is worth noting that social trends thinking has become "target" thinking when it comes to kids' emotions. Social trends theories make us worry about specific emotional patterns in children, and target those for change: boys should cry, we are told, or shouldn't cry; girls mustn't ever have low self-esteem; boys must talk about their feelings to be whole. In contrast to this target thinking, children's natural development is inborn, and its flourishing depends on the patience and wisdom of the various caregivers who understand the child.

Fifth Tool: Hormone Assessment

Deborah Sichel, a physician who specializes in female hormonal development, has shown in studies of thousands of girls and women that hormonal biology is "the cornerstone of emotional health." Her book, *Women's Moods* (coauthored by Jeanne Watson Driscoll), greatly influenced my own book *The Wonder of Girls*. It is a great read for girls and women and for the men who love them. It helps everyone understand how women feel, from a biological viewpoint. Louann Brizendine, a neuropsychiatrist at the University of California, San Francisco, has recently published another very strong book, *The Female Brain*—it is a must-read if you have daughters.

The need to understand how hormonal biology affects health and emotions is not by any means just about girls and women. Jed Diamond, a family therapist who specializes in male hormonal development, has conducted research in both the United States and Scandinavia and shown the importance of hormones in mood and emotional development of boys and men. Although male hormonal biology is not as complex as female, it is one of the most powerful determinants of behavior and mood—a crucial part of core nature—during two specific periods, adolescence and midlife. Diamond's book *The*

Irritable Male Syndrome, is a powerful assessment of what happens to men when their hormones get off balance.

If you have a child of nine or older, you might want right now to make sure you've asked your physician for advice concerning hormone levels and hormone balances. Much of the flow and experience of these are a part of your child's core nature, especially as that nature is affected by the foods the child eats and other developmental factors that have immediate implications on hormonal flow.

Our society is so focused on social trends in the way it looks at childhood and adolescent mood that it neglects the chemistry of core nature. Some of that chemistry cannot be discovered except through simple and intermittent blood tests. This was the key for Alicia, in our story at the beginning of the chapter. It was also the key for another family, the McCrarys.

The McCrarys had three girls, two of whom were having difficulty with focus in school, depression, and rage behavior. Ultimately it was discovered that these two sisters suffered from irregularities in their progesterone and estrogen balance once puberty started. In fact, when the family and professionals looked at this, they discovered that a grandmother and aunt had suffered in the same way, but for much longer in life, the grandmother having been committed to a mental hospital and later committing suicide. Fortunately, this family was able help the girls through the use of estrogen and progesterone patches so that they could live normal lives.

If in looking back at your ancestry and at the timing of when your child's mood swings began you find a possible link to hormones, ask your pediatrician to facilitate a simple hormone blood test. Consult an endocrinologist or neuropsychiatrist who specializes in the hormone biology of boys or girls.

Sixth Tool: Strengths and Vulnerabilities Assessment

Now that you've taken steps to look into the core nature of your child, it's time to ascertain some of the inherent strengths and vulnerabilities in your child's core nature as that child lives, loves, works, and succeeds in his or her world. Take a moment to decide which of these statements fit your child.

My child:

Often chooses active play—art activities, make-believe
Often chooses passive play—TV, video games

Enjoys reading and can sit quietly for extended periods to do so
Needs some activity or movement while reading or listening to words

Seems to have favorite activities and returns to them often
Seems to like change, trying new activities all the time

Seems to have a vivid imagination and likes telling stories
Seems in live in the present, real world much of the time

Seems to focus on completing a task before moving on to something new
Seems to enjoy being in the middle of a variety of tasks

What would make each of these into strengths or vulnerabilities? Your daughter or son might go through a phase of passive play, especially during a time of rapid changes in brain development, but then move more toward an active life and stay active for years. Or your son might go through a phase of liking to sit and read, but then start needing more physical movement as puberty takes over his life, and his testosterone affects him. Under these circumstances, core nature is doing its magic—experimenting, trying on new ways of being, gaining gifts from each. All these might be strengths *or* vulnerabilities for a period of time. Should they worry you as a parent?

Generally not. But these behaviors do become vulnerabilities to worry about if they directly impede life success. If your child's grades suddenly drop, or if your child stops doing important athletics or becomes depressed, then there might be symptoms and even triggers in the behaviors you just analyzed. Now you are called on to see if the problem is in the child or in the social system (school, community, family) within which his or her core nature is growing. If your child is right now struggling in any of these ways, take a moment before going on to decide on one or more of the behaviors for deeper investigation. Make a note of what part the social system might play in these.

Share your assessments with others whom you trust. They may say, "Wait a minute—what you see as a vulnerability, I see as a strength."

This kind of exploration can lead to wonderful discussions and bonding in a family and community. If your child is able to understand, show these tools to him or her and engage in discussion. This is especially useful for adolescents.

A mom wrote to me, "I thought it was a weakness that my adolescent boy didn't show much emotion, but when I asked him about it he just gave me a hug and sighed, 'Oh Mom.' I said, 'What?' He smiled. 'I'm not like you,' he said. 'But I'm okay. Really.' He does well in life, so I guess he was right."

My own daughter Davita gravitates toward drawing pictures—more and more complex as she gets older. When she has free time, she doesn't pick up a book to read; she goes to her "art place" in her room and makes graphic art. This is her core nature, a clear asset; it's who she is. At the same time, when Gail and I as parents gauge possible vulnerability, we look at the school system and how reading oriented it is—how much less graphic. Seeing her strength as also her vulnerability in society, Gail and I make sure to help Davita concentrate on balancing art time with reading time so that she fulfills her assignments. At the same time, because we understand her graphic artistry to be core nature, we don't worry that she will somehow fail in life because she is not the best reader. We know she has her own innate talents well in hand.

Your Essential Parenting Blueprint

The tools you've employed in this chapter have joined your parental toolbox. I hope this helps you sense your child's core nature. I hope that out of this sense will come the foundation for your essential parenting blueprint. Already you might want to do some things differently than you once did.

• You can now change your expectations regarding your child's behavior. You can look differently at expectations you've had for your particular child that came from "outside" and are unreasonable.

Perhaps you've blamed yourself for certain "deficits" you've seen in your child. Now you know that these are not deficits or that you are not to blame, or you understand that if they are deficits, they need a different kind of attention than has been given up to now.

• You can alter the way you and others provide love to this child. The attachment, bonding, and supervision roles of mother, father, extended family, friends, and peers can now clarify themselves.

• You can see the search for meaning, purpose, mission, and morality in which your child's core nature is engaged in the world. (We will discuss this further in Part Two.)

• You can reach a greater sense of personal security and confidence as a parent, and thus can enhance your sense of humor.

Now that you know your child's core nature—its shiftings, plasticity, adaptability—you can supervise, guide, direct; you can back away, let go. You now can have the confidence to say, "This is my son, this is my daughter, warts and all, and I know how to help answer his or her question, 'Who am I?' "

"Who Am I?"

An eighth-grade girl handed me a funny, very useful story when I was working in her school. She said it came off the Internet—a supposed argument via radio communication. I have shared it with many parents and professionals as a deep metaphor for looking at children's core nature.

U.S. SHIP:	To avoid collision, suggest you turn 15 degrees to the south.
CANADIAN REPLY:	Suggest *you* turn 15 degrees to the south.
U.S. SHIP:	This is a U.S. Navy ship. *You* turn 15 degrees to the south.
CANADIAN REPLY:	Understood. However, still suggest you turn to avoid collision.
U.S. SHIP:	This is the *U.S.S. Coral Sea.* We are a large aircraft of the U.S. Navy. Turn 15 degrees right now!
CANADIAN REPLY:	This is a lighthouse. It's your call.

Of course, the particular countries in this story can be changed. To me, what is important is the metaphor of the lighthouse—a wonderful metaphor for human nature. Think about it for a second.

The lighthouse is just *there*—much less movable than the ship. Like human nature, the lighthouse will be in that spot much longer than the ship; the ship is more like our social trends: ever moving, ever altering course depending on the wind or new stimulation. Both the ship and the lighthouse are necessary for the world to exist, to be safe, to be productive, but when the ship thinks of itself as all-powerful, human nature must always remind us that the safe light in the night seas comes from the lighthouse.

After a workshop in which I shared this lighthouse story, Amy, a mother from Virginia, wrote this of her son. His story is a wonderful example of the core nature, the light, of a child shining through—and everything that caring for it entails. Let me end the chapter with this wonderful story, and I hope you'll enjoy, too, the wisdom-of-practice story provided by my friend Dr. Judith Kleinfeld of the University of Alaska that follows it.

I am a mother of a thirteen-year-old, Tim. Since he was born he's constantly been building "stuff" (Legos, working on antique tractors, motors, electronics) or reading manuals related to this stuff. He loves these mechanical activities and views them as a "job." He scores in the 90+ percentile on the standardized tests at school, gets invited to those "Who's who" and Johns Hopkins seminars for kids, is very smart in a school way, *but* he was flunking homework! When we would get a progress report, it showed fifteen items of homework outstanding. It would usually take less than an hour for him to complete the entire list! But he was so bored he just wouldn't do it. So he was constantly on the brink of getting an F.

With a great deal of anger, punishment, suspension of specific activities, and even some pretty big carrots, he was able to step back from the precipice and pass the course. To illustrate who this boy is: I made him walk two miles for not turning in homework (we call this "walk detention"), and when he reached the end he let me know exactly how long to the fraction of a second the trek took! The trek seemed to become a challenge! If that isn't part of Tim's lighthouse, I don't know what is.

This kid is just built the way he's built—he's so *himself.* What we had to understand as a family was that the school is just not set up for his nature. We also noticed that he generally relates better to men, particularly those with strong mechanical skills, and to learning through doing things and building—not, obviously, through doing the paperwork and busy work of homework.

So what we did to keep our sanity—and to adapt to the system and save him from sabotaging his chances for higher education—was to bring our whole family together to help our son follow his passions for gadgets and motors. We live near farms, so we have access to facilities for him to take advantage of his interests. Now we say to Tim, "If you do your hour of homework, you can then go the farm, and help Nate with the tractor." This is helping a lot, actually, because now he does his hour of homework, then gets to do everything else he wants to do. And my husband is becoming more generous with his time and getting some friends to do the same. It was the best we could do to build a new parenting system that keeps him enough in the loop in school and yet lets him be himself.

Wisdom of Practice

MY DAUGHTER RACHEL HAD FROM BIRTH AN UNUSUAL TEMPERAMENT. She didn't like to cuddle. She refused to nurse, insisted on drinking milk from a cup at eight months, and would not wear dresses. She was intense and focused. When her grandma sent her dolls for her birthday, she told her father and me if her grandma liked dolls so much she would send Grandma her entire doll collection.

Rachel was passionate about taxonomy. She loved to classify and organize everything. At six years of age, she labeled all her dresser drawers, with the one at the bottom called "sets that do not match." Meanwhile, her abilities in mathematics made me think I had a Future Female Scientist in my family. She participated in Math Counts, and we got her a special tutor. We got her a summer job working with a female scientist at the University of Alaska, counting organisms in water from the Bering Sea under a high-powered electron microscope.

Then, suddenly, when Rachel was a sophomore, she said to us, "I am not a guinea pig for your project to advance women in science. I want to help people. I do not think counting organisms in Bering Sea water is important to humanity." She was fierce! And we, her parents, got it!

So we backed off. We (and she herself) found others to mentor her in her own passion. A few years later, she became a Rhodes Scholar. She is now completing her dissertation on rule of law at Oxford—developing a taxonomy of rule of law projects! How human nature shines through!

I've learned a lot from Rachel. With her nature, the key was to read the signals as she grew and evolved. With all three of my kids I also learned that unless they have a lot of free time, it's hard to see who they actually are. My husband and I have encouraged each child to define and follow his or her own paths.

All three of my kids are grown now, and I guess most of all I've learned to let them bloom. You may not get the flower you expected, but it will be beautiful.

Nurturing the Nature of Your Child

"There are some things that are universal and basic to all children. Then there is a particular child's own nature—boy, girl, introvert, extravert, tall, short. Meeting the needs of both universal human nature and an individual child's version of nature . . . this is a wonderful juggling act. Succeeding at it through the stages of childhood has to be one of the most satisfying jobs on earth."

—KATHY STEVENS, MOTHER OF TWO BOYS,
GRANDMOTHER OF TWO GIRLS AND A BOY

3

Nurturing the Nature
of Your Infant

The whole world has changed around us in terms of workforce requirements, mothers and fathers in the workforce, divorce, and family makeup. The whole sort of social and economic fabric has changed dramatically . . . but the needs of babies haven't.

—MATTHEW MELMED, EXECUTIVE DIRECTOR OF ZERO TO THREE

AS GAIL'S PREGNANCY WITH OUR FIRST CHILD, GABRIELLE, MOVED toward full term, I often thought I heard our child whispering to me from inside Gail. "Daddy, are you ready?" "Daddy, I'm coming." "Daddy, I need you." This mysterious experience increased my devotion to our unborn child and to Gail. As the months passed, Gail had a difficult time, and I supported her—cleaned up after morning sickness, took on greater workloads, learned new lessons in compassion. I also began to write my first book about parents and children. The whispers of my unborn child inspired me to engage more deeply in the world—to get out of myself, to be useful. When Gabrielle was born, and I held and cared for her, I was a changed person, a person filled with love and hope. As Gail and I cared for our first infant, Gabrielle, and then later, Davita, I felt strongly that it is our children who compel us most of all to a powerful destiny. They have made me want to be a more creative, productive, and helpful person. Our children's infancies give parents our universal and essential purpose in life.

Preview of Essential Developmental Tasks

As a guidepost in every chapter of Parts Two and Three, we'll consider three universal developmental tasks that are essential to the core-nature development of all children in the stage of life featured in the chapter. Each chapter will then go on to provide scientific information and techniques based on research, insight, and anecdotes that will help you take the essential tasks into your care of *your* particular child. In this way, I hope to provide you with both the necessary background and foreground for child care—the essentials of human nature in general that must never be forgotten—and the particulars of individual children that must always be factored in if we are to accomplish the great task of nurturing the nature of each of our children.

For this chapter on infancy, I hope you'll always keep in mind these necessities:

- *Know your child.* Begin a lifetime of parenting by paying attention to your instincts regarding the lighthouse: who your child *is.* In every stage of your child's life, beginning even before birth, you can see traits of his or her core nature, temperament, personality, hopes and dreams. As you care for this infant, celebrate every moment of "Aha" as you tune into the light *this child* is already making in the world.

- *Let your child know you.* Getting to know your child's core nature is the natural result of bonding and attachment. Be there with lots of touching, stroking, cuddling, soothing, singing, smiling, kissing. Bonding and attachment not only will develop your child's brain but also will develop in you a new self, the self of "parent" that has been waiting in you to come fully alive all these years.

- *Protect your child.* Begin a lifelong journey of protecting this child from environmental toxins and distracting social trends. Be a revolutionary parent, open to new information about child safety and healthy development, but also a parent who says, "No information or activity will enter my family's life without my deciding that this is right for *my child.*"

These, then, are three essential tasks I hope you'll keep in mind as you begin parenting your newborn infant. Everything you learn in this chapter will help you flesh out these essentials, beginning with some detailed scientific information about that infant you are holding in your arms.

Information Essential to Nurturing the Core Nature of Your Infant

As the Gurian Institute team and I gathered nature-based information to give you regarding your child, beginning with infancy, we realized just how much good information there is! As professionals and parents, therefore, we've made the decision to choose seven essential pieces of information about brain and body development in each chapter, for each stage of life. We've chosen information essential both to understanding the core nature of your specific child and to gradually deepening your sense of that child's particular needs. Following are the seven points for this stage of your child's life.

1. In getting to know the unique and wonderful core nature of your infant, remember that this baby comes into the world with nearly all of its brain cells, but many of these cells are inactive, unless the child gets your love and attention, your bonding and attachment. The way you care for your baby activates connections (synapses) between the cells. These synapses "glue" the cells together, make them sing together. Your child is not a blank slate—his or her brain cells for temperament and

personality, for instance, are already in place; his or her genetic legacy and inherited potential are already in existence—but it's by your hugging, holding, and talking to this child and caring for this child that you'll be helping him or her activate this personality, legacy, and potential. I think it is liberating to understand that the child's natural assets are already inside that child, in the inborn brain cells; it is liberating to know that if you and others provide essential bonding and developmental help to this child, he or she will take care of growing up—or, as psychologist Leslie Cohen, an infant development specialist, recently put it, "Babies are natural learners. Let them be your guide." This statement holds the wonderful and even revolutionary sense of liberation we can have as parents who bond so well with our children that we can read their cellular signals. We don't necessarily need external and constantly fluid social voices to tell us how to bond with "a child." It is when we are fully bonded with *our* child that we can read the map the child has been born with and follow it to the child's fruition.

2. New scientific research shows that in its natural development, your baby's brain will so enjoy growing and being cared for by you that it will grow more synapses than it needs! The child will then prune the excess cells. Your child's mind, heart, body, and soul will explore, feel, love, and be loved, and in all this *make internally important decisions* about what is useful to his or her core nature and what is not. As this little brain prunes away synapses it does not need, it will be whispering to you, "Thank you so much for exposing me to this stimulant or that stimulant, and I will keep this one but not that one. Please let that be okay with you. I am finding myself in my own way."

I love knowing this about the brain because what comes with knowing it for me as a parent is the idea that as you and I love our children, our children's brains make the choices *they* need to make, according to *their* own nature. This pruning is a natural and inherent independence toward which the child is always moving—the "I am who I am" that will take this child into and through a healthy adulthood.

3. The brain sciences now show us that attachment and bonding are not just "important," but as essential as food, shelter, and clothing. Lack of attachment and bonding will mean fewer synapses in certain

key areas of this baby's brain, such as the frontal and prefrontal cortices—parts of the brain that later will control behavior, ability to learn, aggressiveness, emotional literacy, and social success. An infant can't get too much love, but he or she *can* get too little love. Each child who suffers from too little love during infancy will later manifest the consequences in his or her own sad or angry or lonely ways.

4. Emotional literacy and a child's particular emotional style show up early. Crying is an example. Have you noticed that some babies cry more than others? Some babies cry for longer periods of time and more intensely than others. Some babies hardly cry at all. Each baby has his or her own "crying signature"—evidence of core nature showing through early. A child's wails (especially a colicky child's) can scare us, irritate us, even bring out in us parts of ourselves we wish were not there. At the same time, your baby's crying signature is his or her natural call for help. It is your baby's way of keeping you empathic, attentive, attached. It is your baby's way of shutting out sensations that are becoming too stressful or intense.

Through your attentiveness and love, you will experience the wonder of learning the subtle signals of *your* baby's fussing—which crying signal is your baby's core nature saying "I in particular need food at this time," "I in particular find that kind of contact overstimulating," "Maybe another baby would not be scared of that toy bear, but I am," or "My core nature needs to de-stress by crying loudly now."

5. Just after birth, your baby will usually sleep around sixteen hours a day. There is of course variety in infants in this regard. Each individual child will have his or her own particular sleep needs within the general need for long hours. These long hours will divide eventually into naps of about three to four hours, and may often follow feedings. This schedule will shift to fit *your* baby's core nature needs over the course of the next months and then years.

The latest hyperdrive social trends parenting styles may not necessarily value your particular child's getting as much sleep as he or she needs—there is a lot of stimulation out there that takes all of us (adults included) away from the sleep our particular mind needs. That's why it's so important to be cognizant of *your* baby's sleep needs. If your baby doesn't get the appropriate amount of sleep, attachment and bonding may not be enough to protect his or her brain as it builds necessary synapses. Later in life, healthy sleep patterns will be crucial to the child and adolescent too.

6. What your baby eats really does matter to his or her particular body, heart, mind, and soul. It is quite normal for some infants not to eat as much as others. Each core nature brings its own genetically determined metabolism. If your child is resisting feeding or is not feeding on a regular schedule, ask your physician about this, and ask others who have raised kids.

Your child's infancy is a crucial time for setting good eating habits for a lifetime. Here's just one example of why. In providing information on breast-feeding of infants, Dr. Ruth Lawrence, vice president of the U.S. Breastfeeding Committee, recently reported this fact: mothers who continue to breast-feed when they return to work (through pumps or on-site feeding) have a better attendance record at work than mothers who don't. Why? Because their babies get the colostrum (an immune system asset) and other natural chemicals in breast milk that lead to fewer illnesses in the babies; the moms, in turn, need not take as much time off work as moms whose kids don't breast-feed. Admittedly, there can be many reasons for a child's illness, but what is telling here is the idea we probably all have instinctually known: *nature matters!* There are certainly times when nonbreast milk is appropriate during infancy, but the social trend of a few years ago that told us that artificial milk is as good as breast milk was not based in natural science, and we now have, fortunately, universal information about breast milk that can help each of our particular children be healthy.

7. Protect your infant from visual toxins. I feature this seventh essential element of infant care in the Did You Know? box to highlight it more fully. Our social trends system has thrown a great deal of visual stimulation at us over the last few decades. Is it healthy for your infant's developing core nature? Will it lead to or impede the synapses development *your child* is trying to accomplish in life? Answering this question for life is of major significance to the brain and begins during your child's infancy.

Did You Know?

In the first year of life, your baby's brain grows its particular set of necessary connections through *reciprocal relationship*. In other words, synapses grow through *interaction with living things or objects animated by the environment*. Your child has a natural need to touch and be touched, listen and be listened to, smell, taste (put things in the mouth), see and be seen. Television, videos, and other screen stimulants can derail this brain development—they are not natural! The American Medical Association and every other medical association that has studied this issue are adamant that before a baby is two years old, the safest care of his or her brain is to *avoid screen time*. Every few years, new videos and TV programs come out for infants. Two of the most famous are the Baby Einstein and Brainy Baby videos. You must decide whether these are social trends parenting products that can harm your child. (See the Notes and References section for more information.) Unless you can prove to yourself scientifically that a baby video is good for your child, be wary of it. Scientific proof, of course, must come independent of the company that manufactures the product.

Making sure to care about the issue right now, while your baby is an infant, sets you up to care about it during childhood and adolescence too, when your child's core nature will still need you to be the authority on screen time.

I've chosen to highlight these seven essential elements of knowing and caring for the unique core nature of your infant for two reasons: not only because they lead to greater love and care in general but also because each one acts as a subtle signal of your child's core nature, directing you (and the community around you) to set a foundation for the future of your particular child's development. If you can move through this infancy stage—this sleepless, busy, confusing, hopeful, and adoring time—with these essential elements in mind, you'll not only be promoting your child's health but also helping the genetic legacy, the personality and temperament, of your particular child feel most alive in this wonderful world.

And as you are facilitating this wonder, you'll notice quite quickly that you don't just have "a child" in your arms but a *boy* or a *girl*. This gender identification brings with it a whole other set of essential aspects of your particular child's core nature.

Natural Differences Between Infant Boys and Girls

Even while still carrying their child in utero, moms have said to me, "I know it's a girl; I can just tell," or "I know it's a boy; watch how he moves around." Thus, even during pregnancy, human beings can sense how natural it is that boys and girls are somewhat different from each other. In sensing this, we are also sensing what will turn out to be a great asset of a particular child's core nature—the degree of male or female characteristics.

As I explore scientific information about boys and girls of all ages with you throughout this book, I want to start out by saying that of course we all know that not all boys are one way and all girls another. Any scientific generalizations are just that—generalizations made knowing that boys and girls can enjoy a variety of characteristics and choose any career they wish. "Gender roles" are not what we're talking about when we sense our fetus's or infant's gender differences. What we're talking about here is that the core nature of a boy and the core nature of a girl develop differently. Their synapses, the various parts of their brains, the progression of their hormonal development—all exist and proceed differently. It's important and indeed quite liberating for both parents and children when we respect this gender difference in our parenting from early on. We must set a foundation for both the boy and girl by noticing our children's male and female "light."

Did You Know?

Here are some fascinating prebirth and early-life differences between boys and girls:

- The X and Y chromosomes hardwire gender into your child's brain.
- The chromosomal signals stimulate your fetal boy or girl to develop a male or female brain through hormonal surges in utero.
- There is certainly immense variety among "male" and "female" brains (stereotyping all girls one way and all boys another is a social trend—not a science), and there are exceptions to every rule regarding gender; however, as of 2005, scientists have identified more than one hundred structural differences between the brains of girls and boys. These are not stereotypes; they are aspects of human nature.
- By a few days old, boys look their caregivers in the eye for shorter periods of time than girls. This difference lasts throughout life. Girls and women hold eye contact longer than boys and men.
- From a few days old, girls generally hear better than boys. This difference lasts throughout life, with most women hearing better than men all the way through old age.
- From early on, boys tend to fidget more than girls, whether in the parent's arms or, later in infancy and childhood, in the stroller or in the classroom chair. Moving less serotonin through the frontal lobe, boys and men tend to be more fidgety all the way through life.
- From birth, girls may have more P cells and boys more M cells. These cells relate to our ability to see. P cells are particularly linked to seeing color, M cells to seeing objects move around in an environment. Beginning in the first few days of life and continuing throughout, most girls will process more colors, and most boys will process more physical movement.

In the next six chapters of this book, we'll discuss the newest scientific research into differences between girls and boys. As your child grows, you'll be able to care for his or her particular nature by having scientific information regarding "boyness" and "girlness" in your parenting toolbox. This knowledge can help you resist any social trends theories that say your girl or boy must be a certain way. You can set up a life in which being a boy or girl is the basis of success. As you navigate school, home, media, peer groups, shopping, fighting, emotions, work, and play with your daughters or sons, you will be better able to protect them (and help them protect themselves) by constantly looking in their eyes and saying, "What does *this girl* need? What does *this boy* need?" Often, the boy or girl will need resources and assets that are boy-friendly or girl-friendly, and in helping provide those resources, you will feel the joy of caring for not only a child's heart and soul but a boy's or girl's.

A Revolution in Parenting

The issue of gender is just one of the "politically charged" issues you will be faced with and perhaps even come to enjoy as you hold your infant in your arms. I have found over the last decades that for many people the gender of the child—and caring for a girl's or boy's natural needs—becomes revolutionary to discuss and to fulfill. Gender differences wired into the brains of infants are just one of a number of complex but crucial themes I will look at with you as you get to know and nurture the nature of your beautiful child over the next seven chapters.

Here are three revolutionary themes we must look at when our kids are infants:

1. The wonderful assets of both Mom and Dad
2. The wonderful assets of parents-beyond-parents
3. Protecting mother-infant attachment

These essential themes are crucial not only to helping you with a developmental element of your child's core nature but also to protecting your child from chronic stress throughout life.

Essential Mothers, Essential Fathers

Gail once said to me, "Mike, you are a good father, but not a very good mother." She was not insulting me; she was talking about *gender typology* in parenting: one of the key elements of the natural diversity in parenting systems that we must, as individual families, protect from the day a child is born if we are to fully nurture the nature of the child. She was saying that men and women bring complementary gifts to their marriage. Although fathers and mothers can cross over into the other's way of seeing the world, living, and parenting, the social trends theory that fathers and mothers are interchangeable is not based in natural fact. The latest research has shown us the unique and separate gifts mothers and fathers naturally bring to parenting. As you come to understand those gifts, you will see even more clearly why your kids need them both for core-nature development.

For example, a fascinating study of parents' neural responses, reported in the *Journal of Marriage and Family,* provides a starting point for understanding the nature of our complementary male and female gifts. It showed that fathers of boys feel less neural stress in their relationships with sons than do fathers of girls. Mothers of girls also feel less neural stress in their relationships with daughters than do mothers of boys. Obviously, fathers and daughters experience great joy together, and there is certainly tension between fathers and sons—similarly, mothers and sons and mothers and daughters—but the study is using stress hormone and neural stress indicators to show a gender typology inherent in human growth and development. This is not gender stereotyping—it is typology. There's a big difference. Stereotyping is the product of social trends analysis of what a specific group of people assume that male and female "should be." Gender typology is the scientific study of who males and females actually are, with all variety and diversity assumed and noted.

A number of very powerful studies on maternal and paternal assets have come out over the last decade. I highly recommend the work of anthropologists Susan Hrdy and Helen Fisher, who published two seminal books, *Mother Nature* and *Anatomy of Love.* Psychologist Shelley

Taylor followed in 2002 with a very powerful book, *The Tending Instinct*. We are able to explore the gender typology of mothers' and fathers' assets because of the work of these and other scientists. We can also be guided by brain research regarding the differences between men and women, and by observed real-world applications in families. Many of these observations come from the Gurian Institute's wisdom-of-practice research, conducted over the last ten years, on parents' gender-based assets.

As past and present research comes together, I hope you'll see meaning and usefulness in the model of *symmetrical parenting* that my colleagues and I teach. You have the power, of course, to decide the extent to which specific maternal and paternal assets fit *your* family, *your* child's core-nature needs and development.

One thing that might immediately stand out to you as you ponder the gifts that parents naturally bring to their child raising is the incompleteness of one set of gifts without the other. There is no perfect world, but as brain development specialist Pat Crum has put it, "Children flourish best when they get the best of both worlds during the span of childhood."

Symmetrical Parenting

When you put this information about mothers and fathers together with insights you've gained through the assessment tools in Chapter Two regarding your child's core nature, you have proof of how essential *both* mothers and fathers are, and how important it is that parents provide the key elements of maternal and paternal nurturance *in balance*. It is this balance of the elements that I call *symmetrical parenting*. Neither parent needs to possess all the gifts of maternal or paternal parenting styles; rather, the child naturally needs *both* maternal and paternal parenting assets (even if he or she must receive them from other caregivers); furthermore, the child is most assisted in core-nature development when these assets are provided in symmetry and coordination, not in parental competition.

Did You Know?

A mother tends to

- Bond with children in *long bursts* of connection, both physical and emotional (lots of hugs, touching, talking).
- Provide constant *hands-on* and *needs-based attachment* to the newborn and young child.
- Emphasize complex and multitasking development of *sensory enjoyment* in the growing child.
- Work constantly and intimately toward helping a child express his or her emotions in *words*. (Some dads talk a lot with children about intimate things, but generally moms do more of this in every country of the world.)
- Teach *direct empathy* when someone is hurt, even at the expense of other goals, games, tasks, or work. (Moms are more likely than dads to encourage the child to immediately see and try to alleviate the "hurt" in what happened.)
- *Relinquish personal, daily independence* in order to care for children's various needs. (Moms multitask in complex ways, which include altering their schedules and diverting minute-by-minute concentration in order to address the child's immediate needs.)
- See the child as an *emotional extension of herself,* and thus is unlikely to distance herself emotionally from the child when the child does wrong.
- Promote the child's development of skills and talents through an emphasis on *verbal encouragement.* (Moms themselves tend to like and need a lot of verbal encouragement, and they tend to give as much of it as they can.)
- Try to help the child quickly resolve inner emotional conflicts and stresses so that the whole bonding system can *feel better.* The child's immediate sense of distress or anxiety triggers the release of chemicals, especially oxytocin, in the mom, which directs her to try to relieve these symptoms as quickly as possible.

Did You Know?

A father tends to

- Bond with children in *short bursts* of connection, both physical and emotional ("short-touch" bonding, rough-and-tumble play).
- Focus on teaching children *order, pattern thinking,* and *ritualized action.* (Dads will tend to care less about the minutia of the child's needs, but care more about larger structures and tools the child might need for future survival.)
- *Downplay emotion,* even at the risk of hurt feelings, in order to *"up-play" performance.* (Males are chemically and neurally directed toward immediate rewards from performance, and they prod children in this direction.)
- Promote *risk taking and independence* in the growing child. (Many moms promote independence, but in general, dads push children toward separation from caregivers and encourage them to "grow up!" faster than moms do.)
- Expect and enforce discipline and *provide contests and tests of skill.* (Dads tend to be more competitive than moms, especially in their assertion to children that being able to compete in tests of skill against others is the key to future success.)

Have you seen this in your own life? Perhaps your children generally go to their mother when they want to feel thoroughly what they are feeling, especially if they want to feel it using words. The female brain can have more verbal centers and more linkage to emotive centers than does the male brain, so moms often not only process more of their sensory, emotive, and relational experiences—and talk about them—but also tend to help children feel and verbalize their own experiences more than their dad might.

At the same time, we generally find "islands of emotive discussion" in which the dad participates—for instance, if a daughter has a close relation-

- Teach the child to *fight against personal and group vulnerability*. (With less of the male brain's blood flow devoted to emotional processing than the female, fathers tend to deny any emotional vulnerability or try to problem-solve quickly to avoid such vulnerability.)
- Guide the child to sacrifice his or her own thinking in deference to *"authority thinking"* until the child has *proven* his or her own core nature to be mature enough to become authoritative. Although there are certainly exceptions to this, fathers tend to employ more authoritarian parenting styles than mothers and retain that authority well into the child's adulthood, waiting for the child to prove himself (this generally applies more to sons) worthy of being respected as an adult.
- Direct the child's search for self-worth toward the larger society (that is, encouraging less introspection and more *immediate action*).
- Try to help the child *feel stronger* in the long term even if the child does not feel better in the moment. Fathers tend to care less than mothers about whether a child "feels good." Fathers tend to want obvious shows of strength from children. This is especially true in their attitude toward sons.

ship with her father, she might go to him with questions about her interactions with teenage males. This is a good form of symmetry for the child.

Another area of important symmetry has been noted by psychologist Kyle Pruett, author of *Fatherneed*. About discipline styles, he writes, "Mothers tend to discipline by emphasizing the relational and social costs of misbehavior. Fathers on the other hand tend to emphasize the mechanical or societal consequences of misbehavior, bringing more emotional distance to disciplining as a whole."

Pruett points out that mothers might say to a child, "Did you think about how Susie felt when you said that mean thing to her?" The direct intention of the mother's style is to get the child to think emotionally. The father, in contrast, might say, "If you do that again, you lose your cell phone. Period." The paternal style of nurturance is more directly consequence oriented; there is less stopping to "think in feelings." Both styles are useful to the development of the child's core nature. It is not necessary for the father to parent like the mother or vice versa. The parents can give both assets in symmetry (and, to repeat, we are generalizing about these maternal and paternal assets—your household will have its own unique blend of parenting assets).

Right now, when your child is an infant, if you think about the core-nature development of older children in your neighborhood, perhaps you'll notice an underexpression or lack of development if some maternal or paternal elements are missing or have been taken away. As you look into your infant's eyes, you begin a lifelong journey of trying to connect maternal and paternal ways of being for the good of this child. If the mother or the father is gone from the child for significant periods of time, whole areas of developing nature—emotional expression, self-discovery, personal motivation—may not open for the child. For more information on this, you can see the Did You Know? box on page 101.

Parents-Beyond-Parents

Whether or not your parents and other relatives live close by, it is crucial to carry on a conversation in your family and community about how important not just two people but five to ten people are to your child's natural development. These parents-beyond-parents will help protect and develop your child's core nature throughout the stages of life. You will have to specifically target potential "second mothers" and "second fathers" and other extended family and community members right now, during your child's infancy. These caring individuals can become your "parent-led team."

Perhaps Grandma will say, "Check this house for lead before you buy it." Grandpa might say, "You don't give that kid enough consequences." Uncle or Aunt might say, "When you were that age you did that too, so don't be so hard on the kid."

Did You Know?

There is rigorous debate in our culture about gender roles, including the appropriate roles of the mother and father in raising children. We are all now aware that mothers can do a lot of what fathers used to do, and fathers can do a lot of what was historically "mother's work." There is a new flexibility to gender roles. It is essential to celebrate each of these advances.

At the same time, mothers and fathers are also "naturally different" and are thus "naturally needed" in a child's life. Remove one parent's core strengths, and problems can occur. For instance, when scientists study what happens to children whose fathers are not active in their lives, they find a higher probability of mental, emotional, and social problems.

Boys without the substantial presence of a father are 70 percent more likely to commit violent crimes, and each year spent without a dad in the home increases the odds of future incarceration by 5 percent.

Girls without the substantial presence of a father are 150 percent more likely to become pregnant during the teen years and will experience 92 percent more marriage breakups than girls raised with two parents.

Both girls and boys raised without fathers are substantially more likely to be sexually abused than their peers in two-parent homes.

This doesn't mean that every father (or mother) is good for a child, nor that there is fault in being a single parent. Many children are being raised wonderfully by single mothers (and single fathers), people who are adapting heroically to circumstances in their lives. But even in our admiration, we must also be careful to fully nurture the nature of the child.

Parents-beyond-parents give your child access to any number of models for living. Thus the child's nature receives a wider variety of social and interactive mirrors by which to develop the various aspects of his or her nature. Human beings are by nature polyfilial (rather than monofilial); that is, gene expression takes place in a "multifamily" system. And given how much time youngsters are now spending away from their parents (for example, after school, during the latchkey hours), the role of parents-beyond-parents in transmitting values and promoting emotional development will become ever more crucial as your child grows. Given how much diverse technological (nonhuman, artificial) stimulation children are receiving from our culture, diverse *human* involvement is even more crucial for the filtering of information and for basic supervision of the child.

Here's a wonderful example of how parents-beyond-parents can protect and nurture children's core-nature development. In a recent study of Asian households, when one parent was found to be "too hard"—with behavioral expectations and discipline techniques so severe that the child's core nature could be damaged—it was not the removal of the too-hard parent that improved the situation; rather, it was the increase of attention from the other parent *and other family members* in providing close, intimate, and diverse forms of attachment with the child. The assets of the other parent and the parents-beyond-parents balanced those of the difficult parent.

Assessing Your Own Family Team

Take a moment to really focus on building a parent-led team for your family. In your journal or in your thoughts and discussions, look at how to create alliances with the adults in your child's life:

- *Nuclear and blended family.* Seek constant connection with parents, stepparents, siblings, and others who clearly care about the child's core nature and can help develop it. You may not want to force connections with stepparents or others in blended families who do not care deeply about the child's core nature.

- *Extended family.* Seek constant connection (even if over the Internet and telephone) with grandparents, aunts, uncles, and other blood or adoptive relatives who care about the core nature of the child. If there is a particular relative who does not clearly care for the child's core nature, who is unhealthy for the child, or who has done significant harm to the child, you may want to sever relations with this person for an appropriate period of time. Generally, however, most extended family members are underutilized assets in our busy lives today.

- *Parent coaches.* Seek coaching support among the adults in your community, especially if you are raising children alone or feel significantly confused by one or more of your children. Parent coaches can include therapists, school counselors, clergy, and older friends. As the parent, you "lead" these relationships by selecting parent coaches who will become close to your family in some therapeutic or insightful way; avoid relying on professionals who dole out advice without getting to know the nature of *your* children and family.

- *Teachers.* Seek constant connection with teachers who understand your child's core nature. Most teachers a child meets in school will be good for the core nature of the child. When, however, a teacher or a whole school system is not healthy for the core nature of the child, then it is important to advocate for improvement in teacher performance and to move your child to a different school if necessary.

- *Mentors.* Structure specific and concerted tutorial and master-apprentice relationships for your child. Wherever the child shows an ongoing interest—be it drawing, learning, reading, athletics, love of animals—he or she ought to spend free time in connection with a master in that field. By establishing relationships whereby your child spends less time with electronic entertainment and other passive ways of fighting boredom, and more time with masters in trades, you encourage the core nature of the child to express itself more fully.

- *Members of spiritual and religious communities.* A number of recent studies have shown the benefits to children's core-nature development of involvement in these communities, which provide values affirmation, a sense of reverence, and a pool of parents-beyond-parents. It is a given that within these communities you may encounter a few people and values that you wish your child did not experience. If those few become too substantial, that community is no longer healthy for your child—your intuition generally trumps all other frameworks—but it is nevertheless true that generally a religious environment built on respect for the dignity and divinity of a child's core nature will be healthy for the development of children.

The Importance of the Mother-Infant Bond

In an attempt to define the depth of natural connection a mother has with her infant, Carl Jung wrote that the mother possesses "the magic authority of the female principle, the wisdom and spiritual exaltation that transcend reason, all that cherishes and sustains . . . inescapable like fate." He spoke about all mothers and all children, for every child needs the mother, and each particular child needs his or her mother in a particular way. Jung was referring to the complex ways in which the mother is the carrier of the child and generally the first source of food and natural sustenance for the child, inseparable from the early life of another being that is growing within her and then emerges from her. As Shelley Taylor, UCLA psychologist and author of *The Tending Instinct,* has recently shown using new scientific studies on oxytocin and other brain chemicals, "An early warm and nurturant relationship, such as mothers often enjoy with their children, is as vital to development as calcium is to bones." Children who are well tended in utero, at birth, during infancy, and through childhood by the mother grow up with better social and emotional skills for meeting the world head-on.

We sense this instinctively. While carrying a child a mother may think and say aloud, "There is nothing as important now as this child."

She will make immense sacrifices—stop drinking, stop smoking, do whatever the doctor asks—in order to keep the mother-fetus bond strong. She knows that the health of her fetus is *her* health, as if two roots are now completely intertwined.

After she gives birth to the child, she feels the power of this essential connection again. She is as if completely one with this child, this boy, this girl. (Even if she adopts an infant, there is still oxytocin flow—bonding chemical flow—commensurate in the mother to the necessary bonding with the child.) She knows instinctively that what she does really matters to this infant, that she is supremely responsible for this tiny body, this great new soul. When a few months go by, and she perhaps can't continue her moment-by-moment bond with this child on a daily, hourly basis, she may feel she's losing a blissful feeling of unending connectedness. She may find herself weeping as if she were suddenly losing this child, this part of herself. She may stand outside a day-care facility or her own workplace and feel as if she herself were being torn apart, for her child is not in her arms for six or eight or ten hours of the day.

My wife and family experienced this circumstance during our children's infancies, so I have felt and observed it both as a professional and as a parent. When our infants were born, we were torn by our struggle to protect our parental bonds. Gail was especially torn. We had very little income, so we both had to work outside the home. We chose a high-quality day-care facility for half-day care, and experienced firsthand how much pressure there is on moms of infants in this culture to tear themselves apart from their children. We came to understand intimately the social trends culture we live in—a culture that has sacrificed the priority of the mother-infant bond for the sake of workplace needs.

Gail and I became revolutionaries, joining many others around us, by fighting for corporate day care and other essential protection of infant bonds with primary caregivers. Information on mother-child bonding and attachment supported our instincts with the science to fight this fight. I hope you'll find this information essential as you set up a life and parent-led nurturing team that will make the best decisions about the development of your infant's core nature. This information does not negate the father-infant bond, and I as a father know that I played an essential part in my babies' infancies.

The Science of Bonding

During the last decade there have been some amazing studies regarding the chemistry of bonding itself. Both oxytocin and vasopressin are involved in the essential mother-infant connection. In a study published in *Proceedings of the National Academy of Sciences,* Seth D. Pollak of the University of Wisconsin showed that bonding with infants creates synapses bursts (these are good things!) via these two chemicals. Without appropriate bonds with mothers and with primary caregivers who "stand in" for mother, the nature of the child does not fully grow.

Using brain imaging technology, neuropsychiatrist Allan Schore has been able to show certain exact areas in the brain (for instance, in the frontal lobe) that do not grow synapses without the mother-infant bond. This lack of growth can lead to chronic stress in the child's life later, as well a social and cognitive failure or lack of academic focus.

If you could put a heart monitor on an infant, you would notice how "stressed out" that infant becomes when the mother leaves for a dangerous period of time (or when no second mother or other attached parent stands in). When a baby doesn't get the feeding, holding, singing, cuddling, walking around together, communication, and eye contact from the mother, the baby's heart becomes agitated. This agitation affects adrenaline, cortisol (stress hormone), and even the operation of neurotransmitters and cortical development.

A few hours here or there without mom is not dangerous, but two to three sleep cycles and feeding cycles without mom per day for days and weeks on end can have an effect on that baby's synapses development and stress level—a profound effect, therefore, on the development of that baby's core nature.

As we explore this science, it is essential to remember that "mother" can and must indeed also mean other caregivers. If a mother dies, others will step in. Fathers who become like "male mothers" during the child's infancy can provide a great deal for the infant. When a child stays with

Grandma or goes to high-quality day care, the "second mothers"—the child-care providers—can form bonds that are like the mother's and thus are successful, as parents-beyond-parents.

At the same time, the phrase "like the mother's" is telling. It is a phrase all men need to hear, especially during these infancy years. The highest standard of infant care is, in most cases, the healthy mother's. To engage in social trends that make us politically shy about paying ultimate respect to the mother is problematic. This was recently made clear to me by a court case in which I decided not to become involved. A father, a man whom I believe was a good man at heart—competent, kind, hard working—was suing the mother of his baby son (the couple had divorced right after the child's birth) in order to make the mother give him care of the three-month-old boy for one week a month. His argument, based on present social theory connected to fathers' rights, was that he as a father should have equal rights to the infant. I was approached as a known advocate for boys and the author of *What Could He Be Thinking?*—a book about men.

I believe this father was shocked by my refusal to help him. I am an advocate for fathers' rights as well as mothers'—I don't see them as competitive, but as symmetrical. In this particular case, however, I based my refusal on my understanding of the science of the infant-mother bond. Although I probably would have fought hard for him if his child were older (the science of the father-adolescent bond, as we'll see in later chapters, asks us to become quite revolutionary regarding fathers' rights to bond with adolescents), and although it is certainly true that infants need their fathers, I pointed out that his request for one week of solo care for a three-month-old ran contrary to the natural needs of his son. At his age, this boy needed his mother's breast milk, holding, touching, and consistency of contact more than he needed a week per month with his father.

We must be revolutionaries in fighting for the mother-infant bond. Science backs us up, but so do our instincts. Think about it a moment. Is not the mother's bond with her infant "magical," as Jung asserted? Don't most children yearn in a special way for the mother? Don't most mothers feel the pain of leaving their babies, if they must go away for long periods? Don't most fathers see the pain a mother's separation from her infant causes her and the child? Perhaps the new brain research is redundant for you, as you already make nearly any sacrifice to stay close to your baby. Yet the new nature-based research will, I hope, give new evidence for overcoming the political and social ambivalence about motherhood that exists in our social trends society.

As we fight this fight, it is useful to remember two things:

- Since the Industrial Revolution, mothers have often had inadequate support from extended family and "tribe" with which to answer their infant's natural call for bonding, attachment, love, and learning—thus mothers today need even *more* of our support now, not less.
- Since the Industrial Revolution, mothers have been too rarely allowed to take their children to work with them. Prior to the Industrial Revolution, all mothers worked (except the very rich) but they carried their children on their back or chest or belly, or had them within hearing and touching distance. Now, workplaces are often alien to child raising; they don't accommodate the sustenance of the mother-infant bond.

This is the world we live in, and this is the world in which mothers have to juggle their love of their infant—their "second self"—and the requirements of the workplace. As we work together to support mothers under these circumstances, a statistic can help us clarify the difficulty working mothers face in postindustrial society. Kristen Rowe-Finkbeiner and Joan Blades, in their book *The Motherhood Penalty,* note that 82 percent of American women have children by the time they are forty-four years old, with 72 percent of these women working outside the home. The fact that they are mothers carries a penalty—women without children make ninety cents for every dollar a man makes, but working mothers make seventy-three cents. Before the Industrial Revolution, young mothers died in childbirth much more often than they do today. We have basically dealt with that form of destruction of the mother-infant bond, but have now substituted a more subtle "attack" on motherhood. The life of Lisa Brown, who is now the majority leader of the Washington State Senate, provides a telling example. Thirteen years ago, when her infant son was just born, Brown was a junior senator who breast-fed her infant son at her workplace—during the legislative session. She did it with a blanket over the child, with all discretion, but many of Washington's state senators—who were elected in part to create healthy policy on family issues!—did not understand the nature of the mother's bond with her infant, nor that the normality of that bond is crucial to community health, corporate health, and the safety and thriving of a human workplace and civilization. Instead, many of them publicly castigated this mother for caring for her young child.

If you as a mother of an infant (or as a husband or other person supporting a mother of an infant) understand how essential the

Did You Know?

When women are polled, they put care of their children above the money that comes from having to leave their children. This was recently confirmed in a joint study done by the University of Connecticut and the University of Minnesota. The two thousand mothers surveyed (of whom 41 percent worked full time and 21 percent part time; the rest stayed at home) answered the question "What would be your ideal work situation?" this way:

- 33 percent said working part time.
- 30 percent said working for pay from home.
- 21 percent said not working at any job except care of their children.
- The remaining percentage did not respond or were satisfied with working full time.

mother-infant bond is, I hope you'll join in a social movement to give motherhood and infant bonding the priority it deserves. Check out organizations like Mothers and More, Nurturing Parenting Programs, and Practical Parenting. Without mothers and fathers joining as advocates for mother-infant bonding, our social trends culture is unlikely to understand the science and nature (and thus the essential nature) of the bond. If your children are no longer infants, still I hope you'll join in what you might consider something of a crusade. I hope you'll fight in your corporations and neighborhoods for these practical strategies:

- Corporate day care. Fight for corporations to provide child care at or near the location of a mother's employment so that the mothers can see and connect with their infants at regular intervals during the day.
- Twelve months of paid leave, subsidized as necessary (though not only by the small business employer or the government, but through other incentive programs).
- Motherhood sabbatical—if you've worked someplace for five or more years, for instance, you could receive a half-time-pay sabbatical for a set period of time, perhaps one year, as is done in Canada.

These are just three creative solutions to what has become a significant social issue—the loss of respect for the mother-infant bond. If as you parent your child you become inspired to act toward these or other similar goals, I hope you'll read a very important book, *Ghosts from the Nursery,* by Robin Karr-Morse and Meredith Wiley, which provides amazing scientific evidence (and frightening follow-up research) regarding what happens to people who, when babies, did not get adequate mother-infant bonding.

A story, a chapter, a book—these words cannot solve all the problems you might face (or did face) in building your young family, but I hope these last pages have at least helped you and your family team feel in your own heart and soul that a mother's instincts about her infant

Try This

In your journal, or in the privacy of your thoughts, ask yourself these questions:

- Do I as a mother feel torn between my infant's needs and the demands of culture around me?
- Do I underparent my child because I am not around enough to give the child what he or she needs?
- Do I have a particular infant whose core nature is "pretty independent," or do I have an infant who needs me around even more than others do? If the latter, do I spend adequate time with this child?
- Do I have two or three other caregivers in place who can help guide me, hold my infant, and provide eye contact and bonding cues, so that I'm not trying to raise this child mainly on my own?
- Do I spend enough time every day getting to know the core nature of my infant?

If, once you've answered these questions, you see any issues regarding your own mother-child bond, I hope you won't blame a particular person—whether yourself or a spouse or even a culture. In fact, it's normal for us to constantly rethink what we're doing as parents—to see flaws and make changes. I hope you'll feel inspired to fight for change. Gail and I did this quite early in our relationship. We relied on quality day care for four mornings a week after Gail returned to work (she was given two months' maternity leave), and we alternated afternoon care. She also cut back her work hours to part time. We lived on very little income during those infant years, but we've never regretted the changes we made.

are profoundly important. If our civilization is willing to accept and follow those instincts, we will indeed be able to say, "We care about our children."

Burning Question:
Can Vaccinations Harm My Infant?

In this and every chapter that follows, we'll consider a hot-button issue that parents frequently ask me about. I call these "burning questions."

I am frequently asked whether vaccinations are safe or harmful for infants and young children and specifically whether the mercury found in vaccinations (thimerosal) can be the reason for the astounding number of brain disorders, such as autism, that we are now seeing among our children.

The issue was put to me recently by a mom and training professional, Patricia, this way: "The dramatic increase in the number of vaccines given to children directly correlates to the rise in autism and learning disabilities. These vaccines contain thimerosal—which is 50 percent ethyl mercury. Mercury is a neurotoxin and cytotoxin." This mom provided me with Web sites (including www.gnd.org/autism/overview.htm and www.vran.org/vaccines/mercury/merc-tox.htm) that explain this hypothesis very clearly, with compelling evidence.

Should you vaccinate your child? Dr. Boyd Haley, a biochemist at the University of Kentucky, has argued that boys are especially at risk from possible toxic effects of thimerosal mercury because of the way that testosterone exacerbates the chemical reaction. Should mothers of sons especially turn away from vaccines?

Over the last five years, I've been watching the public and scientific dialogue on what might be causing the increase in autism spectrum and learning disorders. Is it vaccines? Is it genetic? Are diagnostic instruments improving and thus identifying more children with these disorders? Are these disorders being overdiagnosed—are they actually just a broad range of behaviors that are not really autism?

I queried Dr. Harold Koplewicz of New York University, Dr. Howard Schubiner of Providence-St. John Hospital in Detroit, and Dr. Daniel G. Amen of Amen Clinics, each a member of our Gurian Institute Advisory Board. Each are well-known specialists, and they all gave me the same answer to the question of vaccination: "You can vaccinate your child without fear."

Dr. Amen pointed out that vaccinations being made now don't contain mercury anymore. Dr. Schubiner also noted that "we've taken out mercury from vaccines, but the rates of autism have not declined." He pressed further to dispute the thimerosal hypothesis. (See the Notes and References section for a pertinent article.) Both he and Dr. Koplewicz agree that more study is needed regarding why the number of autism spectrum and learning disorder diagnoses is rising, especially among boys, but also that thimerosal does not now appear to be the major causative factor. Furthermore, even if mercury were proven to be a causative factor, it is, as noted, no longer a part of the vaccine.

This information was welcome to me. My children fulfilled all the vaccination protocols suggested by our HMO.

As you make your decisions, I hope you will look at the scientific research in the Notes and References and consult your pediatrician. Vaccinations are essential for our children's health. To overreact against them without conclusive proof that they are harmful would be to engage in a social trends approach to core nature—a tossing out of something of great value without fully understanding the science. At the same time, it is important to question and examine any science-based child-care technique—such as vaccinations—and I thank those parents who have asked about them. In part, because of caring people like Patricia, mercury is not a factor in most vaccines anymore.

Parenting as a Spiritual Discipline

Frank Lloyd Wright said, "I believe in God, whom I know as Nature." I keep this statement taped to the wall of my office to remind me that to explore nature and human nature ultimately is to explore activities of the spirit and the universe even beyond our grasp. Hence, I feel that the journey of parenting you have set out on as you hold an infant in your arms is a spiritual enterprise. It is "holy work" to nurture the nature of the child. I believe that whatever your religion or creed, every sacred practice or text values parenting in this way.

As a parent and professional, I remind myself daily to look deeply into the eyes of children and see what is *really* there—to see the nature of the infant as also the divinity of the whole child. Every day, as a parent and a professional, I remind myself that like prayer or any other spiritual discipline, parenting is a relationship between individuals who humbly learn as they go their unique places in a larger mysterious system.

As you parent your child from infancy forward, I hope you'll pause for breath when you hear or see a social trend that isn't based in strong science and steady intuition or that suggests you mold your child a certain way that seems suspicious to you. I hope that as you grow with your child, you'll keep hearing your child's wonderful voice, actions, and signals saying to you, "Thank you so much for helping me develop *my* core nature in this safe, healthy home."

Wisdom of Practice

ABOUT TWENTY YEARS AGO, A COLLEAGUE OF MINE FROM WORK, whose wife was expecting their first child, told me he had studied the way Asian parents raise their kids from infancy, so as to understand why many Asian children achieve a high degree of academic success. His conclusion was that instead of trying to stimulate their infants and then older children, Asians have the opposite approach. They keep the home very quiet and spare as a way of enabling the child to focus and concentrate on one thing at a time.

I remembered this because years later when I had my babies, I came to agree with this colleague of mine. My instincts and observation brought me to disagree with the conventional wisdom at that time, which was that you must provide your baby with as much stimulation as possible. Remember those black-and-white toys you hung up above the crib? The idea was to provide stimulation in such a way that a tiny baby could process it.

In retrospect, the "as much stimulation as possible" idea seems crazy, given that so much competes today for every adult's attention, and given that children are more often overstimulated rather than "understimulated." If anything, we ought to be teaching our kids how to shut out stimulation.

I know this is a "different" point of view—maybe it is even a bit revolutionary—but in raising my kids, it has worked. They are quite successful young people now.

4

Nurturing the Nature of Your Two- to Three-Year-Old

There was a child went forth everyday, and the first object he looked upon, that object he became, and that object became part of him for the day or a certain part of the day . . . the lilacs became part of this child, and grass and white and red morning glories, and white and red clover, and the song of the phoebe-bird, and the third-month lambs and the sow's pink-faint litter, and the mare's foal and the cow's calf. . . .

—WALT WHITMAN

DON'T WALT WHITMAN'S WORDS PROVIDE A BEAUTIFUL DESCRIP-tion of a toddler? Don't two- and three-year-olds seem to have endless energy for "becoming" objects—holding things, grabbing them, throwing them, listening to them, lifting them, swinging them, smiling at them, feeling as if smiled back upon? Doesn't this still-diapered child, this walker and talker, this tantrum thrower and deep sleeper, this boy or girl want to touch leaves and wind and salty dirt and shadows from sunlight through high trees, and doesn't this child yearn to engage in the natural world?

This is the inward and outward nature of a two- or three-year-old child. It is a nature of the beautiful inner chaos that wants direction, distraction, and the power over decisions, but actually can't accomplish much yet without some help. The toddler years are years when your child's core nature will shine through, though not without a bit of exhaustion for all!

Preview of Essential Developmental Tasks

- *Continue to observe and learn to know your child.* Thus you can develop a deeper, more detailed profile in your own mind and for your family team of who *your* child is. In this period of sharp learning curves (walking, talking, potty training, socialization, the beginnings of separation), provide playtime, order, and discipline that is right for the nature of your particular child.
- *Protect this toddler from harm* by providing healthy nutrition and a safe environment. One important aspect of protection is to be aware of your own "dark side" as a parent. The toddler years often bring out anger in adults, and our self-awareness can be crucial in helping us make sure we or someone close to us does not traumatize this child's core-nature development.
- *Continue strong bonding and attachment*—even as the toddler begins to toddle away a bit—and add new stimulation to this child's bonding system as fits your child. These are crucial years of tailoring stimulation to the individual child—years when the social trends parenting system throws a lot of conventional expectations of performance at us—so we must stay focused on who *our* child is.

Information Essential to Nurturing the Core Nature of Your Toddler

As you raise your toddler, you will be involved in mysterious and wonderful brain and body growth. Here are some aspects of toddler development that you can help unfold in unique ways in your own child's nature.

1. Your toddler's brain is a sponge. That child is absorbing nearly everything. At the same time, your toddler is also forgetting most of what he or she has just absorbed! This is why you will constantly repeat yourself, in actions and words.

The toddler's brain is involved in an accelerated process of making dendrite connections and then pruning them and then making them again. Each two- or three-year-old's brain is like a fingerprint—no two are exactly alike! Your toddler will learn, remember, and require repetition in his or her own way, and some toddlers need far more repetition than others. You will definitely be seeing your child's unique core nature by now. For instance, your "observer" child may be different in certain situations from an "active participant" child.

2. Your toddler's development is susceptible to a broad variety of neurotoxins in the environment (home, day-care facility, neighborhood). Although some kids are born with sensitive skin, allergies, a tendency to remain thin or to become overweight, and other genetic predispositions, all children are vulnerable to obvious environmental toxins, such as lead or radon, and less frequently discussed neurotoxins, such as junk food and TV or other screen time. Each toddler will have his or her own tolerance. Some toddlers can become more overweight than others through exposure to junk food and too little physical activity. Those with higher metabolisms may not become overweight. As you set up your home and other assets for your toddler, look carefully at everything in his or her environment. There are more dangers in its unnatural components than any of us may have realized before. (We will further discuss neurotoxins in this and later chapters.)

3. Attachment and bonding are absolutely crucial to the toddler. Now that your child is no longer an infant, much of attachment and bonding will involve not only cooing and generous hugging but also conflict and discipline. I'll discuss this in detail in this chapter.

4. A toddler's brain is generally starved for brain-friendly nutrients, such as omega-3 fatty acids in fish, protein in general, and iron, niacin, and zinc. Some toddler brains don't need these nutrients as

much as others. Your toddler might process protein more slowly than another child, thus not needing it as much or as often. So it is with every food. As you and your team raise this child, watch closely the child's needs for specific brain-friendly foods.

Our social trends parenting system negatively affects how we feed young children. Advertising and the free-market system have increasingly taught us to feed "branded foods," such as fast foods and peanut butter, to children. Peanut butter, of course, can be a good protein, but because branding has not worked as well for fish as for peanut butter (and because fast foods so dominate toddler eating), we've neglected foods like fish, which actually help brains grow well.

5. Food allergies can be a bigger issue than we realize. They can affect growth and behavior. Our social trends culture has neglected to look at food allergies as vigorously as you might want to. Science is now weighing in on the relationship between foods (such as wheat and yeast) and the behavior of children, and on foods' impact on mental health in general. If your particular toddler is evidencing severe behavior issues, you will undoubtedly add doctors and other experts to your family team; you might ask them to look for a possible food allergy. This can be a good thing to keep in mind throughout your child's life. Food allergies can correlate with genetic vulnerabilities. For instance, I am allergic to yeast; my father is allergic to wheat. We carry this vulnerability to food allergies genetically in our paternal line.

6. Toddlers are highly susceptible to the subtle harms of emotional and behavior labeling. One example shows up in preschools, especially with boys. Their core nature is confusing to relatively untrained and quite overwhelmed professionals, who may label them as suffering from ADD or as hyperactive or as oppositional-defiant or as learning disordered. Each year, nearly five thousand of these kids are expelled from preschools. Many of these children do not have a behavioral disorder; they just don't fit the social trends expectations of the school, and the school does not have time to deal with the core nature of every child. Our effort to make the social trends system fit *our child*, not vice versa, begins strongly in these toddler years.

7. Germs are both good and bad for toddlers. For instance, your kids might have significant problems if they are allergic to a pet. If this is the case, you'll become very protective—asthma symptoms or a constantly runny nose might be a clue to this genetically carried allergy. Simultaneously, our culture in general has trended toward overprotecting toddlers from germs. This is a logical outgrowth of the increase of medical care available since the Industrial Revolution. We learned that hygiene is crucial to human survival, and we've run with that idea. In the process, however, we've lost some of the crucial assets many of our toddlers need in order to fight disease later in life. Scientists have discovered that children exposed to moderate levels of germs in the toddler years (for example, in day-care facilities) have less chance later of developing asthma and other respiratory problems. Parents instinctually seek to protect the toddler, but core nature may well need more germs than we have assumed, and a little dirt can actually help our children develop stronger immunity to germs.

Did You Know?

Words are like a "second milk" for your toddler's brain. Reading to your toddler is therefore a crucial part of bonding, attachment, brain development, and family quiet time. The toddler can't understand many of the words yet, but the child's future success depends to some extent on the number of words he or she hears, in being both spoken to and read to. The shy child is not defective because he or she does not use a lot of words, nor is the child who can't yet read. The child's production of words is not as important right now as the parent's and community's immersion of the child in reading and words. Read to your toddler!

Natural Differences Between Toddler Girls and Boys

Try this experiment some time. If you have a daughter, give her three metal trucks to play with; if you have a son, give him three Barbies or other soft dolls to play with. Over a period of a day, observe what your child does. Without stereotyping, and taking into account all the possible exceptions, I can assure you that although most of the time the child will play for a while with the objects in a way appropriate to the objects, in a relatively short time the boy may try to take the head off one or more of the dolls; toss the doll(s) in the air, laughing with his friends as they bounce around the room; or use them as weapons. The girl, for her part, may try to talk to the trucks, humanize the trucks to fit into whatever bonding game she's playing with her friends (for example, hospital or house), or set the trucks aside and return to playing with her dolls.

These differences show up so clearly in toddlers that parents of older kids look back at the time they did this experiment and laugh.

"What was I thinking?" a mom of a son told me. "Did I really think my boys would play with dolls like a girl?" She realized instinctively how different toddler boys are from girls, yet she also worried when her son treated the dolls so "badly," even "immorally." She remembered thinking there was something wrong with her sons who tore the heads off the dolls. To her, the doll was a human representation, but she realized later that to the toddler boy, the dolls are often not "human"—they are play objects made of plastic.

A mom who is a physicist told me, "When my daughter was so doll obsessed at two and three, I couldn't get her to do anything that looked at all like science. I thought, 'Whose genes does she have?!' Now, by the way, she's studying to be a science teacher. I guess I didn't have to worry."

As both these moms found out, there is no specific way that a toddler boy or girl must play. These children will play in their own way. What is crucial for both sexes is that they play, play, play! They'll play and do much more, all somewhat differently by gender.

Did You Know?

- Regions in boys' brains that are used for mechanical and spatial manipulation (playing with blocks and trucks, moving constantly) develop earlier and more copiously than similar areas in girls' brains.

- Regions in girls' brains that are used for verbal fluency and recognizing familiar faces (and later, for writing and for emotion talk) mature earlier and more copiously than similar areas in boys' brains.

- In the toddler years (and beyond), girls tend to develop their fine motor skills more quickly and fully than boys (more and various hand manipulation of small objects). Boys' brains develop more connectors for gross motor skills (more and various physical movement of the whole body).

- Human children share these gender-specific brain differences with other animals—showing them to be all the more natural. Hanne Smith, who worked in Africa under the direction of Jane Goodall, told me about young gorillas: "These nonhuman males do just like the human: they begin dropping female behaviors from their play, and the females begin dropping male behaviors until they reach a point when their play is mainly gender appropriate. This happens just as they lose their infant coloration [the toddler years]."

- Girls' brains in general develop connectors between the amygdala (an emotion center) and the regions of the brain that handle words earlier than do boys, so even during the toddler years, girls tend already to be better than boys at "talking out" what they are feeling. This difference will increase by the teen years, after puberty, then into adulthood. This is a reason that mothers and other

caregivers instinctively try to get boys to talk things out—
why adults try as best they can to encourage little boys to
"use their words."

- For girls, the toddler years are important years for adults
to put blocks and other objects in their play circle. Of
course there is nothing wrong with playing with dolls,
but especially for girls who don't show a natural proclivity
toward blocks and building things, it doesn't hurt to say,
"Here, can you have Barbie building a bridge? Let me
show you how." This helps girls develop connections in
the brain that might lead to greater spatial skills.

As you live with and enjoy the gender of your toddler, you may instinctively try to help your girls and boys compensate for areas where
you feel they're weaker (such as word use or spatial skills). This is a wonderful thing to do. Just because a particular child doesn't start out with
a dominant proclivity in a certain area of life doesn't mean we can't
help the child try to develop other abilities. Core nature comprises a diverse set of talents and skills. As long as we're respectful of who the
child is, we ought to follow our instinct to open the child to opportunities that might compensate for any possible vulnerabilities. The child
will naturally take the lead in an activity at some point. For instance, if
you give a child blocks twenty times and she (or he) just doesn't want to
play with them, the core nature of the child—at least for this period of
this child's development—may be saying, "Let's focus on something else
in our play—the blocks don't do it for me."

In suggesting that you let the child take the lead, I might be running counter to some recent social trends. Often parents worry today
that if a toddler girl isn't spatial or a toddler boy verbal, these children
will fail in some way in the future. In the social trends approach to parenting, gender differences are considered potentially dangerous if they
are not erased from childhood. It's unclear exactly how this point of
view developed, but it probably came from the idea that men will grow

up to abuse and oppress women if they aren't socialized to become more like women, and women will not be able to compete economically if they don't become more like men. It was probably also intended to compensate for older views of women as inferior to men, and "different" seemed to mean "inferior."

In the nature-based perspective, women's equality is an assumed right: nature is set up for women and men to be equal, and oppression of women was not and is not naturally necessary. Where nature-based theory differs from social trends theory is in its rejection of the assumption that natural gender differences "cause" inequality. In the twenty-three years I have collected research in gender dynamics, I have noticed that an understanding of the natural differences between girls and boys and women and men actually helps create *more* gender equity—in the workplace, in the family, in the world. It is not the differences between male and female but rather disrespect for the natural strengths of each gender that is a root cause of oppression. When we don't understand each other, we try to manipulate and mold each other into an object of our own, rather than nurturing the nature already there.

As you notice interesting ways in which your toddlers play, feel, think, and learn differently, if you feel anxiety and worry that your boys will become hurtful to women or that your girls will become unable, later in life, to perform well in science class (and thus in the workplace), please let the scientific research on gender differences allay your fears. There are many parents who, like me, have daughters who played constantly with dolls as toddlers and now, as teenagers, get A's in science class. There is no proof that gender-specific play in the toddler years causes a lack of scientific acumen later in life.

Do what your instincts tell you to help your boys be more verbal and your girls more spatial, then let the children play. They will teach each other a great deal of what they need to know about gender and the brain, even though they play differently. These little girls and boys are, in fact, very wise, especially about dolls, trucks, and even gender equality.

The Importance of Play, Order, and Discipline

A toddler is a walking contradiction. A toddler needs play—and order. A toddler needs chaos—and discipline. A toddler needs loudness, vitality, exuberance—and quiet time. Core-nature development during these years is paradoxical, so we struggle as parents to keep up with the competing signals and needs of this child. When we add in our own child's specific and particular manifestations of the paradox, we can become quite overwhelmed indeed. Parenting this toddler is good practice for parenting adolescents, who themselves will often act like toddlers.

Gayle, a mom in Sacramento, told me about her three children. "When he was a toddler, Jonah loved to play on his own for hours. Patty, on the other hand, could only play on her own for a little while, then she needed friends. Toney was kind of a middle ground between the other two. I think, being the youngest, he loved the attention he got from playing with his siblings, but then I think he got overwhelmed. He'd pull away, into himself, for a while."

As you experience life with your toddler, you'll notice preset inner patterns of play and order in your children. Also watch carefully for preset inner patterns of self-discipline (and need for discipline) in your particular child's play and exploration.

My first daughter, Gabrielle, was very "internally ordered" as a toddler. She was more able than her sister to play independently, then lie down to sleep when she got tired. Davita, in contrast, overwhelmed herself at play and needed her parents and family team to help her return to order and self-discipline.

As your own toddler plays hard and then sleeps hard; as he or she begins to "act out," push at you, disagree with your commands (or ignore or not hear them); as he or she engages in dangerous actions and breaks things during play; as this child grabs at the world in his or her own unique way, you have the opportunity to notice what kind of order and discipline system *your* child needs. You can focus on a discipline system in your parent-led team that is a fit for your child.

Should You Spank Your Child?

The great majority—90 percent—of Americans spank their children. I've never done so and never will. (My parents hit me too much as a child, in my opinion, and I have chosen not to continue that practice.) My wife, however, did swat our toddlers on their bottoms when they were unruly or doing something dangerous. Gail and I represent many households (and indeed the cultural debate in general), wherein some people practice spanking and others don't.

The social trends parenting system has told us that the issue of spanking can be resolved as an either-or: spanking is either right or wrong. This trend toward simplification is yet another kind of thinking that doesn't take into account the diverse nature of particular children. Although physical abuse is dangerous to child development as well as morally reprehensible, basic physical discipline of children is a natural part of human development.

Gail never abused our toddlers. She practiced appropriate spanking: a swat on the bottom, no use of weapons, no shaming, no pulling pants down, only a hard touch of a hand on the child's buttocks or pants in order to reorient the child toward safety and clarity. She did not use this practice more than a few times a year during the toddler years. She knew that to overemphasize it was to risk its becoming abusive or ineffective. She knew that when a child is spanked frequently (every week or more, for instance), he or she can develop a dangerous enmity toward the parent and an immunity to discipline of any kind.

Spanking is, of course, not the only form of physical discipline possible. A mother in Michigan wrote me, "I decided not to spank our children, but I physically picked up my toddlers during their incorrect behavior and moved them to their time-out chair or their rooms. I also used a harsher tone with my children than Tom did. Sometimes I feel guilty about it—I wish I had absolute and perfect patience—but as I and my children look back now (my kids are in their twenties and have children of their own), we can see how natural my physical reactions to their bad behavior were."

As a parent with a nature-based perspective, I, like this mom and like Gail, believe physical discipline is a natural part of human development. What do you believe? While your child is a toddler, it is crucial that you decide. Are you prepared for the "physicality" of disciplining your particular child? Have you made value decisions about it? In a later section of this chapter, we'll discuss how you can integrate these questions into your self-awareness as a parent of a toddler; we'll also discuss strategies for providing discipline to children who throw intense temper tantrums. Right now, in your journal, you might make a few notes about what kind of physical discipline is okay with you, and what is not.

Creating Your Family's Essential Discipline System

Once you have spent some time focused on the theme of physical discipline, write the words "Discipline System" on a journal page. Providing discipline in the toddler years and throughout life needs to be systematic not arbitrary (and involves, obviously, more than spanking). As you note what kind of discipline system you want in place, I hope you'll look carefully at essential areas of discipline that can provide simple solutions to daily issues with toddlers. These will actually decrease the need to punish the child. I recommend *Positive Discipline for Preschoolers* (see the Notes and References section) as a resource that helps you use time-outs and taking away privileges—two very effective and well-known discipline strategies. Meanwhile, here are some further suggestions for your discipline system:

- *Help your child sleep more if he or she needs it.* Much of a toddler's core-nature development involves energy bursts and lags. If he or she is not getting enough sleep, this toddler will appear to "need more discipline" than he or she actually needs. In these cases, sleep is the culprit, not the child's core nature.
- *Help your child eat right.* Junk food, long lag times between meals, sugar, and foods your child is allergic to (dairy, wheat, yeast, nuts) all can affect mood and temper, thus affecting the child's behavior and his or her incidents of punishment.

A father of a toddler boy wrote me about his son's need for punishment when the three-year-old ate sugar or drank sugar juices. "I know everyone has a theory about sugar. Some folks say it has no effect; others say it has a big effect. I can tell you this: with Jeremy, just a glass of apple juice could make him get really hyper and act out. His mother and I decided to cut sugar out altogether. Once we did that, wow, he just didn't get into as much trouble—not at home, not at Grandma's, not at day care."

• *Teach your child specific developmental steps only when the child is ready.* Often we feel we must discipline a child because he or she is not fitting our mold. A mother wrote,

> There was a lot of pressure on me to teach my daughter to tell time when she was three. When I tried to teach it, though, I kept getting frustrated, and so did she. I even thought she was being resistant, and I put her in time-out. I think I got afraid that she was behind in her ability, and she picked up on my anxiety about it, I guess, because she would get really angry.
>
> Finally, I just backed off. I didn't try again for months. Then suddenly I heard the word in my head, "Now!" I trusted that, and put the clock in front of her and taught her. She understood it in five minutes! I learned an important lesson here—timing is everything! I was trying to force something that just wasn't there yet.

For this mom, the "forcing" had led to a kind of overpunishment and overdiscipline. This can happen in any family. You may well see a readiness (or lack of readiness) in such areas as toilet training, and notice how punishment gets connected to "unreadiness." Your child's core nature is a little brain and body developing in its own time. Every "little thing" you are teaching this toddler is a big thing in his or her small life. Sometimes, if you want this child to go to a certain day-care facility, you must accelerate learning (for instance in potty training). And sometimes there is no harm to your child in this. Kids have to adapt. Kids have to try to force some issues in life and face obstacles. However, if you find yourself trying to accelerate a lot of learning, you might need to look into this child's eyes and back off on some things.

- *Seek out older role models.* Toddlers learn a great deal of self-discipline by sensing around them the inherently self-disciplined nature of people older than themselves—and having to adapt to it. "Grandpa doesn't like you touching that," you might say, or "Grandma doesn't want you to be so loud." This is great for the child's developing nature. If your child is in day care, you might ask your provider if perhaps there is a way to involve the elderly in part of the child's day. In many cases, the day care simply needs to reach out to a nursing home. Elderly women and men can come into the preschool to lead reading times with the toddlers. They help calm children beautifully.

- *Avoid screen time as much as possible.* For children under three, TV, computer, video, DVD, video games, and other screen stimulants can be potentially harmful—even if the programming is considered educational. Researchers at the University of Washington, publishing in the Journal of Pediatrics and Adolescent Medicine, confirm what we've been learning for the last decade through brain studies: "Watching even really good educational shows is bad for children under three," says Frederick Zimmerman, one of the coauthors. This study confirmed previous studies by Dimitri Christakis and his colleagues, who discovered the link between screen time and the increased probability of a child's being diagnosed with ADD or ADHD. Although your child certainly may be one of those who can tolerate more screen time than his or her sibling or friend, you must be vigilant about screen use.

Not only can screen time in the toddler years translate to lower reading and short-term memory scores for these children, but it can also create increased discipline problems. If you are going to allow screen time, one of the ways to determine what your child can tolerate is to notice what happens to his or her moods after watching an hour of TV. Does the watching time make your child more aggressive (or more lethargic and passive)? If so, he or she might be one who should not watch much TV.

Generally we parents are not going to cut all screen time out of toddlers' lives—TV sure does seem to calm some toddlers down!—nevertheless, if you have not looked at the research, please check out the references to the studies on screen time my team and I are providing you in these chapters and in the Notes and References section. You may be shocked to see how much a toddler's life can be affected by screen time—in terms of behavior, sleep, future obesity, and moral development.

• *Avoid hovering.* It is important to let your child develop, play, and learn in his or her own way. You can avoid a lot of discipline problems by doing so. At the same time, you can see the areas of the toddler's play and life that really need discipline.

Harvard psychologist Jerome Kagan has devoted over two decades to studying how children's core nature—especially temperament—is affected by hovering and anxious parents. In studying anxiety levels in individual children, he discovered that "what creates anxious children is parents hovering and protecting them from stressful experiences." Using modern technology, he has been able to measure core nature by measuring heart rates. About 20 percent of children, he discovered, are naturally "high strung" (fast heartbeat). This inherited characteristic is then "aggravated" by a same-temperament parent who tries anxiously to protect the anxious child from getting into a situation of anxiety— thereby encouraging more anxiety! When these toddlers act out as a response to their anxiety, parents may not realize that their child is say-ing, "Back off! Let me develop."

Over a course of a week, consciously observe your child to see where he or she fits in this natural spectrum; the child might guide you to back off more and let play happen, or perhaps to help out more (even hover a little) in a few key areas that need more close contact, but back off in many other areas.

• *Teach right and wrong whenever you can.* Your toddler wants to know right from wrong, and your toddler is naturally altruistic, even at this age. Scientists have been proving this more and more over the last ten years. Felix Warneken, of Germany's Max Planck Institute, recently reported his toddler study of "dropped clothespins" in *Science* magazine. He and his staff dropped clothespins on the floor and observed toddlers moving (at various paces) to pick them up. He saw that the "moral brain" is already trying to shine through in its own way in each toddler.

As you teach altruism and morality to your individual toddler, consider putting less emphasis on words (the toddler won't understand most values-based words), but do make sure your tone of voice fits with "right" and "wrong." When using words and tone, try as much as possible to show the consequences of actions. For example, if your child pinches you, say "Ow! That hurt!" Show the red spot where your skin is hurt. Point out that when a child pulls the cat's tail, the cat gets hurt. "That is wrong behavior. This is right behavior. Isn't it better to do this?" If you keep your eyes open to them, you'll find everyday opportunities to draw the distinction between right and wrong during the toddler years, and you can tailor them to your child.

• *Get your toddler out in nature!* If a child is driving you crazy inside the apartment or the house and you are having to punish this child a great deal, return that child to the trees and ponds and dirt. Henry David Thoreau wrote, "Here is this vast, savage, howling mother of ours, Nature, lying all around, with such beauty, and such affection for her children, as the leopard; and yet we are so early weaned from her breast to society."

Toddlers can indeed be subdued by television or a socially focused DVD, but they will be happier and more strengthened by time in nature—and in the end, that time will subdue them, for it will tire them out with its interplay of chaos and order, things and persons, sounds and sights, feelings, sensations, and natural decision making. Nature is your ally, for your child yearns to touch leaves and see sky and hear birds in his or her own way. Follow that way, and you yourself will find more enjoyment in life too.

If you put these instinctual and nature-based ideas about discipline into a discipline system for the playtime and growing time in your toddler's life, you will be amazed at the results. Even picking just one that's most needed for *your* child—for instance, improving your toddler's sleep schedule or having him or her eat better or going out into nature—can decrease the need for punishment and open up your child's life to less negative stress and more potential self-discipline.

Self-Awareness of Your Own Core Nature

It is during the toddler years that significant physical abuse of children can emerge. Also during these years, any parent—even one who would never hit a child—can be pushed to his or her limits. Let's be honest about this right now. Let's be revolutionary in setting aside any preconceived idea that we have to be perfect parents. Let's look at our dark sides.

What behavior pushes your limits, your buttons, with your child? Take a moment to note these things down. This self-awareness can be crucial to nurturing the nature of your child. In your journal, you might list five things about your toddler that are the most challenging for you. Perhaps your two-year-old always fights against you, cries out "No!" when you just need him to obey. Perhaps your three-year-old cannot stop herself from grabbing things, making a mess, taking what isn't hers. It's useful to focus on these areas of difficulty, useful to communicate about these in your family team. Others can focus on them as well, making sure you are not trying to handle this demanding toddler entirely on your own.

It's also useful to look at some things in yourself that are "rising up" as you care for this demanding toddler. Self-awareness is one of the greatest gifts we give our child. There is not one of us—myself included—who doesn't carry forward into parenting the confused parts of our own nature.

I remember my own dark side coming through during my kids' toddler years. One of my daughters broke something precious to me, and before I knew it, I screamed at her in rage and pushed her into the couch. I am over six feet tall; she was a tiny two-year-old. Until challenged by my toddler, I didn't realize what I was capable of.

Truly, none of us is immune to the dark side of parenting. That shadow is a part of nature and must be self-disciplined. If we don't confront this dark side right now, we will become the person who traumatizes our child's core-nature development.

Right now, take time to write or think about your dark side. Get help if you need it, for your child's sake. As you do this "My Dark Side" exercise, ask others and yourself what your dark side is.

An example of a journal entry might read:

- I am too harsh, just like my mother.
- I become cold like my father.
- I scream at this kid too much.
- I'm too obsessed about my daughter's fingers in her mouth.

This self-awareness of our impatience or inappropriateness (our dark side) can be understood better with the help of our spouse, mentors, and others who care about us and our children. Reach out as much as you can to just a few people you trust. It is powerful to ask them, "What do you think my warts are as a parent? What two or three things do I need to be really careful with?"

Burning Question: How Do I Handle Tantrums?

Does your little girl or boy whine, cry, bunch fists, "hit a wall," both literally and figuratively? This behavior can bring out our dark side. "If I could just understand one thing," we might cry out, "it would be how to stop these tantrums!"

Temper tantrums almost literally light up the brain of the child. Parts of the brain, such as the amygdala, swell up during frustrating moments, and the brain may well have less blood flow between the amygdala and the frontal lobe during this swelling; thus, it's harder for children to calm down without a significant outburst of adrenaline—the tantrum. As your child's brain lights up with his or her own version of this chemistry, he or she is exploring, learning, seeking order as the brain handles anger, frustration, failure, hunger, sleeplessness, and other triggers that your child will certainly encounter again throughout his or her life.

Temper tantrums are normal. But some children are more prone to more severe tantrums during the toddler years. Often we parents think that these tantrums—especially as the toddler gets "out of control," smashing the floor with his fists, screaming at us with her high-pitched voice—are happening because of us. We blame ourselves. Certainly, if we are not securely attached to our child, or if our child is abused or otherwise chronically stressed, then we are in some part responsible for the tantrum behavior. But in most cases, we must develop ways to avoid taking tantrums personally. The child is involved in an internal process that is teaching him or her, in particular ways, about aspects, assets, and even liabilities of his or her own core nature.

By core nature, some kids are already more manipulative and opportunistic during the toddler years than others. Some toddlers are innately better at exploiting parents through the use of tantrums. Some kids are genetically more prone to physical and vocal outbursts. Some kids are more naturally impulsive. If you have a child with this core nature, it's especially important to develop a consistent discipline system for handling tantrums. For any child, the use of distraction is a good tool, but if your toddler is one of the more manipulative or naturally "tantrum prone," you might especially gain from trying to distract him or her before a tantrum starts.

You can't always prevent a tantrum, and given that learning to handle anger is an important part of core-nature development, you don't need to stop them all. However, if you are in the car and you can say, "Hey, look at that cloud! It looks like an elephant," or "Here, do you want to turn the radio on?" try this kind of distraction. Sometimes you will circumvent the tantrum and return the child to play or other stimulation.

Overall, if you realize that your child has learned to use tantrums to get his or her way, you and your parent-led team may need to band together to stop this behavior. You might have to ignore tantrums—no eye contact, no rewards—for a week or two. It might be tough, but it will calm things down around the house, and you'll be giving the nature of this child the challenge and direction it needs in order to fully develop other parts of the self.

Try This

If you are dealing with a toddler who throws severe tantrums, try these steps.

1. Stand back for a while. Even leave the room. Let the child have his or her tantrum if the physical release is taking place safely (that is, the child is lying on the floor crying, pounding fists). If there are dangerous objects around or the environment is not safe or appropriate (in the grocery store, for instance), pick the child up and take him or her to an appropriate place.

2. Decide on a "safe amount of time" for tantrums in your home, car, or other parent-controlled environment. Let's say you have intuited that independent tantrum behavior on the floor for three minutes leads to release of energy, but much more than that seems to exacerbate the tantrum. In this case, at three minutes (some kids will need more), you could lift up the child, embrace him or her, and talk quietly.

3. If the child has used inappropriate words during the tantrum, provide direction and discipline so that those words don't get used again. Profanity at two and three years old is not helpful to self-discipline development. (We must also ask ourselves as parents: Where did my child hear that language?)

4. Don't let children hit parents or other living, animate objects (pets) when having a tantrum. It is fine for them to hit the couch or other safe object that will be unaffected by their little fists, but they should never hit or hurt living things.

"She Was a Handful!"

Thomas wrote:

> My daughter was a handful. She had boundless energy, and she said "No!" to everything. She pulled away when my wife and I tried to guide her. She was in time-out A LOT. We thought, "We are messing up this child, we are stupid parents." I can't tell you how many books we read about how to handle her.
>
> Now she's twenty-four. Guess what she's doing? She's going to law school. She wants to become a litigator. She just won her moot court trial. I guess we didn't mess her up. She's still somewhat wild (her teen years were a constant battle), but when I saw her taking apart her opposing counsel in court, I remembered that little toddler saying, "No!" all the time and I thought, "That's my girl."

Even if you are right now faced with a difficult toddler, enjoy these years. Use this period to set up a strong discipline system, a respectful loving world of play and exploration, and a world of protection against the nutritional, electronic, and other stresses that will inevitably bombard this child—and remember, these years will go by very quickly. Throughout it all, I hope you'll keep writing in your journal, keep thinking aloud, "What parts of this child's core nature are coming through even more clearly now?" Always let your child's cry of "No!" or "Yes!" inspire you to keep looking into his or her eyes. You just never know where that wild (or very shy) toddler is going to end up, but if you create a healthy play and discipline system for this child, he or she will most likely end up making you quite proud.

Wisdom of Practice

TO NURTURE MY TWO-YEAR-OLD DAUGHTER'S NATURE, I TAKE HER outside for a walk every morning. She loves it, she loves to explore, and it really helps her to expand her horizons.

We talk to imaginary friends and have treasure hunts.

We count things—cars, bushes, trees, houses.

We look at flowers and talk a little about them.

We explore in fresh air and wear her out.

We don't watch much T.V at all.

The truth I've found is: to get a two-year-old to walk two miles, all you do is roll a cool rock along the sidewalk and follow along. Life gets discovered along the way.

It's slow, but it works!

5

Nurturing the Nature of
Your Four- to Six-Year-Old

The role of education is to interest children profoundly in activities to which they will give all their natural potential.

—MARIA MONTESSORI

LACEY IS THE MOTHER OF JASON, AGE FIVE. SHE AND HER HUSBAND learned to nurture the nature of their son out of sheer necessity: they had to take on a school system that did not understand Jason's nature. Like all parents of kids four to six years old, they had to face for the first time the interaction of their child's core nature with a large institutional environment outside their immediate family.

At first these two parents were intimidated, as any of us would be when called to take on a big outside organization. But Lacey and Joe became empowered by their need to fight for their son's core nature. In my view, Lacey and her husband became revolutionaries.

My contact with their story began with an e-mail Lacey wrote to our Gurian Institute educational team. Her first sentence was "I am crying as I write this." Then she wrote,

My husband and I just attended a meeting at my son's excellent suburban public school—it was a group meeting with the principal, school counselor, reading specialist and our son's kindergarten teacher. They told us that Jason, our bright 5-year-old, is flunking kindergarten and being placed in remedial reading and math programs. We've known for a few months now that Jason was having problems.

Jason is normally a happy, kind and extremely athletic child at home, but is sullen and disinterested at school. He says he hates kindergarten because, he says, "it's not fun." He refuses to do school work or pay attention in class. He's not hyper, loud or disruptive, he just tunes out the teacher, is joyless and falling farther behind.

Today, the school intervention team suggested we check with his pediatrician to rule out any kind of medical problem—at five years old! They also suggested we find a therapist to help our child deal with what appears to be an emotional issue. We're going to do these things, but I know my son. He doesn't have an emotional issue. We don't understand how he can be one way in school but another way in all other parts of his life. The school team seemed to be saying he is sick in some way. Please help me.

My heart went out to Lacey, and as my staff sent requests for help in her part of the country, we were struck by how many e-mails of this kind we receive: e-mails that show a mismatch between the core nature of a child and the social institution established to nurture that nature.

The years of four through six are an age when the social education of individual core nature becomes central to a child's and family's life. You may have experienced the mismatch between your child who enters school with a core nature in place and an ill-fitting institutional system. Even though the school system is filled with wonderful teachers and staff, it is a huge institution, and quite often a child's core nature does indeed become so mismatched with the school that the members of the educational institution and even we zealous parents wonder if there is a way to alter the child's core nature through medication or by punishing that core nature in subtle, rejecting ways.

Lacey's son entered school with a core nature driven by genetics—his own hardwiring that predisposed him toward learning impulsively and even restlessly, fidgeting, and needing more emotional attach-ment than the teacher could provide. As this core nature was rejected by the school, Jason became listless, joyless, withdrawn, and resistant, and even began to act out with negative behavior. Jason was perhaps a kind of revolutionary leader here, stating in his acting-out behavior, "Who I am is being shortchanged in this system. Let's do something about it."

Lacey sensed that her son was a smart kid. She sensed that he just learned differently than the school was set up to handle. Through her own and her family's zeal, as well as powerful assets in her community, she found support for her work in her family and in the schools. Six weeks later, we received this e-mail from Lacey:

> I have spent a lot of the last weeks worrying about what I feared was my child's doomed academic future, but now I have begun to take steps. The first is that I've begun educating myself and everyone on my school's team about the nature of how boys' brains develop, how they learn at these young ages, and what is happening for them in schools. Most people in the school had not had that information, but they were receptive.
>
> I am also developing a local network to help deal with this issue in our city. For instance, I called the clinical director of the Children's Advocacy Center for advice, and he agreed: if the only place my child is having a problem is at school, then I as a parent have to become a voice for change. By way of coincidence, the director is also the father of a 6-year-old boy. He referred me to other local professionals who are sensitive to these issues.
>
> Already I can see improvement for Jason. Until I began this process of advocating for my son, I did not realize all the resources in my own community. There are a LOT of people involved in this kind of social change. I have much more hope now than I did six weeks ago, and I am already seeing positive changes between Jason and his teachers.

Lacey's story is indeed the story of many parents, many families. And though hers involves a boy, girls too find themselves mismatched in areas of life and school during this stage of development. These early years of learning should be healthy, happy years for girls, boys, and their families. Let's look in this chapter at how to do all we can to make sure they are.

Preview of Essential Developmental Tasks

- *Focus on a deep and visionary approach to the education of your child,* whether from within the family or in partnership with school and community. The child's core nature needs education that fits him or her. A great deal of education goes on between your child and neighborhood friends, as well as siblings (even in sibling rivalries), mentors, grandparents. . . . Anyone close to the child is the child's educator, and each of these people's own core natures can help your child develop his or her unique self beautifully now.

- *Start consciously directing your child toward "a sense of purpose."* A child comes into the world searching for purpose in life—pathways that his or her own core nature will one day follow into a sense of mission and meaning. The early school years are developmentally a foundation-building time when parents and child can set a lifelong course toward the "self-education" that searching for purpose will provide throughout the child's life span.

- *Protect your child from the dangers of materialism* and an unlimited consumerist existence. Children at this age become naturally attracted to "things" and to all sorts of social stimulants. Some children become even more enamored of these material objects and stimulants than others. We can best protect the individual core nature of a developing child of this age by making sure that most of what the child is exposed to has educational value.

Information Essential to Nurturing the Core Nature of Your Four- to Six-Year-Old

You'll be seeing the word *education* quite a bit in this chapter. Maria Montessori's very powerful work in understanding this age group showed parents and teachers that children have a natural proclivity for turning objects, relationships, and environments (indoor or outdoor) into "educational opportunities."

The individual core nature of most children ages four, five, and six is ready to educate itself through the expanding mind. This time in a child's life is a transition period: he or she is moving from primarily being at home or with one or two caregivers toward being exposed to many influences and social trends regarding childhood development. It is essential to remember the following points:

1. Because of the natural variety in synapses development in your four- to six-year-old, there is rarely cause for alarm if your child is not performing in an academic skill the same way as another child. Children at this age develop at very different rates and have a broad variety of skills and behaviors. For instance, it is *very rare* that a child of this age can be (or should be) diagnosed with ADD/ADHD. If the school is suggesting this diagnosis (or if you yourself are feeling pressure to make the diagnosis), the child may well be in an educational or family system that is not understanding his or her core nature.

Similarly, though there has been a recent increase in use of antidepressants for children of four to six, in general, onset of clinical depression comes in later years. Although there could be a genetic exception that would make early onset of depression possible, or a significant trauma to the child (for example, the death of a parent) that might indeed cause significant depression—in most cases, the diagnosis of clinical depression at this age, as well as the use of antidepressants, is likely to be an indication of a mismatch between this child's core nature and the institutional, social, or family system in which he or she is being raised.

2. Certain children in this age group will really be asserting their personalities right now; others will be more taciturn. Our children of four to six educate us about who they are. As one mom told me, "Sure I knew Anna had a personality when she was younger, but when she went into first grade is when she really flourished. She became a leader, and even a popular kid. I wouldn't have expected that when she was a baby."

A grandmother wrote, "My grandson, Ryan, became almost obsessed with drumming when he was six. It was all he wanted to do. It was actually a great way to channel his fidgeting and always running around—although it was very loud! Except for the drumming, he was pretty shy, so I'm glad he had the drumming." Each assertion of "self" in these kids is a part of who they are.

3. In this age group, there is a great deal of wonder and new zeal for learning, but so too can behavioral and neural vulnerabilities in your child's core nature emerge. Autism and Asperger's, as well as obsessive-compulsive disorders, can show up by this age. If your child constantly overreacts to small situations (for instance, when he or she doesn't get a drink of milk immediately, or ties a shoe badly); can't look people in the eye; becomes obsessed with a single activity in an unhealthy way; does not sleep, but instead sits and stares; seems to be entranced internally, but unable to function externally—in any of these situations, professional help is essential. These professionals can help you determine if your child has a significant disorder or is just, by nature, mismatched with his present educational and life environment.

One example I saw firsthand was of a four-year-old boy who lived in the mountains, in relative isolation from other children. He was diagnosed as autistic, but when his parents moved into the city, he began socializing every day and within two months was "undiagnosed"—his behavior lost the characteristics of autism. For the sake of their child, this family changed the environment (moved out of isolation) and discovered that their child's core nature was not autistic.

4. Often I am asked about bed-wetting in this age group. I have also faced it in my own family. It can be confusing for parents: some bed-wetting can be an obvious reflection in the child of significant

stress; at the same time, wetting the bed can also be a part of your child's core nature in this age group. Around 10 percent of six-year-olds have nocturnal enuresis—the technical term for this situation. This enuresis generally carries a genetic component: when both parents struggled with enuresis in their childhood, their children are 77 percent more likely to have the condition. When one parent had it, the child is 44 percent more likely.

Because some children struggle with enuresis as a response to a trauma in the family, school, or community, it is important to get professional help if your child has the condition, but in most cases, we now know that the trend of blaming parenting for the condition was invalid and unnecessary.

5. Nutrition is an essential area of family focus in this age group. Soda, sugars, food allergies—all these become significant parts of the lives of four- to six-year-olds if they get in the habit. Intake of sugary snacks and junk food must be watched carefully so that the individual child's core-nature development is not harmed.

You may already be noticing that some children in this age group are more prone to craving certain foods, such as refined sugar products (the proverbial sweet tooth), than other kids. A great deal of this propensity is genetically constructed in the same way that there is a genetic component to enuresis or hyperactivity. If you have a child who "absolutely craves" or seems "easily addicted to" something that can interfere with his or her development, this is the time to let that tendency educate you to a vulnerability in your child. You might need to be even more vigorous than another family in preventing bad habits.

For instance, some kids crave sugar-sweetened drinks, yet we must remember these have now been causally linked to obesity. To feed a child of this age apple juice or soda pop every day can be like poisoning the child, especially if he or she child craves it and thus tends to ingest even more of it.

6. Each child's brain craves (or does not crave) visual and media stimulants in its own way. Some kids of five can't wait to sit down and watch TV; others are bored by it. Is your child one of those who craves a lot of sedentary time in front of the TV? The prestigious Parents

Television Council analyzed 444 hours of kids' programming and found 2,794 violent incidents—that constitutes 6.3 violent incidents per hour, *more than the number found in adult programming.*

It is critical to remember that in this age of education in your child's life, *everything* that goes into the brain is potentially educating the child. Also, the human brain in this stage of childhood cannot fully distinguish fact from fiction; violent programming can thus lead to desensitization, disruption of empathy development, and increased violence. This is an especial and immediate issue if you have a very "hyper" or "active" child— this child, naturally wired to be more aggressive than another, may well be just the wrong child to stimulate with any kind of violent programming.

The content of the program is not the only thing to consider. As recent scientific research shows, children of this age who watch television more than two hours in a day enter their adult years more likely to experience heart attack, stroke, and other cardiovascular problems.

Of course, your own child's genetic predisposition matters—some kids burn off so much energy that their time in front of the TV is more than offset by their own internal need for physical activity. For those children who appear to have slower metabolisms, however, this link to cardiovascular problems can be a supreme motivation to keep the child from spending too much of his or her education time in front of the tube.

7. The age of four to six is natural developmental period to ask, "How helpful is computer use to the core nature of my child?" Computers are wonderful educational tools for this age group. At the same time, scientific studies show two things about early computer use. First, there is little to no discernible advantage for children of this age who use computers regularly over children who do not. Even if your child does not see a computer until he or she is twelve or fifteen, within a few months of exposure his or her computer skills probably will be on par with kids who were exposed to computers at age five. Second, potential harms from too much time using a computer include arrested brain development due to less outdoor play, less physical exercise, less reading, and less interpersonal interaction. Core nature needs the outdoors, physicality, reading, and interaction with people more than it benefits from prolonged computer use in this stage of childhood.

Natural Differences Between
Boys and Girls Age Four to Six

Natural brain differences between boys and girls become very clear during the years four to six. They can especially affect cognitive development and, thus, school performance. In the Did You Know? box you'll find some fascinating facts about your boys and girls.

Did You Know?

- Boys' brains develop their ability to read and write about 1.5 years behind girls. In the four-to-six age group, boys do not, on average, gravitate as much to reading and writing tasks as girls do.
- Girls at this age do not, on average, spend as much time with cubes, Legos, and other spatial-mechanical objects. The development of their more advanced spatial-mechanical abilities often comes later than boys.
- It's natural for boys already to notice that they cannot carry children, identifying themselves as "boys, not girls." If schools or homes are thinking that girls and boys are emotionally the same, or engaging in other social trend thinking about androgyny, they are not understanding natural gender identification in children. Every child is an individual, and by this age, every child senses some of the ways in which he is an individual boy or she is an individual girl.
- It's natural for girls at this age to feel that certain aspects of boys are "disgusting." This identification of girls with girls and against boys is helpful for future female networking, and also provides opportunity for us, as parents, to teach girls appropriate girl-girl friendship

strategies. (We can help them manage the cliqueishness that is already starting between them.) Throughout life, girls will relate to girls (and women) differently than they will to boys and men. Their way of being competitive, for instance, will by nature be a little different among themselves than it will be with boys.

- Boys of this age tend to process their emotions less immediately through words than girls do. Thus you may notice your kindergarten son still throwing more enraged, pre-verbal tantrums than a girl his age. Quite often, neither girl nor boy in this stage can process as much emotion verbally as we might wish, but more likely than not, boys will have greater difficulty in this area.

- By this age, boys' brains have already begun to compart-mentalize or lateralize more activity (do it in one place in the brain rather than in many places), and girls' brains have already begun to multitask more activity (do lots of activities at once in many more parts of the brain). Thus, although it is not unusual to see both boys and girls occupying themselves for hours with one task, you might also notice that boys get more easily distracted than girls from a set of tasks, preferring to focus on one task at a time.

- By this age, boys and girls have already "discovered their bodily functions" in different ways. This can challenge homes and schools significantly. A first-grade teacher told me, "I caught a little boy wrestling with a little girl and trying to fart on her and gross her out. It made her uncomfortable. I suspended the boy." Although I did not witness this event, I would say that this boy and girl were probably on target developmentally, and suspension might have been too severe.

Handling Sibling Rivalry

As you look at your kids, especially if you have both a boy and a girl, you may see sibling rivalry starting to increase at this age. Let's look at this somewhat trying experience that is also a wonderful educational opportunity for you and your kids: an opportunity to understand two or more developing core natures at odds with each other for resources, attention, and dominance.

Debbie sent me this e-mail:

> My son and daughter are five and six, and they are so different, they fight ALL THE TIME. Sometimes I tell them to stop sniping at each other, sometimes I pull them off each other, sometimes I just walk out of the room. I didn't think sibling rivalry started this early, but in my house it does. I wonder if it's because my kids are of different genders, or because they are so close together in age, or just because their natural personalities are like oil and vinegar. My son is actually very verbal—different than a lot of the boys his age—and my daughter really likes her privacy. To her, he's kind of in her face all the time.

Children's relationships with their siblings are useful to the development of their core nature; siblings challenge and help each other, communicate with each other, get into conflict, and thus educate one another and help one another grow. Sibling rivalry can be a normal extension of living and growing up together, of wanting different things as boys and girls, and of simply being two or more developing natures competing for resources of love and attention. Any child's developing brain at this age moves toward greater self-identification, and some kids, depending on their innate personality, assert themselves more strongly—often to their sibling's dislike.

Many children, of course, will not engage in significant rivalry until later in their development, but now is the time to practice healthy strategies for handling sibling rivalry in your essential parenting system. I hope you'll modify my suggestions in the Try This box to fit the natural temperaments and needs of each of your children.

In many cases it is useful to see if you can "wait it out"—that is, let the kids' individual natures clash and then reconcile on their own. (Clear exceptions would be situations of immediate and obvious physical danger or risk of significant psychological harm.)

Try This

- If you need to enter the fray of a sibling dispute, steel yourself mentally to avoid getting too involved in the *content* of the dispute. Unless you see an obvious need or opportunity to help one of your children explain his or her position, assume that the content of the dispute is not something immediately resolvable.

- Prepare always to treat each child equally, even though there will be times when you must side with one child or the other (for example, if one child has done something immoral or obviously more inappropriate than the other). Remember that "being fair" does not generally mean siding with one child or the other, but siding with "household order." You've entered the fray because household order is at stake. Keeping that order healthy and authoritative creates the best environment for each child's nature to shine through.

- Use your authority freely and frankly. Pull the kids apart physically if necessary. Verbally compel them to stop their verbal sparring. This will become especially necessary in a small space, such as a car, or other area that is within parental control. If, for instance, your children are involved in normal sibling rivalry in your living room, you can say "Take this somewhere else," and they can go to a bedroom or outdoors, where you are not a party to the conflict. But if they are in the car, you are immediately affected and have the parental power to intervene with "Stop that now or face a consequence."

- As the conflict ends, exact apologies from both kids. If one of the children is in a very defensive emotional state, he or she may take a moment before saying "sorry," but the child must apologize for any brutal words or actions. Apologizing will be an important part of conflict resolution throughout your children's future life, and sibling rivalry offers natural opportunities to teach it to them. As a part of the apology, a handshake or even a hug can be in order.

  Again, this may take a moment to achieve, depending on the core nature and personality of each child. There may still be lingering comments from one or both children—but if this apology-and-reunion piece becomes a consistent part of your family's essential parenting blueprint in this stage of your children's lives, it can last throughout childhood, adolescence, and adulthood.

- If the sibling rivalry has been especially rampant over the last week or two, go further than apology and handshake to ask the fighting kids to decide what job or project they can now do together. If they can't think of one, you certainly can! When the car ride is over and you've returned home, they need to get right to the task. Perhaps they should pick up the living room together—one of them dusting, one of them stacking the newspapers, each according to his or her individual nature and passion!

Sibling rivalry will never stop altogether. In fact, we don't really want to stop it—it's an educational and growth experience for each child's individual core nature. Each child will "do sibling rivalry" in his or her own way, and over the years you as a parent will notice, perhaps, how one of your kids is quicker with verbal jabs, another more physical. You may also notice that one of your kids takes everything too seriously, and sibling rivalry is a good way for this child to learn to have a tougher skin.

With my own daughters, I've found such rivalry to be a natural part of their individual development and education. Although my daughters (three years apart) did not engage in painful sibling rivalry until my older child became an early adolescent and left her younger sister behind, Gail and I indeed saw the beginnings of useful and educational sibling conflict in the early school years. In fact, when Gabrielle was five, she hit her younger sister on the head with a roll of wallpaper. We provided significant discipline for this, but this incident is now an emblematic family story, one we laugh over now that our kids are older and their rivalries and conflicts have become far more subtle—more verbal and even more fraught with deeper meanings and deeper educational material.

Helping Your Self-Educating Child Ask, "Who Am I?"

In this chapter we are focusing on how the four- to six-year-old enters the greater world of educational experiences. We've even explored sibling relationships from this "educational" lens because it is in this kindergarten and first-grade age group that children are beginning to set their course of self-education for the life span. Their cognitive and emotional abilities have matured, each in their own way, to enable the child to begin to sense that it is indeed a huge world out there.

It is in this age group that children actually begin a clear questioning of who they are in the world. This is why we send them to school, of course, but sometimes we miss the import of this self-questioning. Especially because it is generally unconscious in this child, we may miss it for years. Yet the child is asking, "Who am I?"

Perhaps you've noticed your young child measuring himself or herself against an older sibling?

Perhaps you haven't heard your young child wonder aloud, "Am I a good person?" but you've seen her focused on inward thoughts as she sits on a swing.

When your six-year-old son obsesses with his heroic quest video game, have you sensed the longing in him to belong, to be the hero, to persevere against obstacles and discover himself, to mean something to someone?

Have you empathized when your five-year-old daughter goes overboard in her in-crowd–out-crowd relationships with kindergarten friends who like her, don't like her, see all her flaws, won't let her belong, call her rude things? The girls are fighting a basic battle to belong, to judge themselves worthy, to mean something to others.

The personal spiritual search of each child gets well under way as the child's brain develops enough, around five years old, to process—mainly unconsciously—why a person is here on this earth, how he or she belongs, what a hero is, why God works in the way God works. These questions are "questions of meaning" and lay a strong foundation for each child to discover, over the next two decades of substantial brain development, what *this* person's purpose(s) will be in life. Thus it is essential that we ask right now, "How shall I shepherd my child's urge to have meaning, to have purpose, to find answers to 'Who am I?'"

Shepherding Your Child's Search for Purpose Through Story

Take a moment to ponder or notice how your particular child is having "innermost thoughts" or wondering consciously over why he or she is alive or if God exists or what to do with all his or her energy. It is sometimes helpful to notice that your child is unconsciously searching for purpose in these essential areas of everyday activity:

1. Discovery of the world through education in nature
2. Imagination, including physical and mental play
3. Spiritual growth, prayer, religious rituals
4. Moral decision making, discussion of values in families and communities
5. Physical and mental work under the training of adults
6. Relationships with the family and society
7. Academic education in school or other settings

If you have any doubt that the activities and environments in which your young child finds himself or herself are replete with your particular child's sense of meaning, you can do a small experiment to prove that in fact they are. Tell the child a story that has imaginative meaning, and watch his or her eyes light up. Stories are great ways to shepherd the search for meaning and purpose in this age group. These young children easily identify with the characters in the stories and answer their own "Who am I?" questions by following the characters on their journeys.

I enjoyed engaging in this shepherding when I was asked to come to my daughter's class and talk to the students. I told them a story from an ancient Chinese teacher, Chiang Tsu. This teacher said, "I dreamed that I was a butterfly flying around. Then I woke up in my bed. Now that I'm awake, I wonder: Am I a man who just dreamed of being a butterfly, or am I really a butterfly who is dreaming right now that I'm a man?"

Of the six-year-olds in the class, I asked, "Okay, so are you a kid thinking about a butterfly right now, or are you a butterfly thinking about a kid who is thinking about a butterfly?" I paused dramatically for a moment and then asked, "Or . . . could you maybe be *both?*"

The expressions on each individual face showed each particular child's processing of this little story. Some kids cocked their heads to the side; some kids closed their eyes. If I had any worries that this story of meaning would be too complex for six-year-olds, my fears were unrealized. A marvelous discussion ensued.

A little boy said, "I want to be a butterfly, but I can't be without magic."

A little girl said, "I like butterflies, but I'd rather be myself."

My own daughter said, "My dad wouldn't tell that story unless he wanted us to think about something."

One little boy actually seemed frightened by the sudden idea in his head that he might not be a child, but instead might be a butterfly.

Later that afternoon, the teacher had the children spend their art time drawing responses to our "butterfly story." Some kids drew butterflies, others drew people flying like butterflies, others drew space ships that looked like butterflies. For an hour or two, the human search for "deeper things," for "the self," entranced each child in different, artistic ways.

It's thrilling to see these young children's core natures become inspired to imagine life possibilities dynamically. As you raise your four- to six-year-old, take time to set your own family's and community's educational assets toward helping your particular child's developing core nature find stories that focus on possible meanings and purposes to life.

Encouraging a Life of Purpose Through Purposeful Action

A mother of two girls, five and six years old, wrote,

> In your workshop, you suggested that if a child drops a spoon at the dinner table, we parents might want to make sure the child picks it up herself. As a mother, I just immediately react by doing things for my children. It's hard to stop. I feel like my kids are busy with school or projects or just with growing up, and I want to do for them what I can. So, I admit, I'm the mom who usually picks up the spoon for them. But I think you were suggesting my children don't gain as much purpose as they could, if I always pick up that spoon for them.

These children are lucky to have this very caring mother. Her "doing for" her kids is part of why her family is filled with love. At the same time, her everyday situation—picking up what her children drop—can be a metaphor for the meaning and purpose we are exploring here.

A child's individual core nature finds meaning through responsibility. A child "means something" because he or she must act meaningfully. A sense of purpose in the child and then the adult comes from small seeds of purposeful action.

A six-year-old child drops a spoon on the floor.

The mother bends down to pick it up.

The child thanks her and keeps eating.

What does the child learn about why he is alive in that moment? The child learns that he is alive to eat and to continue eating. Because his parent has picked up the spoon, the child is not alive in that moment to get out of his chair, bend down to the floor humbly, clean up a mess in the world, and return it to order. He has lost this opportunity to mean something, to be purposeful. He merely eats.

Although there is nothing wrong with the mother's actions, this child may nevertheless feel less connected with what is needed of his particular developing core nature in the world. The mother has perhaps made meaning and purpose for herself, but doesn't give her child the opportunity to find purpose in this little moment. This is a useful theme to discuss in your family as you contemplate your child's budding need to be purposeful and responsible. A story—in the form of an e-mail—that helped me as a dad focus most deeply on this theme was sent by Sam, eighty-four, a retired professor of chemistry at a midwestern university, who wrote his impression of how children's search for personal responsibility and purpose has changed over the generations.

Sam's Story of Responsibility and Purpose

When I was a little kid, we didn't have a lot, and so we really valued every second. When we played together, we figured out rules amongst ourselves quickly, and enforced them.

"This flat rock is first base, this board is second, and this cow pole is third." There were arguments. "I tagged you!" "No you didn't!" "Yes, I DID!" "NO, YOU DIDN'T!"

We settled those arguments and went on with the game. We learned that to get anything done, we had to settle differences and go on with the project, whatever it was, and take responsibility. We grew up, figuring out the world as we went. Our parents took care of us by helping us figure out how to take care of ourselves. Their responsibility to us was to make us responsible for ourselves.

Now let me contrast this with what an old man like me, a great-grandfather, perceives to be the current situation. The six-year-old kid goes to Little League with his father. The adult referee decides all the differences. The parents scream and argue among themselves, and even fight. Little League is mostly for adults. When a kid gets hurt, someone gets sued. What do the kids learn from that?

In raising our own kids, my wife and I encouraged them to get out and play with other kids. We figured each of our kids needed to find his or her own way. We didn't worry too much if our kids got hurt. We deliberately began early to get the kids to make decisions for themselves so they wouldn't always be waiting like scared rabbits for us to make their decisions for them.

At first this was: "Do you want your bath first, or do you want me to read to you first?" Then, later, it became things like: "Do you want the rake the yard or fix the car?"

It was 1960 when I drove with my eighteen-year-old daughter to New York to go live there for a year so she could get citizenship in New York and pay state tuition at SUNY. I helped her unpack and gave her a hug and said, "Claire, you're ready. This is it."

She had nothing, just a few items to get her through, but she knew who she was. She knew just what to do on her own. She was already finding her purpose in life. She had been doing so from when she was very young. Life had been testing her constantly, and she passed. I drove away sad, sure, but I didn't worry about her like parents worry today. New York wouldn't gobble her up, not this kid— and it didn't. She runs her own company now. She didn't have a lot growing up—in terms of material things she just got food, shelter and clothing from her parents—but she had a lot more than people might have realized.

So, what I'm saying is, I think, starting very young, kids need the kind of love that leads to responsibility. They need parents to give them that love and then they need parents to be able to say, "Kid, whatever happens, I trust you to figure out what's right, and what matters to *you* in this crazy world."

I taped this e-mail on my wall by my desk. It was written by someone almost twice my age. I still find it moving to this day.

Redefining Food, Shelter, and Clothing

Sam's e-mail refers to a phrase we've all heard before: *food, shelter, and clothing*. Sam talks about how all he could do for his many kids was give them food, shelter, and clothing, and the love that taught responsibility. As I think about the phrase today, I see interesting differences in its possible meanings for many families as compared to what it meant for previous generations. Food, shelter, and clothing have become more complex for four- to six-year-olds today than they were for Sam in the 1950s.

Let's pause to look at the meaning of these essentials—and the materialism many of us deal with today as parents of young children.

Material Anxiety

For a person of Sam's generation, providing food, shelter, clothing was crucial, as it is now. It was very much a person's, especially a man's, life purpose. There were also precise definitions and boundaries to the nature and quantity of food, shelter, clothing, and other material necessities during the time that Sam's children were quite young. And there was also a tacit commitment on most people's part that food, shelter, and clothing were linked to meaning and purpose. I am generalizing of course, but if you think back just to your own childhood and use the phrase "food, shelter, and clothing" as a lens, you'll notice that perhaps in even your own era (the 1970s? 1980s?), parents were trying hard to make sure kids understood how much time, effort, and life energy it took for each material item, each meal, each piece of clothing, each house to be possible in a family.

Today, for many people, there is a loss of this link. Parents and kids often face a boundaryless world of material goods, including electronic games, DVDs and CDs, videos, fantasy toys, karaoke machines, huge train sets, incredible sport and fashion shoes, toys, tapes, and devices. Material items are parts of fads and social trends—they are not linked to responsibility (quite often). There is an excess to this materialism that can bring some pleasure, but also great pressure. I have dubbed this social pressure (and the loss of the grounding of material things in responsibility) *material anxiety*. I believe this anxiety can invade a child's core-nature development today in ways it generally only used to do to the very wealthy.

Ask some questions with me, if you will:

- Do you as a parent feel anxious about whether you are providing enough "things" and the right "things" to your child?
- Does your child feed your anxiety by complaining to you about what other kids have (and what he or she doesn't have)?
- Do you make purchases for your child that are irresponsible to your family's larger and higher needs, just to quiet (for at least a day or two) your child's or your own anxiety about the acquisition of the material thing?

I think a lot of us would answer yes to some of these questions. This material anxiety today is a new psychological challenge on par in many families with more traditional challenges, such as moral and spiritual anxiety. This material anxiety can manifest not only in anxiety about material success ("Will our family have the right XBox, the right car, the right digital TV?") but also in parents' constant anxiety that they are not doing enough for children emotionally—and therefore must compensate materially.

Take out your journal for a moment if you will. Look around your house, your apartment, your neighborhood. Ask deep questions, helpful questions:

- Is my child's natural search for meaning and purpose distracted by meaningless and purposeless entertainments and things?
- Is boredom setting into my child, one that seems to be "healable" only through new material things—yet one that I know has deeper roots?
- Is my child attaching with me or others too often through material objects, rather than developing meaning through a wider variety of possibilities (noted earlier)—nature, imagination, spirituality?

A mother of a four- and six-year-old wrote in our Institute survey, "Entertainments, things, DVDs, XBoxes—they can be as cruel as they are fun, given how little purpose they bring to children's lives." Her comment was echoed by a number of people in our survey who discussed the anxiety they felt regarding their children's material and social life. These parents felt that the core-nature development of their child—their individual child's natural way of searching for meaning and purpose—was being distracted, even harmed, by our society's over-emphasis on entertainments that went nowhere and on food, shelter, and clothing that became unhealthy. They talked, for instance, about "food" these days as being filled with unhealthy fats, excessive carbohydrates, sugars, and lack of healthy fatty acids; "shelter" as including signals of false safety provided to children within our homes by the blue glow of the TV, the Internet, video, and a continuing flow of marginal celebrities wired into homes; and a lack of interaction and emotional support with living people, hard work, personal responsibility; "clothing" as a new sense of entitlement on the part of children that they have the "right costume" for navigation of peer groups and culture, including inappropriate and constantly changing costumes dictated by the new celebrity or social trend. In some of these survey comments, the term "food, shelter, and clothing" became almost metaphorical of these excesses.

It's a good metaphor, isn't it? What constitutes food, shelter, and clothing has, for many families, changed over the last two generations. Nature-based parenting—the nurture-the-nature approach—asks each of us as parents to make sure we spend little or no time on food, shelter, or clothing that does not nurture the nature of our young child toward purpose and responsibility.

Keeping Things Meaningful

Hannah, a school principal and a mother of three in Houston, "became countercultural" (revolutionary) to nurture her kids' nature.

> From preschool and kindergarten onward, TV and the whole culture taught my kids that they had to dress a certain way, then have certain videos, then later, in elementary school, the cutest boy or girl friend, then in middle school, the thinnest body, the latest whatever, and if you didn't, you weren't worth much. Our kids were learning from the culture around them that they were entitled to instant gratification.

They had a number of friends whose parents were either over involved or under involved. Every moment was a fight—we could hardly go to the drug store without our kids wanting some new toy.

So John and I became countercultural. We said, "No!" We made our kids earn every new toy by doing chores, homework, having a good attitude. Starting from four years old, every time a new toy came in, our kids had to give one away. At five, our kids started volunteering with me and their father in our church program for the elderly—the education director at our church assured us that kindergarten age was not too early to start this, and she was right! Beginning very young, we taught our kids the differences between needs and wants. We told them: you have what you need, not every-thing you want. We became anti-materialism parents during our second child's kindergarten year. If the kids couldn't give us a good reason for wanting something, or even wanting to do a certain activity, we just said no.

Hannah's wise focus on needs versus wants is an important one we can all use with our kids.

There is in each child a powerful momentum not only to learn as much as possible through the early years of education but also to set a course toward an independent, constructive future. Also in each child there are a number of easy pathways to distraction. As parents and care-givers, you and I are called to help the child navigate both.

In my own daughters' lives, big issues emerged in the early educa-tion years as both Gabrielle and then later Davita became intensely focused on clothes. They could not go into a store without begging for some new piece of clothing. With Gabrielle, our first child, Gail and I didn't notice how our daughter was losing track of her own nature—her focus on meaning, purpose, and self-development—by becoming ob-sessed with clothes. (And we considered ourselves, of course, to be such wise parents!) When we finally saw it, and our part in it, we put an end to it.

At first, Gabrielle became very whiny and angry. She told her first-grade teacher she hated us. But of course, after a few weeks of "No!" she adjusted and became less obsessed. By the time Davita was in first

---

Try This

As you focus on "needs" versus "wants" and what you might do to alleviate material issues and even anxiety in your home, I hope these questions will help. Try answering them, perhaps in your journal, in your own thoughts, or in family discussion. Appendix C offers more information and questions to consider as well.

- How do I or others on my parenting team give in too much to instant gratification?
- How do I or others use material goods and possessions to relieve confusion and anxiety about doing the right thing for our kids?
- How do I or others hover or overparent, forcing solutions on children that their own core nature should try to work out on its own?
- In what way(s) is my child overscheduled?
- In what way(s) am I (or another on the team) underinvolved in my child's life (supervising him or her too little in areas of meaning and purpose)?
- What material goods, foods, electronics, even clothes have become dangerous or useless to my child's core-nature development?

---

grade, she tried the constant distraction of "new clothes," but we had learned how to set better boundaries.

It is indeed the little things—an unhealthy food or electronic stimulant, even pieces of cloth—that carry great meaning in the early life of a child. And through them, the themes of meaning, purpose, instant gratification, food, shelter, and clothing . . . all become essential to ponder as we educate our children and help them self-educate during their young years. As we see our child's young core nature flourish imaginatively, in nature, in purpose and responsibility, and in a reasonable schedule with reasonable material objects in tow, we can feel a calm in our home and a deeper sense of purpose ourselves.

Burning Question: How Do I Find the Best School for My Four- to Six-Year-Old?

School is a teacher of purpose, so let us ask a burning question about our young children's schooling. For many parents of children in this age group, few questions burn more brightly than "How do I know what will be the best school for my child?" This is certainly the question Lacey was dealing with in the story with which this chapter began. It is also a question that is sent via e-mail to my staff and me many times a week.

As I provide what I hope is a meaningful answer here, I want especially to thank Kathy Stevens and our Gurian Institute's training team for helping me develop this framework. She and the team have co-trained more than twenty thousand teachers and learned from them what really works in schools. We all strive to develop nature-based strategies for "good schooling" through which the school environment can nurture the nature of each student. To this end, we have found that a school most likely to be aware of the needs of each individual child will be set up as a "nature-based" learning environment, as opposed to a social trends environment.

What do we mean? Nature-based education operates out of these basic principles:

- Clear scientific evidence regarding how the brain and body learn and grow is a primary foundation for the development of the educational environment. (Any new trend is justified scientifically.)
- Learning must engage the entire body—in other words, it must be not just about reading but also about doing, moving, being, experiencing.
- The search for meaning is an intrinsic part of every child's development, and each teacher and classroom must engage this search through story and action and through teaching individual responsibility.

- Each child "patterns" his or her thinking in a unique way, so teachers must be sensitive to unique aspects of each child's core nature from the moment the new child enters school.
- Boys and girls naturally learn differently, and teacher training is thus incomplete if it does not include understanding of the gender-related differences in educational needs and strategies for boys and girls.
- Although learning indeed happens when children focus on a specific task or set of tasks, it also happens when children's minds wander (or when they doodle or when they draw while someone is talking)—these can be very okay!
- Remembering things can happen by rote, but should also be "spatial" and "experiential"—that is, linked to actual things in the world, objects, and manipulatives.
- Emotions really matter a great deal to learning; thus a child's core nature won't learn well if the child doesn't feel emotionally attached to teachers—this being especially the case for more shy or quiet children.
- Learning requires challenge and, when appropriate, clear critique. (Overprotecting a child's ego can be detrimental in the same way that shaming the child can be.)
- Learning takes place both outdoors and indoors.
- Each core nature learns in its own time. Sometimes a mind must be forced to accelerate its learning, but we must also acknowledge that, quite often, the brain of a particular four- to six-year-old is not ready to read or to engage in organized sports or other patterned activity as quickly as we might wish.

A school that follows these nature-based principles should allow for education of what Dr. Mel Levine has called "a mind at a time." This kind of school should be best suited to nurture the core natures of each individual child. This nature-based school may not be the most famous one; it may not necessarily be the local public school nor a private school. It can be any school. It will be the one that helps each of us as parents worry less about what college our child will go to in the future because right now we will feel comfortable that success principles for individual brain development (and therefore the best educational power later in life) are in place in the school and classroom.

Our schools are wonderful places filled with wonderful professionals and potential parent team members, but if the classroom your kindergartner or first grader is entering does not implement many of these brain-based principles, you may need to become like Lacey—an advocate for change. You may also be compelled to look for alternative schooling options that do follow a number of these principles.

The founders of Google credit their Montessori education with being the catalyst for their success. Sergey Brin and Larry Page believe that the Montessori alternative form of education—strongly brain and nature based—helped them develop their individuality and entrepreneurship.

Whether a mainstream school or an alternative one, the nature-based school should be able to help you decide whether to hold your child back from first grade. Many children do need to be held back. Their brain development patterns are genetically designed for slower development—for instance, they don't need to try to learn complex reading skills until age seven—and a nature-based approach to schooling can help you feel relief and a sense of direction as you decide, "I will hold this child back, and I won't worry anymore that something is wrong with him or her."

A nature-based school will also know a lot of tricks for helping children read to their highest natural potential. Especially if you have a child who is having difficulty with reading, refer to the next Try This box for some techniques and guidelines you can use that will not change his or her genetics, but will ensure that your child is more ready for school and for life—and that you have done what you can to care for his or her mind, nature, strengths, and vulnerabilities.

Your child's core nature is what matters the most. Some kids may flourish in a big school that offers a very diverse curriculum, whereas others need a smaller one that focuses on one subject—such as science, math, reading, music, outdoor play, or art—more than others. Some special kids by nature need special accommodations, whereas others can be mainstreamed easily, despite their autism, learning issues, or difficulty focusing.

There will of course be no easy answer to exactly what school is best, and any answer could turn out wrong, but if you pay attention to the nature-based qualities of the school and if you discern how your child's core nature fits with this place of learning, you should find your road to decision making an easier one, and one that leads to more meaningful success for your particular child. Through your vigilance in this regard, your child may not end up in the school others consider "the best," but he or she will be in the school that really is the most appropriate for his or her core nature.

Try This

Some children, by nature, do not read as well at four or five or even six as others do. Often, parents and teachers don't know this, and this circumstance feeds anxiety among parents and teachers (and then kids) about reading skills, especially because adult life at this time in our history is strongly reading oriented. When our child does not read well, we wonder what could be wrong. We think he or she won't read well in the workplace, won't be able to earn a living. Yet in most cases nothing is wrong, nor will be wrong. The child's brain is just developing this capacity slower, by nature, than his or her sibling's or friend's.

By the time your child is six, you'll be able to assess whether he or she is just by nature slower at learning to read (in which case you don't need to worry) or whether you should be concerned about this child's learning or reading disability. If the child has an actual disability (you should probably get more than one specialist's opinion to verify that he or she does), the specialist will start you on a course of adaptation. If, however, you have a naturally slow reader in your four- to six-year-old, here are some practical tips that can help your child develop reading skills in a nature-friendly way. These are fun rather than high pressure, so the child will get education in reading while still "being who he or she is" and without feeling a great deal of unnecessary anxiety:

- Direct the child's eyes to pictures, then associate words with the pictures.
- Help the child to say the words aloud—do it with the child so that you both have fun.
- Help the child break words into their syllables, like a game.
- Ask the child which parts of the words he or she already knows; build on those.
- Read past a difficult word, then return to it.
- Explain words by using examples from the child's life.
- Read aloud and let the child mimic you.

Parents and schools with a nature-based philosophy will together revolutionize a child's learning process by focusing on the child and thus saying to the world, "Patience with the uniqueness of this particular child matters most of all." Social trends and social expectations will not get thrown out, and no school is perfect by any means, but the school and the home that teach children well are those that hear the child whispering, "This is how *I* learn," and bend the educational system as much as possible toward that unique gift.

Moving Forward with Both Peace and Excitement

Just like you, I am raising children in this celebrity-oriented social trends culture. I know how fascinating and useful our culture can be. It is not an ogre, it is not evil, it is not even inherently destructive—if we continue to lead our children. If we give up the control of our four- to six-year-old's life, then our child is in danger—not from wild boar, not from sexual predators, but mostly from the "subtle harms" of core nature's losing its way early on, and probably continuing to do so later in life.

I hope as you move forward in your child's life, you will make sure *you are in control* of the food, shelter, and clothing in your child's life; that your control is healthy for the core-nature development of *your* child; that you are an advocate regarding your child's schooling; and that in all you do to protect this child, you have in the back of your mind the exciting electricity firing through your child's soul that cries out, "I want to mean something important, loving, and wise in this world, and I want to begin finding that purpose right now."

Wisdom of Practice

I HAVE THREE KIDS, ONE BOY AND TWO GIRLS. TWO OF THEM ARE just entering school. I listen a lot to the way my parents were brought up in 1945. I really want that freedom for my kids. When my parents were scheduled to do something, it was either school related or very important for the family's livelihood—like checking the coal fire at 7 A.M. As for my childhood, I was "left alone" in a healthy sense—not overscheduled. I didn't start anything organized until age nine.

Today, my husband and I live in a very affluent area full of four- to six-year-olds taking violin, gymnastics, math camps, soccer, and so on. It is scary to say no to all that my area offers for young children, but I keep a little video in my head of what I remember when I was young. I look at how successful and happy my family is, and I keep my eyes on the good stuff.

As for behavior, I try to keep it simple—it really all comes down to one thing for young children (to me anyway), and that is respect. Nearly every common misbehavior can be traced back to a child's lack of respect for something or someone. Self-control is best gained by my kids when they understand *why* they are needing to gain it—respect for the teacher when you listen, respect for Mom when you respond when she calls for you, respect for nature when you don't throw rocks in the frog pond . . . respect for country when you really *do* put your hand over your heart during the anthem.

My seven-year-old has especially needed help with this but now, I think, "gets it." As I raise all my kids—who are so similar and yet so different each in their way—I keep going back to remembering playing outside until dark and your bare feet would get dirty and the mosquitoes would chew you to pieces and then from way far away you'd hear the parents start to call everyone in for baths. *That* is what I'm most trying to do for each of my kids.

6

Nurturing the Nature of
Your Seven- to Ten-Year-Old

Our children are not machines that need to be repaired through a
series of mechanical steps—they are relational beings whose souls
grow through the mystery of their relationships.

—DAN ALLENDER

ALISON, MOTHER OF BRITTANY, EIGHT, AND BRIAN, NINE, WROTE ME
this wonderful e-mail:

I love having kids this age. There are specific issues for each of these
kids, but there's also such a love of life during these years. Each of
their personalities is really coming out now, my son pretty shy, my
daughter quite vivacious. Neither of them can get enough of me, my
husband, our family, their friends. These kids still love us all! No adolescent tossing us to the wind yet. Our family is all about the day to
day of living together, chores, school work, sports activities, 4-H, and
controlling how much television the kids can watch. We have noticed
one thing for sure: the more the kids watch TV, play video games, or
spend time on the computer, the less they relate to us, other people,
their friends. Because of this, we err on the side of relationships and
away from electronics. Sometimes the kids complain, but not usually.
They know we want what's best for them.

The years from seven to ten are their own distinct stage of childhood. Alison can sense it, can't she? She knows that there are just a few years here to keep the kids close to home, keep them immersed in various relationships, lots of hugs, and family time; keep them centered and not too invested in virtual realms that impede quality relationships; keep them focused on school, the physical body, their family and community.

If we called the infant years the age of attachment, the toddler years the age of order and play, and the early school years the age of education, we would do well to think of our seven- to ten-year-olds as living in the age of relationship. At this age, the human brain is highly active in its growth of synapses and connections between the limbic system, which involves emotions and relational contact, and the cerebral cortex, which does our thinking for us.

Preview of Essential Developmental Tasks

- *Preserve a lot of time for relating.* The years of seven to ten are very much the age of relationship for the core nature of your children, so enjoy and hone your instinct to protect "relating time." This instinct is your own parental core nature coming through strongly in your love of your relational child, and it is your best guide as to what's going to help *your particular* school-age child be successful in life.
- *Work on your marriage* and, if needed, on your divorce. Statistically, many divorces happen before or during this time in children's lives. Whether a couple is married or divorced, they are still "married" in the child's mind. In this chapter, we'll explore ways to make both marriage and divorce most protective of your child's core nature.
- *Hold down TV, computer, iPod, and podcast time.* It is crucial to keep control of TV, movies, video games, computer time, the Internet, and iPods during the ages of seven to ten. Electronic media affect the core-nature development of every child in

some similar ways, and affect each particular child so distinctly that we must constantly gain new information and skills to best control media use.

Information Essential to Nurturing the Core Nature of Your Seven- to Ten-Year-Old

Parts of the brain devoted to learning through relationship really flourish in the child of seven to ten. These specifically involve connections between the frontal lobe and the limbic system and between the temporal lobe and the limbic system. Along these same lines, you may notice some of these other essential features of your school-age child:

1. By the time your child is this age, his or her personality is so "set" that only major and significant trauma (discussed further in Chapter Eight) can significantly alter this child's patterns of emotion and relationship. New genetics research has been able to focus on specific alleles in parts of the brain that control an individual personality's approach to emotions and relating. For instance, parents can now understand their individual child's emotional resilience by understanding his or her genetics. Genetics discoveries in 2003 revealed that about 17 percent of children have two short alleles in the 5-HTT gene, which regulates serotonin (a wellness chemical) to the brain. Children with short alleles have more difficulty bouncing back from negative and stressful situations than children with two long alleles, or even one long and one short. A great deal of how your school-age child handles relationships is wired into these pieces of DNA. (Sources in the Notes and References section can help you learn more about the subtleties of DNA.) As we parents learn more about DNA in our kids, we can often worry less about them generally and focus more specifically on how *this child* relates.

2. Sleep is crucial to the bodies and brains of all children at this age, but as is true of so many other aspects of their lives, each individual child's need for sleep is different, because each child's brain is different.

As you make sure that each of your kids gets the sleep adequate for him or her, you will be helping each child accomplish better memory building, learning, and multitasking; you probably will also better protect his or her relationships. Here's why. Using brain scans, Gregory Belenky, formerly of the Walter Reed Army Institute of Research, now at Washington State University, has revealed that when we don't sleep enough, brain activity decreases; and, he reports, "The biggest drops occur in exactly those areas of the cortex that anticipate and integrate emotion and reason." The right amount of sleep for your child is a boon to relating, and lack of sleep can lead to the kind of negativity that hurts relationships.

3. By the time your child is between seven and ten, obesity can already be a crucial genetic, behavioral, and relational issue. Especially if you see a genetic tendency to become overweight in the parents, you will want to be vigilant with this child about

- Cutting out high-calorie foods when they are not needed. (A treat once in a while might be okay, and carbo-loading before a track meet might be useful.)
- Keeping him or her physically active. If your child spends ten hours a week on screen time, obesity may result, especially if there is any genetic tendency to become overweight.
- Testing of cholesterol, blood sugar, and blood pressure. By eight or nine, your child may already be overweight, and you will want to see a physician for a BMI (body mass index) rating and for other assistance.

4. By age seven to ten, your child's body will need to eat in unique and specific intervals. Some children will need to eat smaller quantities of food several times per day. Others will want a huge breakfast, a smaller lunch, and a larger dinner. There is no one correct way to eat, no one perfect set of habits. Each core nature metabolizes food differently.

At the same time, no matter what eating pattern is best for your child, he or she should eat breakfast. If your child seems to be saying, "I don't need breakfast," this child is probably misreading his or her own biology or might need a physician's attention. Good nutrition is crucial to brain and body development of school-age children.

5. Your child's body at this age needs specific chemicals that are found in specific foods and environments. Not surprisingly, your child's core nature may well differ from another's in this regard. When a child is of school age, it is very useful for parents to see how school performance, athletics, and relationships are affected by the gain or lack of these chemicals in the child's diet and environment.

Dietitian Ruth DeBusk, of Tallahassee, Florida, is one of many people who are calling on families to create a quiet revolution in the care of these specific natural needs. She advises a DNA test (your health provider should be able to perform this) to determine what excesses and lacks exist in your child's nutrition.

How will you know if this is a potentially useful tool for you and your child? You might want to investigate further if your child experiences relationship breakdowns; if your child rages at you or others (for instance, at certain times of the day), he or she may be experiencing a chemical imbalance.

6. By the time the child is prepubescent, around nine or ten, parents tend to realize the "temper" of their individual child. If you have a child who gets angry more frequently (and for smaller things) than others, it is useful to remember that some of this is and has been a part of the child's genetic personality from the beginning; the child's temperament only now becomes "a big deal" because he or she is older, more assertive, and living more "out in the world" and is thus suffering the relational consequences of his or her anger.

If there is too much anger in your home, or if you find yourself with a child who "flies off the handle" all the time, this is a good time to get help so that adolescence can go more smoothly. This is a crucial age for both kids and parents to develop new skills, especially if a child is being disrespectful during episodes of anger. Counseling, specifically for anger management, may be in order.

7. The school-age child's brain is a sponge, but it can get overloaded. Overload can lead to significant stress on the child and on his or her relationships. Indeed, overload over a long period of time can

lead to chronic stress symptoms—depression, rage, withdrawal, and school failure.

Overscheduling is thus a crucial issue to look at with this age group. Generally speaking, for a seven-year-old to play three sports at a time is unhealthy; you might look at whether it is unhealthy specifically for your child. Every once in a while I meet a parent who says, "My child absolutely needs to be constantly scheduled. You call it overscheduling, but for my kid it's just right." The nurture-the-nature approach values this parent's instincts highly, and this instinct about scheduling must be respected.

At the same time, a nine-year-old involved in a long school day, then two hours of tutoring, then two hours of homework every night may actually lose active brain cells rather than build healthy synapses. *Downtime is crucial for the seven- to ten-year-old child's brain.* Thus it is crucial to give your child downtime—even a child whose core nature loves to be highly (even stressfully) scheduled. Downtime of at least an hour a day—reading under a tree, playing, listening to music, "doing nothing"—is healthy for core-nature development of children in this age group and ought to be considered more important than any randomly chosen new activity, sport, or academic pursuit. As in so many areas of life during these school years, a first clue as to whether your child is getting overloaded may come in his or her moodiness and difficulty in primary relationships.

Natural Differences Between School-Age Girls and Boys

The seven-to-ten age group is a fascinating one for observing male-female differences. By the time your child is seven, and moving on through these prepuberty years, you may well notice a number of profound differences between boys and girls.

• School-age boys and girls hear, receive, process, and even need praise in different ways. There are differences in verbal centers and in the brain's reward centers—for example, the caudate in the middle of the brain—that make for brain differences in how boys and girls relate to lots of praise. New research from Britain shows that boys tend not to react as well to excessive praise as girls do. If you notice boys liking to be "praised through challenge" more than girls and girls liking more verbal "Wonderful job!" praise than boys, you are probably noticing biology at work.

• Because boys by this time are well established in tending toward more active physical and spatial stimulation than girls, they will tend to climb more trees, ride more skateboards, put their bodies at more risk, and thus get more brain injuries. Some mental, emotional, and relational issues faced by children are being discovered to correlate with brain injuries. The Amen Clinics have done thirty-five thousand brain scans, and as neuropsychiatrist Dr. Daniel G. Amen recently told me, "A brain injury is something that really can seem to change who you are." This is a trauma, often experienced in this age group, that can especially affect your child's ability to learn and to relate.

If your son, for instance, suddenly seems to be experiencing more moodiness or other significant social or academic problems, it might well be worth asking, "Son, can you remember if you've hit your head really hard lately?" Dr. Amen estimates that around one million American children, most of them boys, have suffered undiagnosed brain injuries.

• Girls' brains process more blood flow through the right parietal lobe, an attention center of the brain. Girls will tend to spend more time attending to the other person in their relationships. And because of this difference in the parietal lobe, boys of this age will by now be more frequently diagnosed with attention span problems.

• The male brain moves through childhood with less blood flow than the female in general, which means that boys may need more physical movement than girls in order to perform at parity on various tasks, such as learning, memorizing, writing—and relating! As one precocious ten-year-old, whose school lets him jump rope in place to start his school day, put it, "This physical activity really gets my brain going.

You need to do this stuff to get through life." These are wise words for all kids, especially for boys in school. You may have noticed that your son is able to talk more about what he is feeling when or after he has physically moved around. The male brain often needs the physical before it can go to the emotional and relational.

• An essential difference between males and females, which shows up markedly by seven to ten and especially affects relationships, is the male brain's tendency to "systematize"—to see the world in large systems and relate to others hierarchically—and the female brain's tendency to "empathize"—to increase social bonds by noticing the emotional life of individuals and valuing it more than the systemization of the large group. In his book *The Essential Difference,* British researcher Simon Baron-Cohen shows the extent of this difference in children's brain biology and provides deep insight into how boys and girls think, feel, and even love. I highly recommend his book.

• By age seven to ten, girls and boys will have established gender-specific relationships with their mothers and fathers. As one mother put it, "My daughter lets herself be more frail and uncertain with me, but acts tougher for her dad." This normal "division of labor" in core-nature development is healthy. It is part of how boys and girls bond specifically with their same-sex and other-sex parent.

If you notice your eight- or nine-year-old, for instance, trying to get both parents to relate to him or her in exactly the same way, it's worth paying close attention, of course; but it is also useful to make sure that your child experiences variety in his or her ways of relating and expressing the self. That way, the child's brain will imprint lots of possibilities and be ready to take on the variety of relationships that the world will throw at him or her later in life.

• By elementary school, girls and boys will learn such subjects as math in different ways. For example, girls may require more schematic drawings of physical science concepts, such as electricity or wind force, in order for them to imagine the physics. Much more of girls' brains are devoted to verbal and emotive tasks by this age than boys' (and thus less is focused on spatial tasks), and these sorts of brain differences may last through life. Schools that help girls (and those boys who need it) use more words during their math calculations are finding improvement in math performance. The group work, relating, and "doing-together" can really help!

• You'll probably observe differences in the way your school-age boys and girls relate to any task, even a small one. As one teacher in Toronto wrote, "When my second grade students build toothpick and marshmallow structures in math class, the girls build horizontally, with a wider variety of shapes, and the boys build vertical towers, with less variety." She notes that when the task is done, the boys like to relate to one another by breaking down the towers they have finished and laughing happily together. The girls tend to want to add more colors and designs to the towers, working among a group of friends, and to keep the towers intact.

The brains of boys and girls are quite different and will be throughout life. If you want to engage in a fun and illuminating exercise, you might set aside a few pages in your journal just to keep a record of how differently the school-age boys and girls in your home, neighborhood, and educational systems approach each task in front of them.

Focusing on the Art of Relationship to Protect Your Child's Core Nature

Debra-Lynn B. Hook, a newspaper columnist, reported that her seven-year-old niece burst into tears after a very busy day of school, piano, and tae kwon do.

"I never have time to play anymore!" Debra-Lynn's seven-year-old son murmured angrily after an afternoon of math club, baseball practice, and piano; "I sure am busy." As both an aunt and a mother, Debra-Lynn could see the stress these children were under and wanted to protect them. She admitted that she is like many of us who "spend our 'free' time, not to mention 'excess' cash, carting kids to events, activities, lessons and tournaments they might not need or even want." She wondered, "Why don't we just pull the emergency plug on the treadmill?" The answer, she decided, was fear with a capital F. Our kids are school-age now, and we sense that they must compete mercilessly in life. We want to do our part by pushing them hard into every available performance and relationship opportunity.

Have you felt the fear? When you look at your second, third, or fourth grader, are you already worrying that he or she won't get into college, succeed, survive? Perhaps we all have succumbed to this fear at one point or another. Perhaps we have all chosen a "new activity" as the way to allay that fear—a way to feel confident (for a little while) that we've done right by our child. This may well be the right choice, of course. At the same time, let's take a moment to look at "relationship" with as much acumen as we might "activity." The brain of this school-age child wants activity, yes—it wants new things, new places, new games—but it also wants and needs *relationship*. In the window available to us during our child's elementary school years, a focus on relationship can help us create safe, protective, and ultimately successful standards for what activities or things our child needs.

A comprehensive study of child success, conducted in 2002 by researchers Karen Mapp and Anne Henderson, looked carefully at high-achieving students from all backgrounds. It found that the common denominator was relationship.

"Their parents encourage them, talk with them about school, help them plan for higher education, and keep them focused on learning and homework." The activity of relationship mattered more than money, more than other "college prep" activities, more than electronics, more than material comfort.

This is common sense, of course, but it is good to have strong proof of it. It allows us to measure the health of our child's life through an instinctual lens—a relationship lens. I hope some of the practical suggestions in the Try This box can help you focus that lens on your child's core nature.

Try This

- Don't overemphasize only one relationship (including your own relationship with the child). Focus on four or five strong relationships in your family and community—nuclear and extended family, faith community, teachers, school personnel.

- Focus on one or two weaknesses, big ones, and let the small ones go. You will see weaknesses in your child by now—some of them, in shy or aggressive children, may be clearly relational. Most issues can be helped if you look for a specific compensatory activity *in which a mentoring relationship will form*. If, for instance, your son or daughter is physically very awkward, you might be searching for a new sport to get the child into. As you search, it might be especially useful to meet with coaches to see if your child will be a fit with *this person*, not just the activity.

- Parents of children in this age group often wonder, "Should my child have the right to privacy?" If you are to remain relationally and intimately involved in nurturing the nature of your child, you might need to look carefully at this issue. Each family must make its own decisions, and certainly bodily functions and nudity issues require privacy, but beyond these, a child of this age should have very little expectation of privacy regarding space, belongings and other objects, or electronics. It is your right to go into your child's room at will, look into drawers, see who the child is relating with and how, ask questions, get answers.

- As you nurture this child's nature through his or her school years, you may well find that your child's core nature comes out strongly if you are not a "sherpa parent"—carting your child and your child's things everywhere all the time. Consider letting your child focus on only a few key activities, so that you are not your child's driving slave, and let the child carry his or her own stuff!

- Remind your seven- to ten-year-old child that you are a parent first, a friend second. Especially if you are a single or divorced parent, this can be essential for helping a child of this age grow—this child needs parenting from you more than he or she needs comfortable, easy friendship. There will be wonderful moments of sensing the future with this child, when he or she will be an adult and you'll be friends, but right now, this child's individual nature needs clear relationships with parents who will guide and teach.

- When your child has conflicts with peer friends, help him or her learn from each little crisis. At this age, the key to friendships is not necessarily to hold on to the friends for many years, but to make sure that the child's core nature learns and hones new relational skills in each passing friendship.

- If your child is shy or has some natural "social skills issues," don't worry if he or she has very few peer friendships right now. Instead, emphasize overnights with the child's godparent or grandpa and grandma. The extended family can be the primary relational system until the child develops better skills with peers.

- If your child constantly becomes angry or is highly aggressive, you will want to use this tendency as a pathway for relational skills development. The Notes and References section lists resources to help you.

- In daily things that go wrong in your child's life or relationships, don't be afraid to help the child figure out what he or she has done wrong. This is a good time to learn that one can't blame everything on others.

Above all else, perhaps most important is to protect family time. Weekends are for relating to parents and extended family. Dinner time (three to four times a week at least) is sacred time. Story time most nights is love time. Every day is a relational day.

If your various daily and evening activities have cut into family time, look carefully at how to eliminate some of them. A very comprehensive new study from the University of Michigan shows that children who lose family time are more likely to abuse substances and fail later. Soon enough, your adolescents will grow away from you. Right now, these preadolescents need you and their families most of all.

Protecting a Child's Core Nature by Creating Symbiotic Marriage or Symbiotic Divorce

Tom was forty-five, an industrial engineer. Toni was forty-three, a part-time marketing consultant. They had two children, seven and nine. They walked into my office ready to divorce. Tom said, "Toni controls me all the time. She can't stop criticizing. She isn't loving." Toni said, "Tom has no feelings. He can't open up. He doesn't know how to love me."

These two good people sat in my office in misery and pain. Tom felt betrayed by his wife's domineering attitude and was in shock at the loss of his children as he set up his new apartment and his children remained with their mother. Toni felt anger at Tom for being so unable to be her friend. She felt sadness and grief at causing her children pain, but she saw no way out of divorce. Tom agreed. These were two people sitting in my office absolutely knowing that this marriage could not be repaired and that despair awaited them, but unable to see anything else.

A year later, Tom and Toni were still married; they had gained a working peace, a truce. Their marriage was not blissful, but, as Toni told me, "We're getting by, and we're on track, at least till the kids are grown."

Why hadn't they divorced? Should they have divorced? Would the children have been better off if this arguing couple divorced? Did they make the right sacrifice in staying married, even though somewhat unhappily?

These are all questions that many of you have faced or are facing. A large percentage of divorces in America happen when the children are between seven to ten. Many couples have noticed how derailed a child's core-nature development can become before, during, and after divorce (whatever the age of the children). At the same time, many couples have said, "Divorcing was the best thing we could have done for our kids."

What is the nurture-the-nature approach to divorce? What might be a revolutionary approach to marriage and divorce in our postindustrial era?

Symbiotic Marriage

To begin answering these questions, it is important to note that the majority of divorces occur for reasons related to lack of emotional fulfillment rather than because of fears for personal safety (for example, domestic violence or abuse). Tom and Toni were not dangerous to one another; they were divorcing because they lacked emotional fulfillment. They were locked in an emotional power struggle, each of them trying to control the other, emotionally rejecting the other in his or her own way, trying to wring from the other more love or a different kind of love than existed between them. Like many couples, Tom and Toni had lived for a few years in a marriage in which they did not trust the other to be there emotionally in the way the other needed. Because they had, at their wedding, tacitly based their future marriage on this emotional fulfillment between two young lovers, they saw no alternative now but to divorce and break free of the emotional betrayal they both felt.

When I began working with them—and without in any way denying the pain of their emotional conflicts—I felt that it was my job to offer to these two good people a different model of marriage and to help them see how they could regain each other's trust or develop a different hinge for that trust.

As a marital therapist, I make a distinction between couples who have children and couples who do not. If a couple walks into my office and does not have children, I see the marriage as primarily a crucible for the emotional development of the two people. Given the freedom with which people marry today, many marriages are consummated for emotional and psychological reasons that are short term, and they may well have been set up for divorce on the day of the wedding. Sometimes I can best aid individuals in these marriages by helping them break free of the troubles they cause one another—all the while (I hope) helping them see how to be more emotionally fulfilled in their future unions.

The situation is completely different when couples with children come into my office in pursuit of marital therapy. I inform these clients of my bias: if there is no immediate physical danger between the spouses—domestic violence, abuse, dangerous addiction—my job will be to try to help them stay together, to develop a *symbiotic marriage* that protects and nurtures their children's core nature. The hinge for the marriage is not necessarily the parents' emotional fulfillment; it is their children's safe core-nature development.

This philosophy shifts the emphasis of a marriage with children away from the lovers' emotional entanglements and toward the development of a union in which the natural need of the child for family stability guides parents. Inspired by the child, these parents form a practical symbiosis from which emotional fulfillment as a couple certainly may grow, but is not the top priority.

Some couples walk out of my office after this first meeting, never to return. Most come back. As one client put it, "Thank you for letting us know ahead of time. That is a different perspective than I've heard before."

It indeed can be a different perspective. It can lead to contention, especially if one or both of the clients in the couple have their hearts set on divorce, as Tom did. It is also a perspective that does not always lead to marital repair or longevity: many of my clients with children do divorce, and my job becomes that of helping them create a symbiotic divorce, which we'll discuss in a moment.

Yet Tom and Toni are an example of a success story in symbiotic marriage. They rethought their marriage and decided that the preservation of a stable symbiotic marriage best protected the core natures of their children. They decided that their children's well-being mattered, at least for a few years, more than the immediate emotional fulfillment of their needs as lovers and a couple. They did not give up their needs, and therapy helped them in their effort to fulfill those needs, but they made a profoundly important decision, in their home and community, to try to make symbiotic marriage work. To help them understand what symbiotic marriage is, I asked them to turn to science.

The Science of Marriage

Every individual couple must make its own decision about marriage and divorce. The individual core nature of each child must be factored into divorce. Some kids by nature can handle the stress of divorce better than others. Some studies, such as those conducted by Edward Teyber, have shown that some children do very well after a divorce. And although any given child may experience trauma from a divorce, he or she may not be devastated. Further, how the parents handle the divorce matters very much (as we'll see in a moment). Clearly, a lot depends on the individual child and the psychodynamics of the divorce. In any case made for or against divorce, it is important to note that studies on the traumatic effects of divorce are often limited by the number of children and families studied, so no one can say for sure exactly which child will be harmed.

At the same time, it is important to note that recent studies have indeed shown that divorce can cause core-nature developmental damage to children. The likelihood that a child's core nature will experience trauma during and after a divorce is high. Divorce is one of the crises in childhood that can lead to chronic stress in kids—not always, but the risk cannot ignored.

A recent study of more than fifty-seven thousand children, conducted by Ruth Stein of Albert Einstein College of Medicine and her colleagues (reported in the April 2006 issue of *Pediatrics*), showed that being raised in a single-parent household was one of the three predominant risk factors for illness—one of the three primary social disadvantages children face in our culture. Some of these single-parent homes had never involved a marriage—but many had involved both a marriage and a divorce. This new study did not show divorce itself to be a cause of illness, whether physical or mental, but divorce is a piece of the puzzle. (The other two primary risk factors were poverty and low parental education.)

Keeping Stein's more recent study in mind, Judith S. Wallerstein's *The Unexpected Legacy of Divorce* is helpful. It showed that although some children did better in areas of natural development after a divorce—from school and athletic performance to emotional and physical well-being—many children experienced trauma in personality development, in their core nature. This damage showed up in differing degrees whether the children of the divorce were infant, school age, or adolescent. In Wallerstein's view, the legacy of divorce is akin to a loss of identity and stability. "Children are exquisitely sensitive," Wallerstein notes. After the divorce, "they don't trust mommy or daddy as protective figures. They feel insecure everywhere."

Wallerstein's findings have been called into question by a number of critics, especially because her sample was small and did not cross socioeconomic lines to the degree it might have. Nevertheless, her findings give us another piece of the puzzle. They have been corroborated by divorce specialist Judith Solomon, and by Elizabeth Marquardt, author of *Between Two Worlds: The Inner Lives of Children of Divorce*. Marquardt reviewed data from around the world on the effects of divorce on children. Working with the children's assessment of the divorce, she was trying to determine what happened to their comfort as children in core-nature development. Beyond the areas of difficulty that can result—drops in self-esteem, drops in athletic and academic performance, emotional turmoil, increased aggression—Marquardt found something that we might not often think of when we think of divorce. Children of divorce, she wrote, "feel they must take care of their parents rather than be taken care of. They feel loss and anger. . . . [D]ivorce divides the inner lives of children. . . . what happens is that the conflict experienced by the parents is simply handed to the child who must then make sense of the two worlds alone."

If you are reading this and are divorced, please understand that neither Ruth Stein nor Judith Wallerstein nor Elizabeth Marquardt holds condemnation. Every parent is doing his or her best. I have never met any divorced parent who cared less for his or her child than a parent in an intact family. Divorce may be the right thing to do in certain situations. At the same time, when I work with couples like Tom and Toni, for the sake of the children, I bring evidence to bear on the possibility that divorce can traumatize them. I remind couples that there is credible evidence that children of divorce don't have *more* problems than children of intact marriages; they just have different problems. At the same time, I ask couples to think back to their own ancestors in order to marshal not only studies and science but parental intuition.

As you make personal decisions about emotional fulfillment in marriage, you might take a moment to look back into your family's history. Whether a genetic system comes from Europe, Asia, Africa, or any continent in our human past, our ancestors did not generally marry in order to find a romantic soul mate (only the very rich did). They married to make economic and political alliances that they hoped would allow for the healthy survival of their tribe, family line, and children. The "divorce debate" today can gain from an anthropological context that looks into our human past, when marriages were generally arranged. I saw this "past in the present" as a boy in India. Living there in the 1960s, I saw marriages that were arranged for the sake of the economic and personal stability and safety of children. This has constantly inspired my nature-based research on marriage systems. For most of human history, our ancestors married primarily to create a healthy parental and family symbiosis for child raising, rather than to gain emotional fulfillment with a spouse.

I believe that it is revolutionary these days to look at social issues and marriage through this nature-based lens—one that puts emotional fulfillment in the context of six primary intentions of marriage:

1. Procreation and the safety of offspring
2. Division of labor between parents and children
3. Healthy increase of mentor (family team) influences in children's core-nature development

4. Transmission of morality, values, and ethics to children
5. Emotional fulfillment, communication, and conflict management
6. Gradual gifting of the child's natural assets to the larger society

In this model of marriage, romance and emotional fulfillment are not thrown out or denigrated, but are simply placed within the larger context of human marriage.

Is There Another Way?

If you are considering divorce, I hope you'll look into your children's eyes and ask, "Is there another way?" If your children are in real danger, there may be no choice but to break up the marriage. But if the root problem facing the marriage is lack of emotional fulfillment for either of the partners, I hope you'll consider setting emotional fulfillment aside, at least for now. This reorganization of priorities generally needs the help of a therapist or other powerful mentors.

There is a deep need in each of us—myself included—to "feel good" in our marriage, and there is always a certain amount of "garbage" that we each bring to a marriage. Marriage can be a wonderful partnership, a place of deep commitment and devotion, a challenge to our inner discipline, an opportunity to build character and selflessness, a call to loyalty, a relationship in which to become a better person. For it to be or become all these things, we generally must avoid overloading it with our vast cache of emotional needs, our unresolved conflicts from childhood, our hope that our spouse will heal our psychological deficits. Some of staying together has to be about just plain maturity and character. Nature, we might say, has set up marriage that way, especially once we have children.

When Tom and Toni checked back in with me after a year of marital repair, they had made peace with the role of emotional fulfillment in their lives. Some of their previous emotional expectations—those on which they had based their first years of marriage—were not being ful-

Try This

Ask yourself, your spouse, and your marital counselor or spiritual and social mentors to help you learn to lower your expectations of achieving emotional fulfillment entirely from your relationship with your spouse. Don't give up on getting your spouse to communicate emotionally as you would like, but pull back from it for a set period of time, perhaps three months. Get support during this time to stop reacting to the feelings of abandonment, anger, and fear your spouse brings out in you. Talk less to your spouse about emotions and more about logistics of children, current events, the lives of friends. Find the many other sources of emotional fulfillment and growth that are available with family, friends, work, and of course your children.

I have supported this process with such clients as Tom and Toni (and have discussed it more fully in *What Could He Be Thinking?*), who reoriented their marriages away from emotional triggers that create a cruel power struggle in the marriage, toward the children who are the ultimate reason for the marriage. As they reorient in this direction, these couples focus on how to make their marriage symbiotic—how to divide parenting labor, accept one another's parenting and gender differences, and work together every day to focus primarily on the care of their children.

filled by the coupleship. Toni said, "I've found a lot of other ways to find fulfillment. Tom is a lot less of it now. And I've realized that much more fulfillment comes from keeping my marriage stable for my kids." With tears in his eyes, Tom said, "Toni and I agree now that it's going to take something more than our own broken hearts to separate us from making our family work right."

These are honest, tough, powerful statements by two caring, courageous people. I think these two people are revolutionary. They do not have a perfect marriage, but they are raising children who they have decided will have a greater chance to find happiness if their parents reconcile and redirect their emotional needs toward marital symbiosis.

Symbiotic Divorce

Having asked you to reconsider marriage, and having done the same in my family therapy practice for many people, I am also a profound supporter of people who are raising children through and after divorce. I hope to help these couples create a *symbiotic divorce*—one in which the divorcing spouses divide the labor of child care and development, and fill in strongly where the other is weaker.

Angela, sixteen, a friend of my daughter Gabrielle, said this to our family at our dinner table one evening: "I actually like it a lot better now that my parents are divorced. Things are calmer and happier. I'm doing better in school. My parents love me more now that they're divorced. I mean, maybe they don't love me more, but they show it more. And they get along better and work together more now that they're divorced."

Angela was a child of a divorce who could frankly thank her parents for divorcing. Her voice is a crucial one we must hear: she feels that her core nature is safer and better off since the divorce. This does not contradict what I've said in the last few pages; rather, it applies to a different population. Angela is also clearly glad that her parents are working together to create a symbiotic divorce, a kind of mirror image of the symbiotic marriage they had wished, years ago, to have.

Simeon, thirty-nine, wrote me this e-mail:

> When I left my wife, I felt really happy and really guilty—happy to get out of a bad marriage, happy that my kids wouldn't have to hide in their rooms from all our yelling, but guilty that I was hurting my kids in a new way now. For six months, my ex and I fought over the kids. Finally, I just gave in. I told my lawyer to let her have what she wanted. I couldn't stand how unhappy the kids were. Now, though, I feel guilty for that, too. The custody agreement isn't good for me and my kids. We don't see each other enough. It seems like everything I do hurts them.

Simeon, like Angela, saw the need for divorce. Simeon, like all parents who divorce, instinctually hopes to enter into a *symbiotic divorce* for the sake of his children. He feels stymied by the process of the divorce, including the court process. He senses he is not in a symbiotic divorce, one that is best for the kids, one in which the parents are working together symbiotically and without rancor—but something less healthy for his children. He wants to find a way of being divorced that fully cares for the core nature of his children.

If you are a divorced parent, see the Try This box for things you can do to set up a symbiotic divorce system and thus make sure that your child's core nature can still receive both the maternal and paternal assets that their nature needs to stay on track.

Try This

- In your journal or in your thoughts, make a list of your ex-partner's strengths as a human being and as a parent. Share them with your ex. Ask your ex to do the same.

- Consider your own strengths as a human being and as a parent. Share them with your ex. Ask your partner to share his or her self-assessment with you. Make agreements on how to bring these strengths to your children.

- Spend little or no time focusing on your ex-partner's deficits. If there is actual danger to a child's core nature from the spouse—drug abuse, violence, or sexual abuse, for instance—this step will generally not be possible. In this case, it is beneficial to try to focus separately on the specific area of danger.

- Express to your children the strengths you see in your ex-partner. If you talk about a deficit, make sure it is the deficit in the area of danger, not in the area of lack of emotional fulfillment. If you find yourself unable to stop talking about your partner's emotional deficits to your children, get help immediately from counselors and other support systems.

- Unless a child is in danger, don't invade your ex-partner's new relationship with the child. Let him or her develop the new relationship that grows organically from the core natures of this divorced parent and child. It will not necessarily be a relationship that fits all your expectations of either your ex-partner or even your child, but symbiotic divorce requires you to step out of entanglements, especially between parent and child, so that the other parent can join with you and nurture the nature of the particular child.

- Create a plan with your ex for how you'd like your children's new lives to look—this plan discusses new routines, the teaching of moral values in common, behavioral expectations, and primary daily activities. This is an "essential parenting plan" that may go into more logistics than the court-arbitrated custody agreement. Work with your children's other parent to agree on the major precepts of this plan. Remember that on all matters related to your children, such as this coparenting partnership, you are still married! Your marriage has transitioned into divorce, but your children have not divorced you as a couple.

- Strive for similar routines between homes. If your ex puts the kids to bed at a certain hour and you see the wisdom of it, do the same. Expect your ex to follow your lead in certain other areas of routine as well. If the two of you have followed the other points in this box, you won't find it difficult to come to agreements on some of these matters of routine. Because of the circumstances of the divorce, you probably won't be able to agree on all issues—but if you follow just a few plans, your children will have a better chance of establishing healthy habits around sleep, TV and video game use, nutrition, and homework—basics of life that are essential for core-nature development.

There are a number of powerful resources in our culture right now that can help you create a symbiotic divorce. One of those is *Helping Children Cope with Divorce*, by Edward Teyber.

Burning Question: How Much Media Is Too Much?

Hannah, a mother in Calgary, wrote this wise e-mail and asked a very powerful question.

> I think sometimes that my kids are involved in hundreds of relationships with people in the media. By this I mean, there is so much influence through the media on my kids' emotions and lives, I for one am very careful. When we go to the store, we only buy something specific, not because we saw it on TV. We buy toys only when the children have achieved 5 stars for good behavior, roughly once per month or so, and TV watching comes with stars, too. We turn off the TV and visit friends who live in the country, all of us together walking and talking and playing. We prefer this kind of relationship. We bike or walk to the park as many evenings after school as possible, making sure not to come home and watch TV immediately. Overall, we limit TV, video games, Internet, computers to a total maximum of one hour per day for our eight- and ten-year-olds. We're following our instincts in all this, and we believe we are best nurturing the natures of our kids by relying on real people to teach our kids most things, but we still wonder all the time: are we overdoing this, are we underdoing it? How much media is right for kids?

Hannah's question has been asked by millions of people over many decades. One of the most powerful things about family-friendly scientific research of the last five to ten years is its call to all of us, now, to become revolutionaries in our approach to media use and screen time for our kids. I have been mentioning this theme in previous chapters in order to give you age-appropriate information for your growing child. Now, in the seven-to-ten age group, our children become immersed in school and various relationships, which can often lead them to become immersed in media "relationships," too.

What standards can you use and adapt to your child regarding media use—whether TV or podcasts or video games?

First and foremost is to notice whether a "perfect storm" comprising three elements is developing in your child's social life:

- *Unreal relationships.* The child's mind can become immersed in screen relationships that are half-relationships, not real—overstimulating, hypersexualized, hyperviolent; these fill the mind with stereotypes and images positioned in the society to stimulate certain judgments and perceptions that will probably never be realized by the child. Unreal relationships distract, to a great extent, from your child's natural development.
- *Isolation.* A sedentary life in front of the screen—even if in MySpace or chat rooms—cuts off a child from relationships with parents, extended family, faith communities, other healthy peers, and many others who are the brain's real food of life.
- *Withdrawal.* Brain and body disorders that emerge in relation to the media use (such as anorexia, bulimia, oppositional defiance) can cause withdrawal from healthy relationships in school, neighborhood, and family.

If you are seeing one or more of these "storms" in your child's life, now—right now, before puberty—is the time to act. Our school-age children need us to help them create not just a consumptive relationship with media, but a "symbiotic" one—one in which media provide what the child can use for core-nature development, and no more.

An hour a day of screen time *after* homework is done—this may well be fine, depending on your child's performance in school, athletics, and core relationships. Each child's core nature will handle different amounts and varieties of screen time more or less effectively. In some cases, as with some kids who have ADHD, playing video games can even develop certain kinds of brain functioning and motor skills. Screen time is not evil. To overreact to it would be to grab on to yet another social trend—this one saying, "All forms of media are bad."

The smart course is to see screen time as both potentially healthy and potentially dangerous, depending on

- The natural personality of your child
- The amount of time spent per day in front of screens
- The content of the programming viewed and listened to
- Whether there is balance with other physical and relational activity
- Areas of special concern, such as a brain or physical problem (for example, ADD/ADHD, anorexia, bulimia, depression, obesity)

How much media is too much? You must decide for your child. See the Did You Know? box for what the latest science-based research is saying.

A father of five wrote,

> My kids are seven and nine. We have no cable TV so reception is horrible. We also put the TV in our room so the kids need our permission to watch it. We password the computer so neither child can use it without our knowledge. Even when they are adolescents, we will use a keystroke and Web site monitor so we know exactly where they go on the Internet and what they are typing. We don't allow our kids cell phones yet and have decided not to allow them until there is a real and important need. Also, our children receive no allowance—the only way they can earn money is to read books. This helps them keep away from the TV, the desire for cell phones, and the Internet.

Online computer and cell phone use is indeed becoming an important media and technology issue in families, and at ever younger ages. There have been cases across the country lately of kids as young as seven and eight going online for hours at a time. Sometimes they go on innocently, sometimes they go on to cyber-bully, and often they end up in dangerous places. Similarly, many seven-, eight-, and nine-year-olds are feeling entitled to a cell phone.

Your instincts about your child's core nature and your family's needs must guide you in your handling of online time and cell phone

Did You Know?

Media use is now one of the most studied aspects of brain science.

- Watching TV can negatively affect attention span.
- Violent video games and TV can increase aggressive behavior.
- The more TV a child watches, the more likely he or she is to be overweight.
- The more time a child spends on the Internet, the more likely the child is to show symptoms of stress, including fatigue.
- Sexual content is becoming increasingly common on television. As of 2005, the Kaiser Family Foundation reported that the number of sex scenes on TV has doubled since 1998, with five or more sex scenes per hour.
- There is a direct link between fast-moving visual stimuli and a number of learning disorders. Not only the content of the TV program or the time spent in front of the screen but also the constant and rapid changing of imagery can affect brain development.
- Relational stereotypes on TV affect relationships in the real world; children grow up to become teens who have an unrealistic understanding of what healthy love looks and feels like.

What we've pointed out here is only the tip of the iceberg!

use. That said, you will probably not err if you consider a seven- to ten-year-old too young to go online without supervision and too young to own a cell phone. Even taking into account the variety in children's core natures, the brains and bodies of these youngsters much more desperately need walking, playing, learning, building, and relating in families and with others in their own home, neighborhood, or school than they need the Internet or the ability to call a friend on their own personal phone.

The Courage of Parents

It is a brave act to have a child, and even more brave to help that child navigate the constantly changing terrain of real (and virtual) relationships. As a parent of a seven- to ten-year-old, you are helping your child's mind, body, and soul imprint right now some of the relational abilities that this young person will have for the rest of his or her life.

You are bravely choosing to do this from within your vision of the actual nature of your child—how shy your child is, how outgoing; how verbally facile in relationships, how verbally inept; how easily angered, how easily swayed from healthy relationship, how easily pushed into too many relationships. Your courage as a parent is the courage to help a fragile young soul find a path of relationship that will ultimately lead to success, for if a child can protect core relationships and develop his or her own style of relating, he or she will never be lonely for very long, and will thus live a healthier life.

In working to help *your* child live, feel, love, and relate in healthy ways, you may well find yourself becoming a revolutionary—a person or family bucking social trends that tell you a child should relate and be a certain way, that a child should do a certain activity, that a child should talk a certain way. By the time your child is ten years old, you know this young person, and you know how to be brave for and with this child.

This is a good thing, because adolescence is on the way, and adolescence is a time when courage and bravery will be required from deep within; when relationships will and must become confusing; when the magical omnipotence of the parent becomes suspect for the child; when crucial limits, rules, and family rituals you've put in place now will protect your adolescent's development; when love of the body and the search for a soul mate become meaningful to each child in ways we cannot predict. Adolescence is the adventure that awaits us, and the years of seven to ten are the transition time in which we set patterns of life for adolescents that will help them (and us) through an amazing time of core nature's flowering.

I TOOK MY DAUGHTER GINNY TO SEE THE "NUTCRACKER BALLET" WHEN she was only eight years old. She was spellbound and on leaving the show told me "I want to put on the Nutcracker."

I told her that she'd have to take ballet first, then perform in the "Nutcracker," and one day maybe she could put it on herself. No, she told me, she wanted to put it on right now. She was involved in a number of other activities at this time, but this was the moment when I thought, "Wait a minute, *this* is a big part of who Ginny is." I knew I had to really help her focus on this part of her nature.

Indeed, it wasn't long before she started rehearsing a group of little girls in the neighborhood and planning her own show. She had to give up some other after school activities to do this, but I could see that these mattered much less to her than putting on this show. One day she came home and announced she wanted to put the show on *in the school's auditorium!* I told her that was unlikely, it would involve a teacher coming in over the weekend, and perhaps paying a fee, and so on. She said, "Don't worry, Mom, I'll take care of it."

Well, she convinced her teacher to open up the auditorium, she rehearsed the show, and a few weeks later, she had an audience of about fifty parents and grandparents for her program! And it was amazingly good—not so good that you suspected an adult was in charge, but she had all the key elements of the ballet and managed to get a dozen little girls where they needed to be at the right times!

This "passion" that my daughter demonstrated at a young age is still something that she's pursuing now at the age of thirteen. She's choreographing her middle school's production of "Grease" this year—something that was handled by professionals in past years. I am so glad my husband and I read her signals correctly four years ago. If we had kept throwing her into other activities like we were doing—driving ourselves nuts in the process, too—we might have missed this passion, this vision of hers, and she might not have learned the hundreds of things she learned through following her own nature: organization skills, leadership, imaginative design, music, negotiation with adults. I think this is your nurture-the-nature in a nutshell.

Wisdom of Practice

MY SON AUSTIN IS SEVEN YEARS OLD, AND HE CAN BE A MAJOR
ful at times. The school wants him put on Ritalin or similar med
currently not on board with this diagnosis. I believe he needs a
tive ways to learn in class. He is definitely a boy who learns w
hands. He also learns best when people are helping him, relatin
him. He can't stand to sit and stare at the blackboard or a book al

I own a woodworking business, and he will stand there and
side-by-side with me learning how to run the tools and equip
He and I are similar this way. My parents put me on Ritalin—
diagnosed with ADD/ADHD, but to this day I think they were v
to do this. I was put in a slow learners class, and my son is on hi
down that road also. I had confidence issues up till early adult
because I thought that I was dumb because I was in that class.
to this day have underlying problems regarding this stuff, and i
really affect my relationships. I think because people didn't
understand where I was coming from, I am vigilant to understand
my son needs.

I'm a den father for cub scouts, by the way, so Austin and I spe
lot of time together. It is great to rediscover through his eyes the s
things that I learned so many years ago. I hope every father of every
can have what I have. Seeing Austin suffer in school and relationsl
really made me get on board with him, and I will never have any reg

Nurturing the Nature
of Your Adolescent

"I think of the California condor, whose babies must peck their way out of tough, thick shells. [Adolescent] children are like that. Struggle toughens them for the future. The trick is to decide which stresses strengthen them and which weaken them."

—MARY PIPHER, *THE SHELTER OF EACH OTHER*

"We cannot just 'construct' a perfect human being. Young people must also 'sprout.' We must plant and wait, and we must have faith."

—LAWRENCE KELEMEN, *TO KINDLE A SOUL*

7

Nurturing the Nature of Your Eleven- to Fourteen-Year-Old

I've had five children, and I can tell you, whether it's boys or girls, raising them through puberty is all about adapting. Every day is different than the last, and there's no way to stop the roller coaster. And you know what? I wouldn't have traded it for anything. It was just wonderful to see each of my kids really show themselves during those years. I could start talking to them like adults, I could give them more responsibility, they asked questions, they disagreed with me, there were battles, there were times when a couple of them just seemed to get lost for a while, but through it all, I kept thinking, "Enjoy it, Pearl, they'll be grown soon." And sure enough, they were.

—PEARL ALEXANDER, GRANDMOTHER OF ELEVEN,
THREE BOYS AND EIGHT GIRLS

I MET PEARL AT A PARENTING WORKSHOP IN NEW YORK IN 1995. SHE was in her mid-seventies, a very short woman with thick glasses and thin gray hair. She walked with a cane but had a great fire in her eyes and a beautiful, wry smile.

She showed me pictures of her children and grandchildren, including her granddaughter, who, she told me, was diagnosed with depression in seventh grade but "is getting the love and help she needs." Pearl told me about her work as a librarian (working part time for about ten years and full time for fifteen) and about how much she missed her late husband and couldn't have raised her kids without him; then she came to the topic she very much wanted to discuss: what she felt was missing in "the public conversation."

Without any intention to offend, she said,

> You therapists talk a lot about self-esteem and adolescence like it's all bad, like everything's falling apart, but I don't think you're having a full public conversation about it. See, I think a lot of what happens to these kids is actually good. When the kids get their hormones, they get sultry and brooding and all that, but they also get so damn proud. Well, I think Nature has a solution to that. I think that solution is "low self-esteem." I'd say, let's have a little more of that low self-esteem in those adolescent kids. They need it! My kids all had their share of low self-esteem and all five of them turned out quite well, thank you.

What a wonderful, even shocking comment this was. Over the next week I thought a lot about Pearl's comment; then, as Pearl expanded on her concepts in a long letter (from which I quoted at this chapter's opening), I had an "Aha." She was talking about the normal narcissistic self-absorption that's so common during early adolescence—a natural part of a child's neural, physical, and emotional transition from childhood to adulthood. She was instinctively making the link between hormone flow, brain chemistry, and expansion of the core personality during puberty. She was further indicating from her experience that each child experiences "pride" a little differently and has individual internal resources with which to cope. I was being called to deepen my therapeutic thinking on self-esteem by a grandmother who wanted me, and all of us, to see all sides of the trend in self-esteem research that was burgeoning in the 1990s. This grandmother seemed to me to be saying, "Don't forget about human nature. It's an interesting new trend, this self-esteem conversation, but go deeper. Look at the nature of each of these kids. Other things are happening in kids, too, that you're simplifying too much."

Indeed, for over a decade, because of comments like hers, my own parenting experiences, and research into pubescent biology, I have found myself constantly reshaping my understanding of early adolescent children. And while raising two daughters of my own, I've found myself seconding Pearl's ideas. These early adolescents who become dark one moment, then want a hug the next; whose self-esteem drops one moment, crests the next . . . each of them is unique, experiencing pride, brooding, toughness, vulnerability, and the whole range of emotions and behaviors in their own natural and particular way. Their whole sense of self is shifting from child to adult with the help of social signals, but from a base of internal experiences that they will probably never again perceive quite the same way. They are in puberty—and they desperately need us to nurture their individual natures.

Preview of Essential Development Tasks

The ancient philosopher Plutarch said, "The mind is more a fire to be kindled than a vessel to be filled." When thinking both about a child's "first birth"—from the mother's womb—and this "second birth"—out of the womb of childhood and into the colder world of adulthood, we can gain from interpreting the science of a child's early adolescent nature through Plutarch's vision.

As we've learned about a baby's brain, we don't need to fill it with cells; the brain is born with all its cells. The fire of synapses between those cells just needs to be kindled. Similarly, the pubertal adolescent's life need not be filled with as many activities and stimuli as we may have thought—his or her mind is already quite stimulated, indeed, from within. What the early adolescent needs is for the fire inside him or her to be kindled (directed) toward the kind of adaptations that will lead to meaningful lives.

- *Help your child adapt and be flexible.* Because the years of eleven to fourteen are very much an age of constant adaptation, and because every early adolescent will adapt in his or her own way to internal and social stimulation, your parental rules need to stay strong—and to adapt. Your schedules need to stay firm—and to adapt. You need to stay true to your preset value assumptions about adolescence—and to adapt. You need to help your child adapt and learn from each failure and success in his or her myriad relationships. Your child needs to fight hard for new aspects of his or her nature to show through—and meanwhile to adapt to the loss of childhood aspects of this nature.

- *Permit self-esteem to rise and fall.* Self-esteem rises and falls constantly during puberty. It's okay for your child to become down; it's okay for him or her to get criticized by peers; it's okay for self-esteem to fall. As long as the child learns new skills, new adaptations, his or her self-esteem will rise again in the way and time that fits *your* particular pubescent child's identity— his or her particular fire.

- *Increase the role of the father.* The father's role often needs to become increased in this age group. The mother's role is not necessary diminished, but pubescent children with active fathers do better, in general, than those without them. Fathers have a certain way of caring for the fire inside a pubescent child. Even more each day, as life for the eleven- to fourteen-year-old gets more complicated, your adolescent may well need more father-nurturing. We can, I hope, all fight hard to make sure our pubescent children get fathering and male mentoring.

Information Essential to Nurturing the Core Nature of Your Pubescent Child

The suddenly on-fire brain of your early adolescent is, like all brains at all ages, divided into the brain stem, the limbic system, and the cerebral cortex. The cerebral cortex is divided into four main lobes: the frontal lobe, which among other things handles decision making; the temporal lobe, which has a lot to do with mood and memory; the parietal lobe, which does a lot of sensory processing and gives us our individualized way of orienting ourselves in space and direction; and the occipital lobe, which is very involved in how we see, and in the process-ing of what we see. During puberty, these lobes are often disconnected from one another, even though we adults might wish otherwise! The fits-and-starts effort of these parts of the brain to achieve connectivity—normal in each particular pubertal time—is the reason I call this puber-tal period the age of adaptation. The adolescent (and everyone around this boy or girl) is constantly adapting to internal and external changes.

1. In the limbic system, deep inside the brain, are two areas trying to connect up: the cingulate gyrus, which is our internal concentration center and a big emotion center, and the basal ganglia, our anxiety and pleasure center. These two parts of the brain are *very* active during this time. Your adolescent will be concentrating on some things well, others not so well; concentration and pleasure will sometimes link up, but other times not. This is a normal aspect of the journey!

Another part of your adolescent's brain called the amygdala be-comes very fired up (filled with the electrical currents of blood flow) when he or she feels slighted, hurt, or scared; in these states, it sends signals to other parts of the brain. In some kids more than others, those signals go upward, toward the frontal lobe, for good decision making. In some kids, especially if hormones are raging, those signals often never make it to the frontal lobe—especially to the prefrontal cor-tex. The kid will do something very impulsive, and we'll wonder, "What went wrong?!" The fire within sometimes rages without regard for ap-propriateness or inappropriateness. About the prefrontal cortex (PFC), neuropsychiatrist Daniel G. Amen writes, "It houses our ability to match our behavior over time to reach our goals. When it is low in activity, it is as if the boss is gone, so there is little to no supervision and nothing gets done." This is a primary reason your pubescent child needs *lots* of supervision. Adolescents want to adapt, often through parental super-vision. You and your family team must, at times, be your child's PFC for him or her. Some kids need even more supervision than others, de-pending on their natural personality. The more inherently aggressive the child, the more supervision he or she may need.

2. Simultaneously, if you have a child whose PFC is overactive, hypersupervision or excessive criticism (or both) by you and others can cause severe stress in that child. Often it is children who by core personality have overactive PFCs that get targeted for bullying and for badgering by parents. They seem "weak" because of their constant self-criticism, and this leads to shaming behavior from others around them. Dr. Amen writes, "When the PFC works too hard, it is as if the boss is micromanaging everyone, and people are left with anxiety and worry."

When your pubescent child's PFC is hyperactive, he or she will go from being immensely judgmental of others ("You're lame") to immensely hard on himself or herself ("I'm stupid and worthless"). This is often your signal to listen empathically rather than to be critical. Your early adolescent's core personality will generally send you his or her particular signals about what is needed (and it's okay if you at times read the signals incorrectly—most of the time, this helps the child adapt to real life, too).

3. Your eleven- to fourteen-year-old is constantly activating and de-activating the brain chemicals epinephrine and norepinephrine. These give him or her the natural "high" of an adrenaline rush. When these chemicals are aroused in the brain and spinal column, a person is more inclined to feel extremes of "Watch out, I better react" and "Wow, I really like that person."

During puberty, not surprisingly, these brain chemicals are being excited a great deal! This is due to flooding of testosterone, estrogen, and other chemicals through the pubescent child's system. Each early adolescent secretes different amounts of each chemical, so each child experiences the excitement differently and will stimulate himself or herself with the excitement differently.

It may take you a year or more to figure out the nature of *your* adolescent's approach to adrenaline and thrill. As you observe and talk a great deal in the family and with your child, you can gradually adapt to this inner power of new desires and excitements and help your adolescent adapt to it as well. As you constantly listen to, watch, and communicate with your pubertal child, and provide him or her with contact time and mentor time, you'll help the fire of this adrenaline find its own helpful burning points.

4. There are some times during the day and week when your pubescent child will be a "walking amygdala." Surges of testosterone in both sexes swell the amygdala, causing a rise in aggression and irritability. In his or her own way, fitting his or her own personality, this child will be dealing with emotionally laden memories and the huge numbers of emotion receptors that flood through the brain.

When you notice that some little thing you say "pushes your child's buttons," that's the on-fire amygdala specifically working in your adolescent. You will have to decide, based on your nurture-the-nature approach toward *this* child, how you should emotionally engage, and you will always want to pick your battles. Some kids in certain moments do need you to analyze a situation emotionally or intellectually. At another moment, or for another adolescent's core personality, it is enough right then to be nearby, to listen, to let the moment pass. As you get to know your adolescent and as you adapt to this constantly adapting being, you may often determine, "If it's not really serious, it's probably just the amygdala learning (and constantly relearning) what certain emotions feel like. I'll just watch and wait."

5. Dopamine is a big deal to these pubescent kids. Their hormones, as well as their normal brain growth, stimulate this powerful neurotransmitter, which is involved in producing a positive mood or feelings of pleasure. The brain and body of your early adolescent take a number of years to learn what will and will not give them pleasure—and each adolescent will be a little different in this outcome, just as you and everyone around you is naturally a little different in what gives you pleasure.

It takes years to experiment with what pleasures connect to the moral system that the PFC and frontal lobe are in charge of; it takes years for this adolescent to discover links and disconnections between what his or her hormones stimulate from within (sexual desire, sensuality, love, growth, power needs, high energy, mood swings) and what social and other natural systems want: self-control, social ambition, an ethical life.

Some pubescent kids will by nature be more inclined to seek dopamine rushes (even engaging in addictive behavior more readily than others). A great deal of the way the brain seeks dopamine is wired by genetics, though a great deal is also the result of family and social nurturing. As you observe your budding adolescent, you will naturally become vigilant and rely on your parenting team in heightened ways, especially if you have a dopamine-hungry eleven- to fourteen-year-old—one who, in search of stimulation, tends toward addictive behavior, intense thrill-seeking behavior, and even a lot of conflict with you or others.

6. A fascinating "second birth" actually occurs in the synapses of the pubescent child's brain, which each particular adolescent resolves in his or her own way. During puberty, the human brain overproduces synapses, *just as it did right after birth*. These early adolescent years are years of intense activity for the brain, as it "uses or loses" synapses. Your adolescent's individual brain is pruning away unused synapses every day, and doing so *in his or her own way*.

You can keep focused on observing and enhancing adaptability by encouraging the activities that clearly bring health and success to your child's nature, and you can get a second chance to help this child make adaptations that he or she didn't make earlier in life. So, for instance, if your child has been a couch potato from seven to ten, you have a second chance to open his or her future up to "No more TV—it's time to do something useful." It's time now to get him away from the video games or get her away from endless Internet use. It's time to get them into music, tutoring, outdoor work or chores, worship and connection to faith communities, relationships with you and the family team—activities that are also a part of the adolescent's core nature, but that you need to encourage, perhaps. Your early adolescent's brain is ready for a second surge of becoming what he or she *does* during these years.

7. The circadian rhythm in your early adolescent's brain is changing. This circadian system sets natural sleep and waking times by use of the sleep chemical melatonin, which is individualized to each brain. Each adolescent's melatonin level will go up to its own degree during the day—signaling the brain that it's nighttime. It is unclear why this

happens in general, though most probably it is a response to the flooding of hormones. Your child's brain is being constantly barraged with new experiences and wants as much sleep as possible in order to help it calm down and adapt appropriately.

Generally speaking, if you help your pubescent child get at least nine hours of sleep, you will be helping him or her set up a good sleep-sturdy adolescence. At the same time, the nature of your particular child will reveal his or her own sleep eccentricities. As you tune in to these, you'll be able to help this adolescent adapt, always with one goal in mind: enough sleep for *this* child.

Natural Differences Between Early Adolescent Boys and Girls

Even if your boys and girls are still prepubescent in this age group—showing no outwardly physical signs of adolescent growth—hormones are already working in their systems. Hormones are nature's growth chemicals. They begin making their fire when children are around nine or ten, and they affect boys and girls differently.

Puberty is a time of natural vigilance for all parents, and if we are parents of boys or girls during this time, we will have a boy-friendly or girl-friendly vigilance: vigilance that fits the nature of *our* boy and *our* girl.

If you notice your pubescent boy mainly wanting to talk deeply about his feelings with you only when these feelings have to do with performance or accomplishment, but you notice your pubescent girl trying to verbalize nearly every feeling, you are seeing how the brain of your girl tends to connect a great deal more of what is happening in the cingulate gyrus to verbal centers in the top of the brain, whereas the brain of your boy tends to connect more of what is happening in the gyrus to actions, especially physical actions that bring social or hierarchical power.

For many decades, our whole society has been grappling with what to do with gender-based emotional and social differences during puberty. Social trends parenting sources have been worried that if boys don't talk about their feelings, they go out and hurt people. Despite all

Did You Know?

- Girls' bodies and brains utilize estrogen not only for growth of the secondary sex characteristics but also as a basic chemical for a great deal of female life and living. Connected to adolescent estrogen increases are changes in progesterone, prolactin, oxytocin, and many other mood-regulating and mood-stimulating chemicals, which girls get in greater floods than boys, making their mood swings often appear more complex and even strident.
- Boys' bodies and brains process between ten and twenty times more testosterone than girls' do. Testosterone is the hormone that stimulates male growth of body hair, a deeper voice, larger muscle mass, and growth of sex organs; it is also responsible for sex drive and quick-burst aggression. Thus, although girls can certainly be aggressive and have high sex drives, there is a tendency—no matter where in the world or in what culture—for boys to be even more sexually active earlier than girls and to try to resolve life issues through more physical aggression.
- Girls' hormones flow in a lunar or monthly cycle, with each particular girl experiencing her flow (and mood regulation) in her own particular way within this cycle. Thus, close observation of your girl over a few months will allow you to pinpoint which times of mood difficulty are hormonal, so that you can "back off" with this particular child at certain times or even "work harder to stay close" at other times.
- Boys' hormones flow in a diurnal (daily) cycle; boys' testosterone spikes five to seven times per day, and each boy experiences the degree of each spike differently. You can observe times of more or less fidgeting during any given day. You can also observe times of more and less concentration, motivation, and "zoning out." In these early

adolescent years, your son is learning how to adapt to his own daily cycle of hormonal fire.

- Girls with eating disorders have higher than average levels of serotonin. People with high levels of serotonin tend to be obsessive and anxious, to be perfectionists, "the best little girls in the world." Puberty is the time when hormones can stimulate significant "serotonin distress" in girls (and in some boys, too). If you notice eating difficulties—too much or too little eating—and if you notice that your genetically anxious, even perfectionist child is now becoming unhealthy in these tendencies, her serotonin may need to be regulated, with the help of a physician or other professional.

- Boys with brain disorders (such as ADD/ADHD) often have lower levels of brain activity in the cingulate gyrus, the "concentration" center of the brain. By nature, boys generally have less activity in that center than girls do, and, also by nature, some boys have even less than others. If you suspect that your son has a brain disorder, you will find in *The Minds of Boys* a five-step protocol for determining scientifically whether or not that disorder is his nature. Given the rampant misdiagnosis and overmedication of boys in our social trends culture today, scientific protocols are crucial. One short pediatrician visit or one quick self-test is generally not enough to determine what is going on in your son's nature.

- ADD/ADHD among all girls, especially among early adolescents, is probably underdiagnosed. Boys tend to act out and fidget when they have hyperactivity. Because of differences in serotonin levels, the cingulate gyrus, and other parts of the brain, girls will tend to think and process their own problems more intensely; they turn inward, masking symptoms and then letting them out in other mood regulation problems (such as depression). If you are raising a girl who is having learning difficulties, it may be useful to consult a professional who specializes in female brain biology.

the scientific and empirical evidence that boys feel their own fire in their own way, we've thought of them as defective. In your home, as you raise your early adolescent boy or girl, you'll be experiencing both your own child's natural gender traits and your society's confusions and ideas about that nature. Every step of the way, you'll tailor your care of your pubertal adolescent boy or girl to what nurtures this particular child's nature, and thus you'll be revolutionary.

Helping Your Pubescent Child Through Early Adolescent Adaptations of Core Nature

Terence wrote me about his philosophy of raising two girls during the pubescent age of adaptation:

> My daughters are now 26 and 29, both nurses, successful, one of them married, both well-adjusted. Their "puberty years" were key years. My wife and I were believers that you treat your kids maturely, and at the same time, you don't ask them to grow up too fast. That may sound like a dichotomy, but it's really not. For example, my wife and I expected them to behave maturely in public, say at a restaurant. But at the same time, we would not ask them to make decisions that they were not prepared to make at their age. I did not let my daughters decide at 11 that they were ready for make up. I also personally believe that the best and most successful thing I ever did was to make sure I was involved in their lives. Not in a way that smothered them—but to make sure that I as a dad knew what they were doing and where they were at. And both my wife and I believed very strongly in the "teaching them to fish" method of life. We wanted them to learn how to think, and to think critically.

Helen, a mother of two sons, twelve and fourteen, gave me her philosophy of raising two boys during the age of adaptation.

> My experience as a parent has been about getting out of the way, helping them to manage their time, and giving them encouragement and support. We set limits, such as "You have to choose between

hockey and skiing. You can't do both." We keep the lines of communication open so we can work through anything that may discourage them. We encourage them to make their own decisions, even if we don't agree. Our boys are required to contribute financially to some of their recreational activities. For example, we split the cost of camp, some competitions and their dirt bikes. If they want a nonessential item, they pay for it themselves. Finally, we attend events they participate in as spectators and dedicated fans, not as coaches.

Terence and Helen are nurturing the nature of these young adolescents. These parents and their spouses are providing appropriate limits so that the nature of each child can breathe safely. Helen ended her e-mail with a quotation from John F. Kennedy that seems very appropriate. His words, for her, embodied the spirit she wanted to see inspired in her kids. "Some people see things as they are and say 'why?' I dream of things that never were and say 'why not?' "

I vividly recall being twelve, thirteen, fourteen and seeing the world through this dreamy lens. What every early adolescent of every generation needs is a safe and secure family base from which to feel the natural freedom to dream in his or her own way.

As you parent your early adolescent, I hope you'll find the following nature-based insights to be useful. I have gathered them not only from personal and professional experience but also from surveys of parents like yourselves, who have helped my staff and me identify areas of concern for parents of early adolescents.

• Your early adolescent is hungry for push-pull connections with others and you. The pubertal brain naturally experiments, explores, engages in trial and error. It needs relationships with people in order to complete this development. Your son or daughter will push-pull with you in his or her own way. In order to encourage this natural dynamic, media use needs to be controlled. If the early adolescent spends his or her relating time with the box, that's what he or she will learn—how to relate to a box—and it isn't adequate for individual core-nature development. Human relationships are challenging and complex, stimulating and important to the brain, yet adolescents watch approximately twenty-three hours of TV per week (fifteen thousand hours of TV by the middle teens)—more time than they have spent with teachers, friends, or parents. When they get addicted to TVs, iPods, or MySpace, they are not learning to read actual human emotional signals. They will be less adept at living than you wish they would be in the future. For some kids, individual core personality types will require even more of your vigilance in this regard. If you have a very shy child, for instance, he or she may need extra help disengaging from the TV and discovering real relationships.

• Be careful about addiction to activity and stimulation. Your early adolescent child's individual nature may lend itself to taking on five different activities at a time. Your child may love being stimulated every second. But use your instincts here—help your adolescent child choose and direct his or her energy. How do you know if there is an unhealthy addiction to activity? You may see signs of too little sleep, too little family time, "taking on too much," and "not knowing how to set his or her own limits." In these cases, you may need to cut out activities right now so that you can protect this child from chronic stress later in adolescence and adulthood.

• Sex education is crucial for pubescent children. Honest sex education best allows the sexual nature of each pubertal child to emerge in healthy and moral ways. If you were brought up in a repressive family or religious environment, you remember how hard it is on both boys and girls to have family and spiritual team members refuse to talk honestly about sex.

Sol Gordon, a psychologist who specializes in helping kids and families understand their newly discovered sexual selves, has written several books, including *Raising a Child Conservatively in a Sexually Permissive World* and *The Sexual Adolescent*. In the Try This box are adaptations of some of Gordon's basic rules for raising sexually responsible adolescents; they fit very well with a nature-based philosophy.

Try This

- If you are a parent, be the primary sexual educator of your child. Your children grew naturally from your own nature, so you are the best natural sexual educator of them. Schools and other family team members will step in to help you with information and wisdom you may not be able to provide, but as the natural nurturer of the child, you should help the child with sexuality.

- Be prepared for any question at all, and answer first with something encouraging and welcoming like "That's a good question." Remember as you are listening to the question that if you filter out "stuff" from your own past and upbringing—even from overbearing religious and ideological approaches to sex—you'll probably be able to hear your child asking a very logical question.

- Make sure the child knows that anything that has happened to him or her will not be made worse by talking to you. For instance, if your child has participated in oral sex and you have specifically talked about your family's values against this behavior during puberty, you may provide natural consequences for the inappropriate behavior, but you will not shame or attack. "I'm glad you're able to talk to me" is a good sentence to use. Or even, "Yes, I'm disappointed in you, but I'm glad we can work this out together."

- Sexuality is not about being perfect. Expect your child to make some "mistakes" in sexual behavior. If your early adolescent pursues a "first kiss" experience or other sexual contact and then feels ashamed, help the child turn everything sexual into a growth opportunity, an adaptation to a new self. Gordon has a wonderful phrase: "Failure is an event—it is never a person." Your child is not a failure because he or she masturbates, for instance. Most of what an adolescent experiments with is within the range of normal for puberty. Especially if your particular boy or girl is physically and emotionally an "early maturer," you can expect more early experimentation.

- Bring up sexual topics—sexual fantasies, erections, menstruation, penis and breast size, masturbation—with your adolescent when he or she seems naturally ready. (Remember, your child is probably ready a year or two before you may assume him or her to be!) Some of these things will have never been discussed earlier in the child's life, but discussion of each of them now is usually appropriate at this early stage of adolescence. I can think of no child who makes it to fourteen without having heard about or thought about all these things.

- Emotions and moods are a big deal during the age of adaptation, but they can often be the source of parental overreaction, too. Talk in your family team and with your child about hormones, moods, and emotions. Make a strong pact with your children not to overreact. Maybe you'll say, "I get what's going on inside you. When you go on the verbal attack, I'm going to try to hold back" or "When you get depressed and moody for a few hours, I'm going to wait to react. I'll see if you can come through independently. But know that I'm always here for you."

Let your kids adapt to themselves, and let them know you are trying to adapt to them. Often we make early adolescence much more difficult than it could be by trying to "read something into" moods and flares of emotions. You and your team (to say nothing of your child, who is becoming quite wise now) will know when something truly distorting of nature and self is going on in the child's life (such as bullying, abuse, school failure) and when a mood is just a mood. You will together be able to engage in the big things and stay out of the mood swings that really are your child's to grapple with, not yours to solve.

• What your early adolescent eats and how much exercise he or she gets are still (and always will be) crucial to nurturing the nature of your individual child. If your particular child is showing signs of obesity, get him or her checked, and set a new eating routine, with your doctor's help. If your child is not getting some form of exercise every day (beyond twenty minutes of physical education class), his or her core nature is not able to fully emerge. You may need to be sure to "send the kid outside" for at least one to two hours a day.

• Rites of passage are natural and essential. During puberty, epinephrine, dopamine, and other internally stimulated chemicals trigger blood flow surges into areas of the temporal lobe that are, as we've discussed, linked to religious and spiritual yearnings and to heightened awareness of the self as a part of the world and universe. The whole brain of this child can suddenly light up with an insight about the mysteries of life and about his or her own position in the mysteries. This is one reason video game manufacturers make spiritually fascinating games like the Final Fantasy products. Nature has set up hormones and brain chemistry to make each child, in his or her own way, more physically and emotionally aggressive at the very same time that each brain grows more of its own capacity to see deeply into moral consequences and spiritual awakenings. Our ancestors provided rites of passage at this age for these very reasons; you can too.

I've listed resources in the Notes and References section that can help you form a rite of passage for your early adolescent. This is a time in your child's development to look closely at your own particular family's involvement in faith communities, which can provide access to visions, insights, and mentors who can help you nurture your adolescent's nature.

• Significant traumas can happen to children in early adolescence—or may have happened in the prepubescent years—traumas that can cause the child to act out in new ways. We are going to cover these crises in more depth in Chapter Eight, and you will also find in the Notes and

References section a number of books and Web sites you can utilize should your child suffer from abuse, bullying, mental illness, physical injury, or brain injury.

• Puberty is a time for linking natural development with earnership and "able-ness." As a father put it to me at a workshop, "I think kids are less able to do and learn things today than they were when I was young, especially in those confusing puberty years, because they don't have to earn what they learn. It's all given to them or force fed. But kids learn naturally by exploring, by doing, by thinking about what they've done. That's what I had to do in my early teen years—I didn't have the distractions my kids have."

This father's perspective has been supported by new research, recently published in the *British Journal of Educational Psychology,* on eleven- and twelve-year-olds who are learning math and science. The head of the research team, Michael Shayer, professor of applied psychology at Kings College, University of London, put his findings bluntly: "Eleven and twelve year olds are now on average between two and three years behind where they were fifteen years ago."

Certainly, there are many reasons for this drop in our adolescent's "able-ness," but one I want to highlight is the lack of earnership. This issue is one you can do something about at home. If you have not already done so, you can institute a system of rewards for service in your child care and discipline. As you talk in your family about how to do this, it is good to remember that social trends today can often push us to infantilize our adolescents: to extend their childhood artificially by not giving them responsibility, not allowing them to develop at the unique pace of their own core nature. Often we make sure our young teens experience constant entertainment without even earning that privilege through daily work and service.

Puberty is exactly the time to help young adolescents adapt their particular core nature to the requirement of earning everything good by doing good. The Try This box gives you some practical tips on how to set up a system that encourages earnership.

Try This

Discuss five things in your family team that you want your early adolescent to "earn." Discuss five hands-on activities that they can accomplish so that they can earn those things.

In my own family, my eleven- and fourteen-year-old daughters had to (1) do chores, without resistance; (2) clean their rooms once a week; (3) complete all schoolwork; (4) complete all family and social obligations (for instance, engage in appropriate family time and complete their bat mitzvah classes); and (5) choose one physical activity per day. Through these tasks, they earned (1) their allowance; (2) an appropriate amount of TV and screen time; (3) the right to stay over with friends on a weekend night; (4) the right to stay awake longer; and (5) more special items, such as a dress they yearned for or a new CD.

As you find what items and activities are right for *your* family and *your* child's nature, discuss how you plan to institute and enforce these policies. For example, you could have your child create a written chart to put on the refrigerator for the first week of this new practice. He or she can do this for the next few weeks as well, although after a few weeks, the new policy may well become so institutionalized in the family that it just "is."

Joining Together to Link
Fathers and Men to Early Adolescents

Over the decades in which I have been gathering ideas from parents and caregivers and seeking scientific bases for understanding our lives, I have noticed a gender trend in the kinds of letters and e-mails I receive. Mothers and women tend to write me the most about children and child care in general. Men generally don't write as many words, e-mails, letters, emotions, or thoughts. When they *do* write me about child care, however, they write twice as much about parenting adolescent children as they write about raising smaller children. In this chapter, in fact, I have featured a number of male voices, as I also have in the wisdom-of-practice stories. Although women's voices still fill this book more than men's, I am bringing you a number of men's voices as I explore the nature of your pubescent child with you because this is, indeed, an essential moment in natural child development when we must listen very carefully to men. They have particular insight into our particular adolescents.

In *Democracy in America,* Alexis de Tocqueville wrote, "The father is the natural and necessary tie between the past and the present, the link by which the ends of two chains are connected." Michael Meade, who works with adolescent boys in the prison system, has said, "At the root, our fathers connect us to a mysterious spark. The father must be sought in questions that penetrate the past, and in footsteps that we inevitably follow, not knowing where."

Something deep, mysterious, and very natural is going on between fathers and their adolescent children as the children become hormonal (grow into adults). This natural process goes so deep into human biology that new studies have shown this amazing fact: pheromones of biological fathers help a girl start puberty later. When a girl is raised by a stepfather, his pheromones compel earlier puberty in her. (Her body unconsciously—at a cellular level—sees him not as "father" but as a man who is a potential biological mate.)

When I read this study, I was amazed by how congruent our science and our instincts can be. Although of course stepfathers can be great for children, and male mentors in general are crucial for children, we probably sense that something important goes on between the biological father and his adolescent offspring and that there can be natural confusions between a stepparent and stepchildren. Every relationship matters, and I think the new pheromone research on stepfathers is yet another piece of a nature-based vision that shows how biologically connected and needed fathers are.

In Chapter Three, regarding the nature of your infants, I asked you to form a nature-based movement that will specifically take the dialogue about "women's rights" into a dialogue about "mother's rights."

Here I ask you to join together as revolutionary parents in encouraging a fathers' movement, one that will use cutting-edge science to call attention to the need adolescents have of their fathers.

As always, nature loves diversity, so these movements are not contradictory or oppositional. Indeed, I get a great deal of e-mail from mothers and stepmothers who write different versions of these words: "Why have we come to so disrespect the father that a man's children can barely find him?" or "I'm a woman, but I know how important a father is to his kid. How did we take fathers so far away from their children?" Indeed, first the Industrial Revolution, then certain aspects of social trends parenting have taken away a great deal of the father's meaning and purpose in adolescent children's lives. Let's understand this, and fight it.

Early adolescents raised without close and active fathers often lose their way. They are unable to develop key aspects of their own core nature. The chronic stress of the lost father interferes with their own natural development. They adapt, but they adapt into a more limited being, losing parts of their nature to negative stress. Although in some rare cases fathers are dangerous, in most cases fathers are essential, and their relationships with adolescents compel the children to do the hard work of being "reborn" into adulthood through puberty and through the father's guidance.

One of the mysteries of the father's relating style with his children—a relating style based in less oxytocin and more testosterone; less verbal-emotive centers in the brain and more spatial-kinesthetic; less direct empathy and more nurturance through aggression—is the way that his role grows from his psyche's constant attempt to close distances between himself and his children. As de Tocqueville and Meade were suggesting, the father's arms are very large, closing distances between mountains of past and present, failure and success, falsehood and truth, good and evil. In order for the father to do this magic, he must be active in the adolescent's life; he must be respected by the family system and by the society.

The mother is constantly close to her children; the father is constantly striving to be close by making the child come to him.

The mother is constantly attentive to the child; the father makes the child earn his attention.

The mother takes a longer time to give her children independence (the distancing of the child's core nature from the mother's); the father expects that independence constantly, even if, often, too soon.

All exceptions must be noted, of course—sometimes a child has a very cold, unattached mother and a very "maternal" father—but in the main, and throughout the world, the father's identity is one gained from battling the angels and demons of emotional distance, so he brings closeness-from-distance to his adolescents. He is a paternal nurturer, not a maternal one—this is his nature. This is at the root of his nurturance of hormonal, on-fire, constantly changing and adapting adolescents.

The father sees the fire in the child's core nature and says, "Cry tears with that fire when you must, but in the end, you will have to rise up out of that fire into something tough, strong, unafraid."

He sees the child's constant exploration and says, "No! You can't explore that way or that way or that way. I want you to explore *this* way." He seems to be limiting the child, even shutting down the child's feelings (and sometimes he may well be doing these things), but at the same time, he is in his own way helping the child focus, mature, direct his or her energy, be strong in a way that will not be broken by the harsh world.

A fifteen-year-old girl who was just asked onto an Olympic development gymnastics team read a book I wrote for teen girls and wrote these powerful words to me in respect of her father's form of paternal nurturance: "It's my father who makes me and my brother independent. When we cry, he always says, 'Cry for the count of 10 then it's done.' I'm glad he does this. It's one of the reasons I can do what I do, especially in athletics." This young woman understands the value of her father's way of "doing emotions"—she lets her core nature flourish through his harsher-than-Mom love.

In the preindustrial world, the father's way of parenting was sustainable and functional (though certainly not perfect!) because fathers tried to take adolescents (mainly boys) to work with them on farms or in other apprenticeships; but even when the father was absent or dead, a number of linked men (grandfathers, uncles, cousins), not just the father, were responsible for the paternal protection and nurturance of the father's offspring. Fathers and men of his family and tribe were regarded as natural links in the chain of paternal nurturance and transfer of identity, power, and well-being from past into present. There was a clear respect for the father, especially in the life and safety of adolescents, who desperately needed his and the grandfather's, uncle's, and mentors' care.

Today there is a lack of understanding, and even of respect, for the role of the father and men in general. Many social trends have led us to this cultural denial of the vital importance of fathers. Among them, three are most hardened in our culture; they require the most resistance and transformation, especially if you are raising a pubertal adolescent:

- *Fathers now often work in locations away from their children,* rarely seeing them—especially when those children are adolescents who desperately need paternal nurturance at the deepest levels in order to help them develop their core nature, their passions, their self-control, their ability to love, and their sense of order.
- *Grandfathers, uncles, male cousins, and other natural male assets who are "like fathers" are frequently disconnected* from the lives of boys, especially adolescent boys who lack fathers—these father-hungry boys often end up in "father-substitute" systems like gangs or entangled in high-risk behavioral trends that cry out for men to teach them how to behave.
- *Unnecessary divorce is rampant,* taking the father out of the picture by the time the child is pubescent. Both boys and girls are left psychologically confused and alone to some extent, especially as they begin internally and psychologically separating from their mothers in order to discover who they are as independent beings.

There is a burgeoning fathers' movement in our culture. It is dealing right now with politics in order to lay its foundation. I hope that fathers, mothers, and stepparents will band together in a grassroots nurture-the-nature movement that, for instance, forces workplaces to include children at least a few hours every week at the father's office or job site. This particular innovation was less possible early in the Industrial Revolution, when most men went into dangerous mines and factories and thus had to protect their children from their own work; now, however, most jobs do not involve danger, and children's presence can again be what it always has been: natural to the process of fathering.

Burning Question: How Do I Protect My Early Adolescent's Self-Esteem?

As this chapter began, we started talking about self-esteem. We moved that topic into the even larger nature-based topic of *adaptation*, yet everything we've discussed affects adolescent self-esteem. Perhaps this is why so many people verbally or in writing ask, "How do I best protect my child's self-esteem?"

A father of two grown children asked the question in this way:

> I was raised by critical parents and I was pretty critical with my kids. My parents rarely said "good job" to me, and I said it more than they did to my kids, but still, I didn't say it all the time like I see today. In a park the other day I saw young parents saying "good job" to their four and five year old kids for every little thing. The four year old kid would walk from a jungle gym to the parent and that would be enough for the parent to cry out, "Good job!" I don't get that. Maybe it's just not my nature.
>
> Anyway, I guess my question to you is: does all this "good job" really help these kids? What does science say about it?
>
> Although, I will say this, too—maybe it will contradict what I just wrote—but when I grew up, my brother didn't take as well to my parents' criticism as I did. And with my own kids, one of them sure needed more "boosting" than the other. So maybe the point is that self-esteem boosting, especially all the "good job," is better for some kids than others?

Try This

Here are some ways for fathers to remain constantly active in protecting the essential core nature of pubescent adolescents' everyday lives.

- Read your children's e-mail as needed—that is, if you even vaguely sense danger. Your pubertal children do not have the right to privacy from the father (or mother).
- Learn the names of your children's friends, and talk to your children about these friends. If your child says, "a friend gave me this Gameboy," close the father-child distance by finding out who that friend is.
- Meet with coaches, clergy, teachers, and anyone else who takes an interest in the child. Be a part of the adolescent's mentoring community. Talk to the adolescent and these other mentors as needed about crucial life issues.
- Be a vigilant force in looking closely at "demons" many of us wrestle with today as parents of early adolescents. Don't give up your paternal parenting to the mother; do your own parenting. This means looking at these questions:

Am I overparenting or underparenting?

Am I too materialistic and therefore creating in my adolescent the anxieties of undue entitlement?

Am I overscheduling my children's (and my own) time?

An active father myself, I explore these questions constantly, and I never let myself off the hook. I feel it is part of the honor I earn as a dad to stay self-aware regarding these essential elements of fathering. I believe it is not enough for me to be a man or even a father: I must be an *active* father.

These are powerful observations and questions. When does a child need a boost, and when does flattery do more harm than good? How much of the answers to these questions has to do with the unique core-nature needs of the individual child? These are important questions to resolve throughout your parenting years, but especially urgent by the time puberty comes. Adolescents need more than just the "good job" approach.

The new sciences and nature-based theory can help us understand self-esteem development in powerful ways. Let's look under the surface, into human nature.

First, what really does constitute self-esteem development in early adolescents? Researchers reporting in *Psychological Science* have discovered that adolescent self-esteem (children's holding themselves in high esteem) rises and falls depending on whether a specific goal is gratified (for instance, if they feel they look good or buff on a given day and then someone tells them they do indeed look good), *but* that the rises and falls are so temporary, just as the constant "good job" is temporary, that they have little long-term effect. In fact, two of the researchers, Jennifer Crocker and Katherine Knight, point out that some of the most unsuccessful and antisocial adolescents in your neighborhood would test out with high self-esteem. Thus, it really is important to try to understand how an individual adolescent's own core nature needs self-esteem development to occur.

For us parents, how we look at self-esteem can naturally depend on what we are trying to help the child accomplish. Do we just want to make the child "feel good" in the moment or make sure the child develops his or her core nature so that he or she can take care of this "feeling good" and "feeling bad" within himself or herself independently? Although there may be moments when the individual core nature of a child really needs to hear something nice and flattering right now, nature-based theory leans toward the long-term approach. When researchers at UCLA and UC Santa Barbara studied how the brain and body actually respond to high and low self-esteem, they looked at cortisol (stress hormone) levels of adolescents who are experiencing both high and low self-esteem. They discovered what it was in the child's core nature that actually had the most effect on stress levels at a given time (with control for interruptions or distractions, such as traumas). Their discovery was that "values affirmation" (the adolescent's ability to access his or her own internal values, "self-resources") has the most profound effect on long-term stress levels. They also found that response to low self-esteem was not always bad or harmful. The children and early adolescents who could access their own sense of "who they were" were better off than those who constantly heard "Good job!" without gaining the internal critical development of self. The researchers discovered not only that some self-esteem stress actually helps kids be happy and healthy but also that some kids are even more hungry for empowering critique than others.

A kind of parenting discipline I practice and teach is to look at an adolescent's long-term development by nearly erasing the word "self-esteem" from my language and substituting the following concepts of *core-nature development.* My purpose is not to denigrate the concept of self-esteem for adolescents but to shift the parenting dialogue toward the use of more "adult" language as the child moves through and beyond puberty. Thus I suggest that you ask yourself questions about the following "self" aspects of your child's core nature:

- *Self-motivation.* Does my early adolescent know how to motivate himself? How good he feels about himself might not matter at any given moment, as long as he can motivate himself to fulfill tasks and projects that provide a foundation for the gradual revelation of his core nature.
- *Self-reliance.* Does my early adolescent know how to rely on herself in age-appropriate ways? Whether she reports positive emotions at a given time might matter less than whether she acts with strength in a few key areas of core-nature success in her life.
- *Self-care.* Does my early adolescent know how to move in and out of social alliances that lead to self-care? A breakup with a friend, a feeling of loneliness may not in the moment be such a bad thing, as long as my child is showing the ability to adapt into

Did You Know?

To protect self-esteem, we want neither to return to a deficit-based parenting approach nor to assume that every child will respond to self-esteem development techniques the same way. The following are what I believe are the three main findings of the new sciences:

1. Heaping too much praise on kids can backfire, because it does not create the lasting values affirmation a child is seeking—the lasting inner strength that comes not from praise itself but from *specific praise and critique* regarding an adolescent's *specific* actions. And although too much criticism can backfire, especially with specific kids, criticism regarding values and core nature is not as dangerous as we once thought; it can actually *increase* self-worth in the end, forcing the adolescent to get better acquainted with his or her own values and inner resources and to plan for the future.

2. Healthy core-nature development will actually cause low self-esteem for *constructive periods of time* in that specific adolescent. These kids actually need to experience hurt, pain, and poor self-image at certain times. Nature has set things up so that low self-esteem can often provide an inner balance against the inherent narcissism and self-absorption of adolescence.

3. What works for one child's core nature may not fit another's. If you are going to read a self-esteem book, choose it very carefully, with an eye to whether it fits your child. Some self-esteem research is about the core nature of children, but some is not—it is generic and based on social trends, and it may not fit the individual nature of your specific adolescent.

making good choices for care of his core nature, and through that, his family and community.

- *Self-awareness.* Does my early adolescent know how to understand what is happening in life around her and how she and her core nature fit in with what is happening? In a time of anger between her and a friend, we may want to help our daughter "feel better" by condemning her friend who has made her feel bad, but it may be that more core-nature development would occur better if we were to listen to our daughter and then point out to her (making her feel bad, momentarily) where she is to blame in the situation.

- *Self-discipline.* Does my early adolescent know how to control himself in appropriate ways? We might think that his self-esteem will be hurt if we tell him to stop interrupting, stop dumping his clothes in the living room, go away from the adults for a moment until he and his friends can calm down—but in fact, his gaining of self-discipline is more important for development of a strong core nature and thus future happiness and success than is his feeling good about his own or his friends' impulses at a given moment.

Moving Forward with Pride

Each of these areas of an adolescent's core-nature development is later going to be linked to a healthy sense of confidence in himself or herself. The journey of your adolescent child's nature through the world will evolve with periods of low self-esteem, yet will be blessed by even greater gifts: motivation, self-care, and self-control, on which, in the final analysis, his or her core nature, a lifetime's success, and sense of purpose actually depend.

By the time your child moves into middle adolescence—the subject of our next chapter—you will, I hope, find yourself saying, "Wow, this is who my son is" or "Wow, this is who my daughter is," with the added words, "Wow, I'm proud of this kid." You'll feel the deep inner sense that you are raising a daughter or son who is nearly able to live, love, and exist independently of you.

You will turn to your spouse or friend and smile, "It's really happening; this kid is adapting, becoming a man, becoming a woman, and learning how to nurture his or her own very complex nature. We've done a pretty darn good job!"

It's good to feel that pride now, during early adolescence (and even if for just a moment a day). The high-risk middle adolescent years are coming. They are some of the most fun and inspiring for parents, and they flow along best if we go into them nurturing the nature of our adolescents with our own sense of purpose and pride intact.

Wisdom of Practice

WHEN MY DAUGHTER WAS ABOUT EIGHT, I DISCONNECTED THE CABLE. Her grades improved immediately. She's now fourteen. I encourage her passions. She cares very little about TV. She loves to ski and snowboard, and as a very good skier myself, I'm in a position to help her there. It's something she can do with her friends, where she can function as a leader. She loves team sports, and is currently playing lacrosse—I encourage that. She's a creative artist and writer, and I encourage that. I encourage her where success is likely, and don't badger her to succeed where it's unlikely. We don't get spread too thin. We seem to be mostly avoiding frustration, self-esteem issues, and depression. I'm a single dad, doing the best I can. So far, so good.

I HAVE TWO GIFTED BOYS WHO ARE VERY DIFFERENT FROM EACH other, yet in some ways they have the same traits. My older son, who is twelve years old, has shown us that he needs to have a quiet period after school before telling us about his day. He needs a snack and then time to just "veg out"—usually some mindless activity like watching TV. He is the type of kid that uses all his energy during the day absorbing facts and information, and filtering out chaos and interactions with his peers.

My younger son, eleven, can be a great barometer for the classroom. Many teachers expect him to sit still and just learn, but he learns by using all his senses, and that may look like a kid who needs to multi-task while listening to the instructions. He is a visual learner and is quick at doing things. He is detail oriented, but you couldn't tell by his actions—he just doesn't like to sit in hard chairs.

By making sure these kids get what they each need, I feel like I am doing right. Some people think both my kids are difficult, and I think my second especially could be an easier kid to handle at school, but because I understand both these guys, I am in that stage where I can just enjoy how they are developing. I can't imagine having these kids become other than they are. They're doing just fine, thank you! They make me very proud!

8

Nurturing the Nature of Your Fifteen- to Eighteen-Year-Old

When I was a teenager, around sixteen, seventeen, I did risky, stupid and bad stuff. I broke the law more times than I can remember. It was as if I was just rolling down a mountain. I couldn't stop myself. I remember I was just seventeen when I wrecked my second car. My parents woke up, suddenly, or something like that. They just said, "Enough!" My license got taken away, my parents made me focus on home life and working with my uncles, and I was grounded, with gradually regained privileges, for six months. That was what I needed. That was when I started really having to become a man.

—ISAIAH, FATHER OF THREE, LAWYER

MARK WROTE ME ABOUT A PROVOCATIVE, CONFUSING, AND VERY TELL-ing life situation. He was in the middle of trying to decide whether to retire early as a high school teacher. He had become embroiled for a year in a school-led investigation of his conduct. In the last week, he had been vindicated, but still, he felt somewhat lost at fifty-three. His story went this way.

In his high school, a year before, four of the junior girls were being especially difficult in two of their classes—English and science. Their teachers and Mark were talking about it one afternoon—the principal had already been alerted—and the teachers asked Mark, who was the basketball coach and had the girls in his gym class, to "read them the riot act." These teachers felt they were not getting through to the girls, and they thought that Mark, who had a certain strength and a certain rapport with many of the students, could "rein these girls in."

That afternoon in gym class, Mark did indeed talk with the girls. He threatened them with suspension; he made it clear to them that they had broken the character and ethical standards of the school through their gossiping, talking back, and relational aggression and bullying.

The next morning, one of the girls and her parents went to the principal's office. There the girl claimed that Mark had patted her on the buttocks when she came off the soccer field. She also claimed that he had looked at her in a sexual way. She and her family were irate and worried for her and the other girls. Immediately, the principal called Mark in, described the complaint, asked what Mark had done—Mark denied these claims—and set in motion the legally required process of complaint and appeal. Mark was investigated for sexual harassment, and because the principal could not tell him who the complainant was, Mark did not yet realize what this was all about—the girl getting revenge for having been chastised by Mark.

Rumors got around, and Mark was accused by parents of being a predator, or at least of being sexually inappropriate. Rumors even flew that Mark had slept with female students. (In one rumor, he was also homosexual and had slept with a boy.) Mark's family was targeted for angry mail, and his own son got in a fight defending his father (for which he was suspended for three days).

As the investigation progressed, Mark did finally learn who the complainant was, and his representative was able to discredit the complaint and even to convince the three girls who supported her in her fabricated story to rescind their support. Six months later, the complainant herself rescinded her accusation. However, Mark's life and the lives of many people around him were irrevocably damaged by a teenage girl whose social violence went unrecognized. The social system in place at the school (in place, of course, for a very important reason: to protect our youth from inappropriate and predatory adults) neglected to look at the kind of supervision this adolescent girl's developing core nature needed from the school. She didn't need more power or "personal empowerment"; she needed more self-control. She didn't need carte blanche to express her anger through social structures she could manipulate; she needed individualized help in controlling herself socially, emotionally, and personally. The social system caring for her did not give her what her core nature needed, and derailed the purpose of a teacher's life, failing both student and teacher.

This case has stuck in my mind. It shows the complexity of what teens and their support systems are going through today. Your teen is trying to become independent, feel his or her power and purpose, manipulate social systems to his or her own benefit, compete, be aggressive, be empathic, be ethical, develop character yet take risks, and, in all this, individuate his or her own particular, inborn core nature—shy, aggressive, impulsive, contemplative, alpha, type A, beta, type B—into the larger world in which he or she will ultimately work, live, and raise a family.

Every culture has wrestled with how to give more privilege and power to adolescents, knowing they need those new experiences for their natural development; and every culture has wrestled with how to preserve order, teach ethics, withhold power and privilege until the individual child is ready for it.

In Mark's story, the social system gave this adolescent girl too much of the wrong kind of power. She abused that power, and the system helped prolong her abuse of it. No one was inherently evil in this—the girl ended up regretful and Mark later forgave her—but in this instance the social system failed to create a nature-based parenting and educational framework with which to nurture the nature of adolescent children.

This chapter is about making sure your family and social systems do indeed nurture the nature of these individual adolescents. Our adolescent children of fifteen to eighteen are dynamos of experimentation, love, truth searching, and, at times, ordeal and struggle. How can we best nurture the nature of fifteen- to eighteen-year-olds whose most intense goal is to become individuals who feel that they don't need us?

Preview of Essential Developmental Tasks

You are now raising an adolescent child in and through the age of individuation. As these young people psychologically separate from you (though they are still quite bonded, of course), they will have lonely moments but also, they will seek to develop their core nature in groups—in organizational systems, such as schools, athletics, and rock bands (and sometimes, unfortunately, gangs) that allow both the solidifying of their childhood and early adolescent core nature as already established and the risky experimentation with new aspects of core nature, aspects they could not risk looking at while they were under the parents' shadow or while they are alone.

The following are key developmental tasks during this period:

- *Help your adolescent manage peer groups,* especially by *integrating those peers into family, extended family, and other relational systems* that have already been established. As we'll explore in this chapter, each core nature individuates differently into peer groups, so each adolescent needs particularized help in discovering himself or herself through peers and peer-family connections.

- *Help your adolescent learn full coping skills for crises and setbacks.* Each of us and each of our children deals with crisis somewhat differently. As you go through this chapter, looking closely at your own children's crises and setbacks, you might also find yourself challenged to look at your own fears and dreams.

- *Keep a strong executive and management position* in your home and family environment so that your adolescent knows the rules, the consequences, and the responsibilities that go along with expanded privileges, pleasures, experimentation, and time away from home. Even the most inwardly independent middle adolescent does not actually want us to let him or her go one day suddenly, at fifteen, sixteen, or when he or she gets a first car or goes on a first date. Our adolescents, to some extent, don't want us to let go at all; they are immensely attached to us (though at times it does not seem that way!). They want to trust us and be trusted by us. They want to be free, but not too free. They don't want the safe mountain of family experience on which they've grown up to suddenly crumble. They want to force that mountain to let them fall freely and make a rolling path of their own.

Ultimately, over at least a three-year period of push-pull with us, they will *force* us to let them go. They will make us say, "Whew! I'm glad that's done." Essential to remember is that if one day we just let go suddenly of these young people at fifteen or sixteen or seventeen, their core natures would shrivel, and they would have to attach themselves to some social trend system or group (such as a gang) as if to a lifeboat. Better for them—and they know this too—is to experiment with social trends and groups, and through those experiments force us to critique, badger, love them despite their errors, relate to their friends, and make emotional and social mistakes of our own, so that gradually they can say, "My parents are okay, but so am I. I can survive on my own. I see what's up—it's time for me to make my own journey. I'm scared, but I'll do fine."

Information Essential to Nurturing the Core Nature of Your Middle Adolescent

If we expect our middle adolescent to "try anything," we will be pleasantly surprised when they try only a few crazy, high-risk, dangerous, and even immoral things. To expect them *not* to take risks or *not* to do something we ourselves have done; to expect them not to try on many masks, personae, costumes (as we ourselves may have also done); to expect them to live by a higher standard of morality or social conscience than we have done—to want any of these things is often to set them up to fail before they get started.

And, of course, they will do all these things in their own particular ways. Some kids will take more risks earlier than others. Some kids will talk about their risk taking more than others. Some kids will be more directly empathic than others. Some will seem to go through a year or more of becoming unempathic, especially to the needs of parents.

1. Sexuality is a big deal in *every* middle adolescent's mind—in his or her own way. As parents, we often hope, quite protectively, that our adolescent children will not experiment with sex; it is natural of us to feel out of control when it comes to our teenager's natural sexual yearnings. It is even protective and instinctive of us to wish sex would somehow bypass the age of fifteen to eighteen. But because even the most thoughtful among us yearned at that age to delve into the body of another (and yearned, too, for the day when the self-satisfaction of our own organs would not be our only means of achieving loving satisfaction), it should not surprise us to find our middle adolescents trying to connect with each other's bodies.

As we answer our individual teenager's questions, listen to his or her particular romantic pains, facilitate safe sex and birth control, we can bring more thought and reason to the frightening, exciting, heart-wrenching journey of sex and love that this individuating self is now making. But with sex, as with most of this middle adolescent's life, we cannot be in control. The journey of individuation is a journey we make with our son or daughter—but also one that this adolescent must now make without us. This can be frightening for all of us (including the adolescent who pretends to know it all already!). If you have an adolescent who is maturing early and whose core nature, you believe, is ready for sex, it's essential that you say something like, "I can't control you, but I want to help you be in control of your body." This help can take the form of your own and your family team's discussions with the adolescent regarding both abstinence and contraception (and assistance in learning about and obtaining contraception), and constant listening to what *your* young person is going through.

2. As we navigate adolescent individuation in our home and community, it is essential to know that many of our teens are doing very well. Social trends thinking over the last decades—especially through

media stories—seems to be showing that most or all teens are rebelling against parents dangerously or having inordinate amounts of sex or doing drugs and binge drinking. Indeed, some teens are involved in constant high-risk behavior and our youngsters do suffer, but we as parents also can legitimately experience the liberation of staying focused on the specific needs of our specific teen's core nature.

3. One of the most intriguing and helpful things brain research (especially MRI and PET scans of the adolescent brain) has taught us over the last five years is the difference between how adolescents and adults process emotions. In her brain scan studies, Deborah Yurgelun-Todd, director of neuropsychology and cognitive neuroimaging at McLean Hospital in Belmont, Massachusetts, looked at what parts of the brain work in adults and in teens when we process emotional stimuli. When shown pictures of people who were scared, 100 percent of the adults correctly identified the emotion of fear, whereas only 50 percent of the teenagers did. Many of the teens read the facial expression as sadness or confusion. Some of the teens said they just couldn't tell what the face showed, and some said the faces showed shock.

Dr. Yurgelun-Todd found that the frontal lobe in the human brain—which controls thought, planning, and goal-directed behavior—is less active in teens than in adults; simultaneously, the lower part of the brain, the limbic system, associated with emotions and gut responses, is more active. Parents instinctively know that their teens are often not reading emotions and experiences in "adult" ways. Brain research now confirms that instinct.

Not surprisingly, this research also confirms that each teen develops the ability to do this emotional "reading" in his or her own way, in his or her own time. To nurture the emotional nature of each teen is a major focus for us, yet much of it we must let our teens do themselves. When our particularly "confused" or "overreactive" (or "underreactive") teen makes mistakes in peer and social groups, we may feel sympathetic and may well try to assuage the adolescent's pain, yet at the same time, we may need to remind ourselves, "These are lessons my child must learn. It is part of his or her nature."

4. The frontal lobe is a big deal in the middle teens for more reasons than emotional. It is also the seat of executive decision making—something we wish our teens would do well! It is the CEO of the brain, in charge of such executive functions as planning, organizing, setting priorities, making sound judgments, handling ambiguous information, putting on the brakes by calming the self. It is, as adolescent development specialist Pat Crum has put it, "the seat of civilization," yet is often "asleep at the wheel." It is one of the last parts of the brain to fully mature in our adolescents! If we keep this in mind when our youngsters do things that even they will later say "were so stupid!" we can be more patient.

We can also remember that this frontal lobe maturation happens best when we keep rules clear, make sure consequences are suffered when appropriate, and practice many of the strategies we'll look at in a moment, which seem to denigrate freedom for our adolescent in the short term, but better assure his or her survival and freedom in the long term.

5. Aldo Leopold, the early twentieth-century century educator, wrote, "All ethics rest upon a single premise: that individuals are members of a community of interdependent parts. Their instincts prompt them to compete for their places in that community, but their ethics prompt them also to cooperate."

I love this statement when thinking about middle adolescents. As their "competitive juices" (amygdala, hormones, limbic system) constantly flow, their ethical systems struggle to form, to include their core nature, their answer to "Who am I?" The general struggle to make connections in the brain between the gut instincts and executive decision making is a basic moral and ethical struggle taking place within each cell and synapse of your unique and growing adolescent.

Sometimes we forget how ethical and moral our adolescents are trying to be—and how confusing it is to have stark urges to compete, have sex, succeed (all of which are urges that our kids must have if they are to individuate, grow, become men and women, become mothers and fathers), yet also be altruistic, turn the other cheek, "stay above the fray," be abstinent, and make ethical arguments with us so unique and well thought out that even a lawyer couldn't figure out how this adolescent just got us to agree to his or her request! In your home right now is living a unique reconciliation of primitive animal and sophisticated Solomon. As we love both selves in this adolescent (and all selves in between), we fully nurture his or her nature.

6. It is essential for all of us to remember that many, if not most, troubled teens can learn restraint, judgment, and compassion. If you are right now raising a troubled teen, don't give up! Sometimes even the troubled teen thinks he or she is doomed, and sometimes suicide or complete self-destructiveness results. Our teens have a lot of resources, and each teen has his or her own internal templates for adjusting to life's vagaries and hurts. When you keep asking yourself and your family, "Who is *this* adolescent?" you will see this young person's unique strengths and vulnerabilities. Past the mask of "trouble" will generally be individualized solutions.

I'm often asked, "Can you save every troubled adolescent? Is the 'tortured' or 'confused' brain plastic enough to change?" Some sexual predators, to name an extreme example, are already sexual predators by adolescence. If they have already raped a child, then their brain is either so rewired from abuse and neglect or even hardwired with deformed genetic markers that they probably cannot be saved; these predators will try to destroy innocence, and the best we can do is contain or imprison them or use hormones to try to rewire them.

But most troubled adolescents don't come anywhere near to fitting this description; most can form strong relationships with a few caring adults and peers and come through. An adolescent's full connectivity of brain tissue does not occur until into his or her twenties. Nurturing the nature of each individual child is a philosophy that requires optimism and hard work. We must never give up on the nature of a unique child, for the human brain, and human nature itself, constantly presses at the adolescent to find his or her own way; nature struggles inside each unique adolescent to succeed, survive, and thrive.

7. It's essential, finally, for all of us to remember that whenever adolescents are questioned, surveyed, or challenged about their parents' roles, they always say, "We want more time with parents." Indeed,

surveys often show that even older teens, not just the younger ones, want more time with their parents. Yes, certainly, teens seek independence and solitude, but they also yearn for parents who aren't so tired, so chronically stressed—they want more of our time and presence! In a moment, we will look at how to make this time and presence work for the core nature of each of our unique adolescents.

Natural Differences Between Middle Adolescent Girls and Boys

By the time your adolescent is fifteen, his or her brain chemistry and brain development, influenced by your child's particular genetics, have brought to your parenting an adolescent who is strong in certain areas, weak in others; then perhaps months later, that child will gain strength in the very areas he or she was once weak. Adolescence is a time of trial and error for both boys and girls, a complete learning experience; at the same time, boys and girls find and face their ordeals differently.

• In reading emotions—in closing the gap between emotion centers in the brain and frontal lobe understanding and explanation centers—adolescent girls are generally more accurate than boys. As Yurgelun-Todd put it, "the males in our studies showed more reaction from that gut region of the brain, and less frontal or executive reaction. The relationship between the gut response and that executive region was very striking for the males, and somewhat striking for the females, but was not as extreme for the teenage females compared to the teenage males."

If your son does not read emotions at sixteen as accurately as your daughter, don't be surprised.

• At the same time, as Daniel G. Amen's SPECT scans have shown, your adolescent girls will tend to read *more* (and even extra) emotions into events, activities, and relational moments than your adolescent boys. (This will continue as these youngsters become women and men.) Your daughter's cingulate gyrus is more constantly active than your son's, so she will run emotions through her mind more constantly and will keep attaching new content to those emotions until it seems to you that she truly is imagining whole emotional scenarios that never occurred (or that did not occur with the power and detail she imagines). You might be quite right.

• Girls at this age tend toward more "relational aggression" than boys, and boys tend toward more physical aggression. If an adolescent boy feels wounded or rejected, his greater blood flow in his brain stem, coupled with his higher testosterone levels, will tend him toward greater fight-or-flight activity: perhaps he will try to "duke it out," or he will simply (in more cases) withdraw, ignore, move on.

Girls have less brain stem flow and less testosterone, but higher oxytocin and more verbalization connectivity in their brains. They are more likely to wreak havoc in relational and bonding systems (through gossip, making things up to destroy another girl's self-esteem, being verbally cruel).

• Adolescent boys and girls tend to do their risk taking differently. This comes as no new news to parents, but now we have fascinating science to watch how risk taking is stimulated and processed in the brain. When dopamine (risk hormone) levels rise in the female brain, the rise in this chemical stimulates oxytocin and other relational and bonding chemistry in such a way that adolescent girls tend to do less overt risk taking than boys. Girls also have an average of 20 to 40 percent more serotonin, a neurotransmitter responsible for inducing relaxation and regulating impulses. Hence, boys will tend to be more impulsive in general. And because girls are not stimulating as much testosterone with their dopamine, they do not tend to take as many aggressively physical risks. (This may be why, for instance, very few adolescent females would want to play football, and far fewer would sign up for infantry combat, even if they were legally allowed to do so.) The higher testosterone stimulated in males leads to more physical and aggressive risk taking.

When we parents look at how to help adolescent boys and girls with risk taking, we often find ourselves asking "What crowd is my child hanging out with?" This is wise thinking. If he is hanging out with a very physically aggressive group of guys, we should expect him to do something physically and aggressively dangerous very soon. If she is hanging out with a group of girls who "keep getting into trouble," we should expect our daughter to get into trouble soon. It may not happen, certainly—but we would be blind not to expect it and not to try to mitigate the trouble before it occurs.

• The way adolescent girls and boys trust other people is naturally somewhat different. New research has discovered that when a young male receives an interpersonal signal from another person that leads his frontal lobe to think "this person isn't trustworthy," the brain and adrenaline system in the male stimulates a testosterone compound called DHT in large quantities.

The exact same situation does not stimulate testosterone or DHT in females. This is one of the reasons males become more physically angry when they feel they cannot trust their parent or another person. Their amygdala may swell up, their adrenaline get stimulated, and their testosterone wash through their brain and body system, and they may then have more difficulty articulating their feelings verbally than a girl.

It may well appear that this boy has been trained "not to talk about his feelings" or "not to cry," and indeed some social trends do train males to avoid these "verbal-emotive" responses to such issues as distrust in a parent, but because the male brain is chemically wired also to process this stimulant in its own way, his family is smart if it tries to get the DHT-stimulated boy to exercise, punch a punching bag, shoot hoops, or otherwise (and safely) process the hormone physically through his body.

• Adolescent boys and girls differ in their ways and styles of learning. We have looked at this in previous chapters, and as you've watched your children grow you may already have noticed that your son is a learner who is more focused on single tasks and who may not read as much as you'd like, or heard your daughter saying, "I hate math; I can't do it!"

Although of course there are exceptions to that pattern, most schools and most parents find that by adolescence, males and females have matured and grown toward two parallel situations: some of the earlier gaps in reading, math, science, and other classes dissipate—that is, some boys and girls have caught up to one another; simultaneously, some boys and girls now need extreme interventions to keep them in school and out of trouble.

More and more parents will find themselves turning away from "normal schooling" as the main emphasis of the struggling adolescent's educational life; many will move toward apprenticeship environments. These focus the struggling girl or boy on specific tasks and work, and often make sure that the child has a same-sex mentor.

The Did You Know? box looks closely at a sexual difference between adolescent boys and girls.

Adapting Your Family to Accommodate Your Middle Adolescent's Individuation of Core Nature

As you look at, revise, and alter your family and community systems to include the risk-taking, individuating adolescent you are raising, you'll probably see his or her core nature mainly clarified by now (certainly by eighteen). I can roughly estimate that right before your eyes, you can see about 80 percent of "who this young person is," warts and all. You can generally see this core nature in two or more of these three categories:

1. Individual personality, emotional style, self-motivation, moral direction, and empathic ability. If your adolescent child is more of a leader than a follower, or vice versa, it will be pretty clear now. If he or she has quite a temper now, that same temper will probably be his or her gift and burden throughout life.

2. Social skills, relational interests, romantic shyness or aggressiveness (or any longings in between). If your adolescent is the one in the group who likes to set dramas in motion, he or she may well become the adult who sees everyone's point of view and wonders how to manipulate it. If your adolescent is the naïve one in the group, he or she may well, by nature, be a person whose interests lie elsewhere than emotional and social sophistication.

Did You Know?

Both adolescent boys and adolescent girls feel quite natural romantic, emotional, and relational anxiety related to sex and love. They often feel these things in different ways, however. One area of difference occurs in relation to the sex act. This difference is especially crucial to teach to adolescent girls, for without this knowledge, they may have difficulty protecting themselves from depression related to postcoital abandonment.

When the boy says "I love you" and tries to exercise his various strategies in order to get sex, he is building toward a relational and physical act laced with testosterone—sex is, thus, quite often a part of his experimentation with aggression and conquest. When a girl says the same things and maneuvers toward the same act, her chemical base most often includes higher concentrations of estrogen, progesterone, serotonin, and oxytocin, along with her testosterone.

If the sex act occurs between this boy and girl (we hope, obviously, that they are young men and women), these bonding chemicals remain high in her, but with a few hours, the male's bonding chemistry—especially his coital burst of the bonding chemical, oxytocin—dissipates, and his testosterone rises again. She will often think, "He just said he loves me, and he has now had me in my most vulnerable state; certainly he will call me tomorrow."

Unfortunately, as you and I know from our own adolescence, he often will not call her. He will promise to text-message her, but

3. Higher abilities in certain talents and skills, including academics, athletics, or artistic endeavors. By now your adolescent will probably not know what he or she wants to do professionally (some adolescents do, but most change their minds); however, you will have a pretty clear picture of two or three areas of life to which this mind and heart are probably best suited.

will "forget" or "get busy." After a few hours of the "oxytocin-bonding high," his testosterone takes over again, and he biologically moves toward more self-development through domination, conquest, and diverse sexual experimentation. Nothing in his hormonal system or even brain system (except the girl's pleadings) is telling him to mate with this one person, at sixteen or seventeen, for life. Her hormonal base, however, can remain high with oxytocin for days afterward; her internal system (despite her frontal lobe's knowing this guy isn't right for her) may be pleading for him to treat her better, not abandon her, tell her what she has done wrong, tell her how she should change—get thinner or fatter, wear different makeup, stop studying in school, leave her parents—anything to bring him back.

Although this is an extreme example, it's not so far out compared to what is going on inside the minds of some rejected girls. Male-female differences in sexual-hormonal biology can lead to a steady derailment of female core-nature development—even to depression and crisis. Thankfully, most girls (and boys, too, who become very depressed after romantic rejections) do indeed get help, and do indeed learn more realistic coping skills; but if we don't teach our young people about the testosterone-oxytocin difference, they will suffer more than they need to. Boys will pursue conquest and remain insensitive to girl's postcoital feelings, and girls will engage in sex without realizing that they are likely, as teenagers, to be abandoned.

A way to put all three of these categories of activity and behavior together is to think about athletics a moment. If your son or daughter is an athlete, you will see his or her core nature shining through in the position he or she plays on a team. For instance, if your son or daughter is an aggressive forward on the soccer team, you might store away that detail; look back on it when this child is thirty and in a profession, and you might well see that same aggressiveness in his or her place in the career hierarchy. If your adolescent child is a fullback on the soccer team, protective and defensive, you may see, decades later, that same quality in his or her profession.

Looking carefully at who this young person is, how he or she is developing, what abilities and temperament are shining through, can be a beautiful and intense exercise, both celebratory and worrisome. As much as we love being able to talk to this kid, see the world through his or her sense of invulnerability (or intense vulnerability), live through his or her accomplishments, so too do we see how tough life can be for any child, even one whose nature we have nurtured. We know that this is the journey, this is what life is all about, this is how a child grows into an adult . . . but still, it can tear at our hearts to see our kid suffer.

Here are some areas of focus you can come together on in your family as you decide how you want daily life to look for this middle adolescent. Your individuating teenager needs to make his or her own mistakes, but if you have these essential elements in place, you should generally be able to trust that you are helping to nurture his or her nature through the tough moments.

1. Ascertain (and enforce) when you want this young person to date (go out alone with a potentially sexual friend). In my home, sixteen is the age that seems to work best for the developing and vulnerable core natures of our children. If you choose an earlier age (given what you read earlier about adolescent brain and biological and sexual development), I hope you'll make that choice because you absolutely know that the core nature of your individual adolescent is ready.

2. Retain family meals, family time, and whatever is you and your adolescent's equivalent to the "cuddle time" you had when he or she was small. "Cuddling" is more verbal now, and more a sense of shared presence in the house, but it is still cuddling. Develop "check-in" rituals, for instance, every day after school: "How was your day? What were the highlights? How did it go with Tom and Brittany? Did that problem get resolved with your math teacher?" Every day, every adolescent needs to check in with you, if only briefly. Each child will use this check-in time

differently, but without it, the adolescent's core nature will lack a crucial ritual, an important opportunity for comfort and connectivity.

3. Be involved in religious communities, extended family gatherings, community events, team challenges . . . make sure your adolescent is involved in two or more of these on a regular basis. Each developing brain can benefit from this kind of support, attachment, mental and spiritual challenge, and connectivity in order to navigate its own particular version of middle adolescence.

4. Share the passions of your own core nature with your adolescent. Chores and grueling homework and workplace details need to be done by all of us, but there must also be time each week for father and son and father and daughter, mother and son and mother and daughter to be involved in deep discussions, passionate work, and times together that go beyond the mundane. If you are a fisherman, take your teenager fishing with you. If you have a women's coffee group, take your teenage daughter with you; let her be one of the women in that group, now, who hears and discusses adult themes you care about.

5. Make sure to do service work together as a family, and encourage your adolescent (and his or her school) to integrate service work into educational and extracurricular life. Every middle adolescent's core nature needs and wants the empathy building and sense of purpose that come from service work. Some young people will need it even more than others, especially those who are highly introverted and pulling too far into their own rooms, computers, video games, podcasting.

6. Find a way of parenting this adolescent that works for you. It won't be the one prescribed by a newspaper article or talk show. It will in fact include some permissiveness, some demandingness, some hovering, some hyperparenting, some underparenting. You may make mistakes—withdraw when you should engage, tell the kid what to do when you should in fact not protect him or her from failure, let the young man go on a date too early, let the young woman be too rude to you. You are not perfect. Like every parent, you learn from trial and error. But you will learn to alter your parenting to fit *this* individuating core nature. Often we hear people say, "Be consistent in your parenting."

That is very good advice. Perhaps added to it, though, could be, "Ascertain the core nature of your adolescent and what it needs, and be consistent in helping *that*." Consistency of rules without focus on core nature is not enough for middle adolescents. It can lead to unnecessary and troublesome rebellion.

7. Though your adolescent is becoming independent, it is still your job to protect him or her from dangerous technologies. New studies regarding teen behavior have revealed that online bullying is happening constantly. The Internet is also a constant source of seduction: adolescent boys and girls are being tricked into meeting predators, into providing live videocasts of nudity and sex. Recently a network of teens was paid to take off their clothes and have sex. Predators watched via video cameras online. The Internet is potentially dangerous, and you brought the Internet into your home: you pay for it; you control it. Your adolescent lives in your house and does not have privacy of Internet. If you suspect any bullying or any other dangerous behavior, you have the right to get on your adolescent's MySpace or other account. Your adolescent needs to know that you are still the parent—you trust him or her, if that trust has been earned, but trust does not mean a blanket right to privacy.

Furthermore, it is only social trends thinking that a child is entitled to constant cell phone use. Cell phone use has recently been linked to teen anxiety—there is some discussion now among scientists about whether too much cell phone use could be affecting neurotransmitters. Look at this research (see the Notes and References section) and make family decisions together with your adolescent as needed.

Be aware also that studies have linked iPods to hearing problems. (You can go to www.dangerousdecibles.org for more information.) And you must decide when your adolescent's core-nature development warrants the right to a TV or computer in his or her room. The later the better, for most kids. As much as possible, we want to keep this developing brain away from too much screen time, especially since it is human relationships that help the limbic system and the frontal lobe create their connectivity. Screen time is a poor substitute, in most cases.

A final and crucial note, I believe, relates to homosexuality. The latest research shows that between 5 to 10 percent of all human beings are biologically homosexual or bisexual. They are born gay or lesbian, in other words. Nevertheless, we live in a society where a large percentage of the population still considers homosexuality something that needs to be "cured." Interpretation of religious texts has been the primary source of this antihomosexual social trend, but the trend also grows from the natural fear in all human beings of sexuality itself, especially sexuality that is different from what most people practice.

My job is not to convince you to see homosexuality as moral or immoral; my job is and always has been to help the children who are homosexual and their families develop a healthy, successful accommodation of their biological reality.

If you have a homosexual child, this boy or girl is not different from other children except in the aspect of core nature called sexual preference. The homosexual child needs your understanding and mentoring in his or her sexuality as any child does; and your homosexual child needs you to pay attention to iPod use, electronics, extended family support, and all the areas of family life we have just looked at. Your homosexual child needs you to be mom, dad, mentor, and leader (and follower) of his or her particular and natural individuation. And with a homosexual child, you may need to take special care to nurture and protect this boy or girl from the fear and hostility of antihomosexual social trends. These young people need you to help them accept themselves within a bitter culture. They need help connecting and networking with other gay and lesbian friends.

Most of all, they need to be loved no matter what. Women's rights and civil rights were fought for and finally won. The rights of your gay or lesbian child to be treated as a biological and social equal are now being fought for in our society. During this tough time, the core nature of your gay or lesbian adolescent needs your love, support, and advocacy more greatly than you may realize. Adolescents naturally face a number of crises in their development, as we'll see in the next section. How powerful it would be for your gay or lesbian child—as he or she faces the "social crisis" of his or her sexual nature—if you could help make it a source of meaning that empowers and shapes the young person toward service and the greater good.

Helping Adolescents Through Crisis

Perhaps one of the most difficult aspects of childhood is the inevitable and painful area of crisis. The crisis can be the death of a loved one, a divorce, an incident of severe bullying or physical assault, sexual abuse, an ongoing condition of poverty, a state of war. The crisis can be the discovery that a child has a mental illness or a brain disorder. A crisis is any major event or condition that heightens cortisol (stress hormone) levels in the child's brain for a period of time long enough to potentially affect or atrophy other developmental functions in that brain.

The Story of Breva

Breva was ten when she seemed to her mother to be "thin as a rail." Given the core nature potential of having a very thin child—Breva's mother was genetically quite thin—her doctor saw no signs of worry yet. He was aware that the age of youngest anorexia patients has declined in the last decade from thirteen to nine; however, ten was the right age to "watch and wait." He coached the family to alter its mealtime habits. He referred the family members to a counselor who could help them with their busy, overscheduled, high-pressure life. These parents wanted to help their daughter, so they looked at their family habits. They kept a vigilant eye.

By the time Breva was twelve, her weight (eighty pounds) really scared her parents. The physician became even more concerned. He set up requirements with them for eating habits, daily journal writing, and a special diet. He looked closely with them at how they were managing the pressures on Breva, her school life, their expectations of her, her behavior, and their own family habits.

A year later, when Breva was thirteen, depletions of iron and calcium in her blood were clear. Her parents were unable to watch her every second of the day, and Breva had been feeding her breakfast to the dog and not eating lunch at school. Breva's doctor now hospitalized her and put her on a feeding tube. A specialist took over Breva's case—a neurophysician who specialized in the nature of eating disorders. He rotated Breva on and off the eating tube for three months, continuing her treatment after she left the hospital. This approach may well have saved her life.

Using brain scan equipment, Breva's specialist discovered what he called "superhigh levels of serotonin" flooding her brain—a characteristic of anorexia. He also found heightened cortisol levels, and through discussion with family he discovered that anorexia was hidden in both the parents' DNA and the family's everyday nurturance of this child. There was a genetic predisposition, a legacy of this illness that others in her family had suffered. Also, the family and cultural dynamic created a psychological etiology (set of circumstances) that triggered the gene that carried anorexia. The triggers in Breva's life were, in the doctor's words, "high pressure private school, perfectionist parents, a divorce, the cruel culture of thinness for women, and depression." Because of Breva's superhigh serotonin and cortisol levels, her brain was suffering from life-altering side effects. Even her memory was changing—and thus her schoolwork was suffering.

The time that it took to recognize and treat Breva's anorexia became a period of change in the family's dynamics, the parents' approaches to their daughter, the child's learning system, the child's physiological functioning, and the child's and the family's search for meaning. Fortunately, Breva, like many of the 2.5 million girls who have eating disorders, became a success story. When she was sixteen, her menstrual cycle began, and puberty got back on track. Her brain chemistry returned to its natural rhythms; her school day was now a more normal one, with fewer high-pressure activities dominating her life. She said to her doctor, "I feel weird, like I don't really fit with most other people, but I know one thing: I sure want to help other girls."

Breva volunteered in peer mediation at school and on the suicide hotline of her local mental health center. Her doctors and outpatient treatment programs helped monitor her progress over the next year as she helped others heal themselves.

And so it was that Breva, by losing herself to disease, had found herself. Her crisis helped her find many aspects of her own core nature that were being lost before. Her family, too, by losing its balance during the severe stages of her illness, had found a new equilibrium in developing a symbiotic divorce and loving her through treatment and recovery. Her family supported her social work, the mother volunteering with her daughter to answer phones on the suicide hotline. This family made meaning and mission out of crisis—supporting an individuating core nature, supporting maturity.

Dealing with Crisis

If we are nature-based thinkers, we must revisit how we feel about crises in our own and our children's lives. My family and I have faced crises in life and, each time, emerged newly born. Because life is inherently difficult, it is worth saying aloud that every child and every family must and should experience bumps in the road, obstacles, dangers, traumas, and crises during the twenty- to twenty-five-year period of childhood and adolescence. Every child must fail from time to time: failure is an important invitation for some new part of a child's core nature to emerge. Every growing and living thing must go through dangerous tunnels, ordeals, challenges, and traumas; through these, each organism embraces limitations and discovers assets in its core nature that would otherwise have been missed.

Nature itself—to say nothing of society—is, in truth, a dangerous place. It is filled with trauma and pain. As physicist Brian Swimme and cultural historian Thomas Berry have pointed out in *The Universe Story,* violence, destruction, and chaos are present everywhere in nature, from geology to organic growth to human development. Disruption is part and parcel of the universe.

If our parenting is nature based, we must integrate the natural destructive elements of our life experience into our parenting. We must admit there is no "perfect" way to raise children away from nature's disequilibrium. Every child will be hazed, teased, and toughened by peers. Many families will struggle with mental illness in their children, and many families will care for children through physical illness and physical pain. No matter how we protect our children—and it is natural, instinctive to do so—we cannot protect them from the very nature of things.

Stories like Breva's remind us of one of the keys to essential parenting: that crisis must not be made into something artificial or alien to a child's and family's development, but instead must be absorbed naturally into a given child's individual life. This absorption may or may not make the crisis less painful in the short term; in the long term, however, it will give the crisis meaning, and from that meaning will come discovery of who the child is—a discovery that will feed the innate strength and compassion in the child; a discovery that will also feed the family, the world, and the society with the assets of the meaningful and purposeful child.

"Why do we fall, Bruce?" asks Bruce Wayne's father and mentor in the movie *Batman Begins.* "So we can learn to pick ourselves up," Bruce responds. Right after this interchange, Bruce Wayne's parents are murdered. Bruce spends a decade and a half in crisis, fear, and grief over the loss of his perfect existence. He eventually overcomes all odds to serve the world through his crisis. He becomes a symbol of steadfastness against destruction. He does not lessen his own pain, but he makes it purposeful in his existence. He becomes meaningful to himself and others. In the end, it is clear, no parents could be prouder of a son, even from the grave.

Batman Begins is, of course, a movie based on a comic book. Yet it's also based on classic stories of core nature's quest to survive and thrive through crisis. It reflects the natural human cycle of crisis-depression-fear-intervention-action-meaning. This cycle is crucial to the development of the core nature of each child. Brain science is presently showing us how and why a crisis in a child's life—a loss, a divorce, even moving constantly from one geographic location to another during childhood—affects the child's growing nature, especially the child's brain.

As reported in *Psychological Bulletin,* the journal of the American Psychological Association, researchers reviewed thirty years of stress research and determined that how we handle crises, stress, and traumas has a profound effect on how our core nature moves through the normal cycle of crisis, depression, fear, intervention, action, and meaning. As you help your child become Breva or Bruce, a person who serves humanity as a result of crisis, you'll discover the ways your child is able, just by nature, to keep pulling herself or himself up from the darkness, and other ways in which your child needs special help. You may find yourself using many kinds of interventions—medical, psychological, educational, parental, nonparental, nutritional, and peer group. In all these, you will want to focus on the three primary kinds of intervention:

• *Medical and chemical,* through medication or change in nutrition, directly affecting brain chemistry and functioning. A single mother wrote me this e-mail: "My husband committed suicide when my son, Jamal, was three years old. Jamal is now in fourth grade and constantly struggled in school. He had separation anxiety and generalized anxiety. Then, last June, his therapist put him on Prozac. He is now like a new child. The temper tantrums are gone, his anger is diminished, and his sadness is so much less. For the first time in his life he is a typical boy. He has really started contributing to our home, to his school. He really likes getting up in the morning now and going and *doing* something."

For this child, medication works very well, healing him by healing the brain's chemistry directly, and the side effects are not too severe. For some children, medication is not the answer, but it is essential to look at medical alternatives when necessary.

• *Relational sympathy.* Psychologically empathic talk, family activities, core mentoring and one-on-one relationships . . . all can help the child and family deal with the emotions and feelings arising from the crisis. Long periods of isolation rarely help a traumatized teenager. In all relational methodologies (such as therapy), the hidden agenda of treatment is relational sympathy. When one or more caring individuals take the time to become sympathetic, the healing assets that are built into human nature have a greater chance of working within the child. Success depends on one or more people's focusing on the child for many months in ways they probably have not before—spending days with the child, tutoring the child, being much more present than they were before.

• *Spiritual integration.* All around us is guidance from wise sources of meaning. These can be integrated into the family so that the crisis becomes a part of the life cycle of the universe, the human being, and the hopeful future. If an adolescent is bullied or abused, or faces parental divorce, it is useful, even natural, for the young person to be led by wise adults and communities (such as a faith community) to understand what part in the life journey this crisis plays. This integration of crisis into the life cycle is perhaps the one intervention we focus on least in our society. In missing this one, we forget the nature of the child. If we nurture the spiritual aspect of our child's core nature, the dark can turn to light from within the very heart and soul of the child.

A microbiologist and engineer, father of two, wrote this powerful, supportive e-mail:

> I am both a scientist and a religious man. I have survived a lot of crises in my life, and I can say life involves choices, decisions, uncertainties, failures, fears, risks, and always the feeling of being watched by God or by Nature, however you want to put it. I think this is obvious to everyone really, but our society tries to eliminate real decisions for children, real uncertainties, risks and rewards, even the Watchful Eye. I see this in school a lot. I don't mean the whole "prayer in school" thing—I understand why a democracy can't have that in public schools. What I mean is the draconian punishments given for the simplest of infractions to enforce an unnatural environment. It's as if we want to take pain out of life and learning. It's unnatural.
>
> Think about it. A kid pushes another kid into a locker. The principal suspends him from school. What the kid needs is character

development; he needs to understand the bad thing he's done and the pain he's caused in the context of how he can be not a warrior against the other boy but a warrior for a greater cause. Kids are going to hurt each other—we have to help them understand and direct their energy. This is nature. As a natural scientist I can tell you it's very rare in nature that anything good happens the first time. We learn best and most naturally from making mistakes and getting hurt and figuring out how to do better the next time and the next. If the world comes crashing down on kids' heads for every simple error, how do they learn who they are? If they are never allowed to take a risk, how do they learn to assess and manage? And if no one ever helps them understand why they feel bad in the context of the greater good, or dare I say it, "God," how will they grow up? Then at the magic age of 18, our youngsters are expected to spontaneously exhibit crisis management skills, impulse control skills, and risk factor skills they have been denied the opportunity to learn. They are supposed to take their place in society, be completely responsible for themselves, and go to war. I'm ranting, but here's my point. We are driving our kids nuts, but blaming *them*. I did this to my own kids, so believe me, I understand—I'm part of the problem—I didn't help my son figure out who he should be in the greater good. I didn't help him find himself, find a relationship with God, or with deeper parts of himself. He turned to drugs. He almost lost his life. He's been in and out of rehab (and I've participated with him), and now I'm beginning to understand him a little bit better. The twelve steps, for our family, have become not only the most natural way to help an adolescent grow up, but also a very spiritual way.

There is such wisdom in this man's perspective. His son, he himself, Breva and her family, and other families that let crisis change them have anguished and wrestled and have won parts of their individual core nature. In the father's case, he understood that his son—and so many other adolescents—needs a deeper look into himself, and a spiritual focus and discipline. As you look closely at your adolescent's core-nature development, I hope you'll become fearless in the face of crisis. I hope you will blame yourself only to the point of self-improvement, never to the point of denial or paralysis. I hope you will look deeply into the eyes of your hurt or broken child and ask not only "How can I help you feel better?" but also "How can I, the adult, help you discover in this crisis how *you* are meant to fight for the greater good?"

Burning Question: What Is the Best Way to Handle Peer Groups?

In response to a Gurian Institute survey on peer pressure, a mother of three—her children all grown now—wrote me, "When my eldest daughter, Lori, turned fifteen, she completely got into her peers. She wanted to spend the night at a friend's house on both Friday and Saturday night (or have one or more friends over to our house for one or both weekend nights). She wanted to talk to her friends on the phone or online *all the time*. Especially with our first child, it was kind of scary to see her go so quickly into her peer group."

Every family notices when a reorientation of the child's core-nature development moves him or her toward peers. At some point in a child's life, peer pressure begins in earnest (and for many kids, the move happens earlier than fifteen). Fortunately, with this scary move also comes peer wisdom, peer alliance, peer exploration, and peer support. Even while the child's parents remain active in the child's life and the child's parents-beyond-parents are still important, now a peer "third family" becomes essential—especially, at this age, a peer family in which there are problems, bad choices, bad influences, *and* a challenging community for the child's development of adolescent core nature.

To equip you to help your teenager manage this peer community, let's look at the full role of peers in activating your child's core nature, then at the role of parents. The Did You Know? box discusses the role of peers.

Did You Know?

There are many important aspects of child development that a peer-group community can encourage and influence in ways that parents cannot. Although parents play a role in all development, peers have a special influence that is essential to core-nature development. Specifically,

- Peers put each adolescent's core nature through necessary ordeals and tests of character.
- Peers nurture adolescents in ways parents are afraid to or are not qualified to.
- Peers help make girls into women and boys into men.
- Peers give physical and emotional safety to adolescents when parents are not understanding or helpful (and even when they are).
- Peers pull teens toward independence (sometimes dangerously).
- Peers often signal to the adolescent and to the parents areas for growth, what parents need to know about (even despite the pain the signals cause).
- Peers compete and want success and promotion, and nurture one another toward that promotion.

Peers are, in short, invaluable assets, and your accommodation of peers is an essential part of your parenting plan—of helping your child individuate.

A nice way to think of this is to consider yourself as the house in which your children learn who they are, parents-beyond-parents as the village in which children gain support for who they are, and peers as the city streets and even the surrounding wilderness in which children become who they are.

In all of our ancestral societies, no matter our continent of origin, peer influence on adolescent children was well managed by family systems. Children's core nature gained biological and social advantage by peers' being "brought into the family" in the years just before adulthood ("your friend Joe is like a son to us"); families didn't "give up their children" to peer groups and gangs.

Making Peace with Peers

The Try This box describes some essential components of managing peer life and energy. These will help you play an essential part in the "peering out" process in which your adolescent is engaged, as peers become a large part of your child's extended family. If you do these things, you will have set a solid system in place for your individual child to explore his or her own core nature safely through peer pressure, and meaningfully in peer groups.

Try This

To manage peer life, try these simple steps:

1. As long as your children live with you, know where they are. If a child goes somewhere he or she has not prescheduled, or does not keep you in communication with his or her changing plans, there need to be consequences. Hold to curfews, with consequences as well.
2. Meet your children's friends, talk with them, shake their hands, look them in the eye, invite them into your home, get to know them. A friend you have never met cannot become one of the family, and that is an isolation that can become a danger to your child.
3. Meet friends' parents and extended family; when possible, do things together with them. Build interwoven, multigenerational family systems in which peer activity takes place.

---

4. With such institutions as community, religious education, or sports agencies, organize peer events for your children. Human institutions that manage adolescence exist in part to help us raise our children into peer influence in "healthy psychological containers": structures (like sports and service events) that contain adolescent energy as that energy expands.

5. Hold as many sleepovers at your house as your children go to at other houses. Become the parent the other kids like spending time with, even confiding in. Suggest shopping, car repair, neighborhood soccer, and other projects that fit the energies of the boys and girls, young men and women, who are, when they are in your presence, in your care. The kids may shut you out, but you'll be surprised at how often they'll invite you in.

6. If you see any dangerous peer activity—drugs, alcohol, inappropriate sexual activities, or other risky behavior—call other parents, counselors, and community support staff. Often if your child says, "Don't get involved, I'll be embarrassed," you need to make the call anyway.

7. Take away privileges when children become overoccupied with peers (especially dangerous ones). As needed, consult with professionals, such as counselors, and other members of your family team for interventions in the lives of children whose core-nature development has become completely dependent on peer groups and peer activities isolated from the family system.

8. Commit to at least one daily check-in ritual with your child regarding his or her peers (for example, "How are things going with your friends?"). Do this even through late adolescence, perhaps once at breakfast and/or another time at dinner or sometime in the evening. Not a lot has to

be said, but at least you checked in. Your son or daughter will register that.

9. Create a relationship where your child can "talk to you about anything." This will often involve "general listening" and only "surgical talking" on your part. Peers are talking about everything with one another, but often in relative ignorance. If you develop a trusting, listening relationship with your adolescent and his or her friends, you can be the comfortable expert for those quick moments when these teens let you give your wisdom.

Provocative Peers

In a workshop I conducted, a father told this story: "Karen [his fifteen-year-old daughter] came home crying yesterday. Some of the girls at school called her 'fat' and a 'dork.' My wife (her stepmother) and I both consoled her. We told her she was fine, that things were okay. We asked her if we should talk to the other kids' parents. To make a long story short, we tried every way we could to help her, but I don't know how much we helped. I know some of the kids are still calling her names, and I'm not sure what to do."

Our workshop participants engaged with this father, asking questions. More information came out. Karen, it turned out, was about thirty pounds overweight. It also turned out that the "dorky" behavior her peers were name-calling her on was behavior the father had himself seen: Karen would say inappropriate things, and she interrupted in class, making the other students (not just the teacher) irritated with her. Karen, in her father's words, "is admittedly not the easiest child."

In the workshop were two grandparents. One of them, seventy-four years old—her four children in their thirties now—told stories of her own kids' peer relationships during the 1970s. Two of them sounded very similar to Karen's. There were ways in which her kids didn't fit the norms of the social group around them, and that social group had unmercifully pointed out the anomalies. This grandmother said wise words (though painful ones): "If you as a father know that the peers are right, then you don't do the kid much good pulling the wool over her eyes. You have to tell her that the peers are right."

"Tell her she's fat?" the father protested. "Tell my daughter she's a dork?"

The older woman said, "Figure out your own language. But use what the peers are saying to help her grow up."

The older woman had already wrestled in herself with just how much pain her own children could take from peers—where the line was that connected truth with maturity of core nature yet still protected long-term self-esteem. Her kids had come through well, and she was trying to signal to the young father that sometimes the peer group is more honest with a child than the parents are.

This may happen to your kid. Peers will point out the social, physical, and emotional "flaws" in your child's developing core nature. It's provocative, and sometimes it's mean. Your immediate instinctive response will be to help your child recover from the initial flood of painful feelings. It's a good instinct. But then, sometimes, you might miss the deeper instinct underneath: that the peer provocation might have some truth to it.

In the case of the father and Karen, our workshop group ended up agreeing that Karen needed her parents and extended family to help her develop different eating patterns. Thirty pounds overweight was not healthy for her. Her peers had been more honest than her parents in pointing that out. When the father came around to focusing on his adolescent's life from this perspective, he immediately saw that Karen needed to stop eating sugar cereals for breakfast, pizza for lunch, and spaghetti for dinner. He saw also that Karen probably did need more effort on her parent's and extended family's part in developing social skills appropriate for her age group.

When Karen's father sent me an e-mail about six months after this workshop, he reported that after a great deal of family deliberation, both he and Karen's mother confronted her about her weight and inappropriate social behavior and then set her up with three months of counseling. Karen came to like the youngish (thirty-year-old) female counselor. That counselor, an "older peer," was able to help Karen understand how her "dorky" behavior was hurting her relationships.

Peers do often bully—attacking a child's core nature by attacking race, sexual orientation, or basic core personality. Almost one-fifth of our children report being bullied. Right now we live in a culture that is, with good reason, looking closely at bullying, and doing something about it. (Good resources on bullying appear in the notes for Chapter Seven.)

But what happened to Karen was not unhealthy bullying. It was peers doing what they have always done in human development: provoking maturity. All families can benefit from this kind of healthy "peer pressure." I hope you'll look closely at this underestimated benefit of peers in your adolescents' lives. Peers are not generally enemies—they are coconspirators with our children, they are assistants to us, they are provocateurs, and they can be wise friends.

Becoming a Woman, Becoming a Man

Keeping kids away from peers or living in fear of peer influence is a negative scenario for families; it generally leads to hyperrebellion or hyperattachment to a girlfriend or boyfriend or dangerous peer group. At the same time, letting kids give up their family and extended families for the sake of peer groups is not a good idea—actually, it is an easy way out for children, and neglects their full growth as individuating beings. So it is with all important aspects of your adolescent's life: each can potentially help and harm core-nature development. Adolescence is the stage of life that, after infancy, can be one of the most tumultuous and risky.

It is also one of the most wonderful. I, like many of you, have enjoyed having young people in my home, not just "kids." I've enjoyed debates with my adolescents; I've enjoyed seeing the world through their maturing (and risk-loving) lens. I've also enjoyed watching my adolescents juggle their desires for their parents' company and wisdom and for their peers' company and wisdom. They live in a constant state of stimulation, so they keep me young! They also exhaust me, as your children may exhaust you, but as my children move toward high school graduation, they inspire deep feelings of hope and freedom in me. I hope your adolescent will inspire these feelings in you.

Wisdom of Practice

I HAVE A SIXTEEN-YEAR-OLD SON. WHEN SOMETHING IS UPSETTING me about my life, I speak honestly with him about my feelings. He usually tells me his feelings about something, too. He doesn't tell me everything I want to know, but we both agree that's okay. Luckily, we've worked out this compromise so that we can talk about anything. We also say "I love you" once a day. I hug him while he's playing his favorite computer game. He knows I hate MTV (because of its objectionable subject matter), so he changes the channel when I come in. We respect each other and kid around about things like "flatulation." We have fun. He's a normal kid, active, driving, all that—but he knows when he needs something, I'm there.

I HAVE A SEVENTEEN-YEAR-OLD DAUGHTER WHO IS ACTIVE IN LOTS of things. I've noticed she has a lot of pride in what she does. It's her nature, I think, to just have to do a thing well. If she can't do it well, she goes to something else. We encourage this in her.

Other parents have said, "She'll be a quitter if you don't force her to finish something she starts." With our kid, at least, this isn't true. She prefers sitting at dinner with us (we have dinner together at least four times a week) and telling us about her successes rather than her failures. Believe me, earlier in her life, she had enough of those—she wasn't very talented in soccer or in other sports. Now she's in karate, which she's good at (teaching younger kids), and she's very academically focused and volunteers in our church. To me, there are no magic answers to raising adolescents, but listening carefully to them is really good. They kind of tell you what they need if you just move to a "I'm here for you" position and get out of the "I have to pressure you" position.

9

Nurturing the Nature of Your Adolescent of Nineteen and Older

We reach backward to our parents and forward to our children, and through their children to a future we will never see, but about which we need to care.

—CARL JUNG

FR. JAMES RYAN, A JESUIT PRIEST WITH A CONSTANT HALF-SMILE AND alert gray eyes, was one of my best philosophy teachers in college. I remember when he stood in the front of his new class in 1978 holding a huge tome, *Insight,* by the philosopher Bernard Lonergan. We nineteen-to twenty-two-year-old philosophy majors stared at a great deal of future reading! "This book is about the search for a mission in life," Fr. Ryan said. "Get to know it. Your whole grade in my course depends on reading this book. Your grade in life," he smiled enigmatically, "depends on understanding this book."

All of my philosophy teachers seemed to think that their own particular course offering would be life changing, so I was skeptical at first. At twenty-one, I had been around the world more than once. I had lived a tough, confusing boyhood, and wanted from college more than hyperbole from professors. But Fr. Ryan was a commanding presence, and I listened. "Even if after reading this book," he continued, "you young folk understand what Lonergan actually is trying to say, I will be quite surprised. Bernard Lonergan is asking, 'Who are we? What will we do with our lives? What can we hope for?' Many young people seem already to know the answers, even though Fr. Lonergan himself admits he does not."

Fr. Ryan, it turned out, was not just a hyperbolist or a critic of young people. As the semester progressed, his class learned how to answer some very profound questions. This philosophy course was taken not only by philosophy students but also by engineering students, social studies majors, and the Jesuit scholastics studying at Gonzaga for the priesthood. All of us young people looked, in our reading, learning, social activities, and dreams, for a mission in life. Each of us sensed our own core nature by now, in our late adolescence and early adulthood; we were starved to know who we were going to *become* as missionaries of our own core nature in the world.

Think back a moment. Were your early twenties a bit this way? Were you wondering more steadily every day who you would become? Were you trying to move out of childhood and even adolescence by "acting like a man" or "acting like a woman"? Were you "living in the moment," trying on many passions, even friends and lovers, all in search of your future place in the world? Many of us moved out of our parents' homes, either to go to college or to work, and set up a life without parents; even if we still lived with parents, we were looking elsewhere, to other places, other mountaintops, other journeys than theirs. It would be a decade or two before we saw how similar our own journey and theirs would end up being—not until we had children would we fully understand who our parents were as they tried to help us discover who we were. For this late adolescent moment, we just wanted finally to be free, finally to jettison ourselves toward the future . . . the fruition in our adult lives of the "who" in "Who am I?"

It is no wonder that people often think of the years between graduation from high school and the middle twenties as the "finding myself" years. These are the years of mission. Given the brain and body chemistry of each young person at this age, I believe even the laziest or least self-aware among us can be coaxed toward some attempt at mission during these years of early adulthood. Some people, like myself, enter therapy during their early twenties, trying to rescue what we've lost in a difficult childhood; others move to a lifelong vocation; there are many fits and starts, many dreams dreamed and limitations discovered. Not everyone runs through this time of life at the same pace. During our last stage of adolescence, our mind and heart are trying to learn, each in its own way, that *our particular core* nature is not locked in one place or time, but rather can fully emerge in the deep longing to do what we are each called by nature and God to do, whatever that is and wherever it takes us.

The young person in your life is in a seventh stage of significant childhood and adolescent growth, one linked specifically to focusing the individual adolescent human brain toward tasks, worth, and mission. I believe now that this is what Fr. Ryan, as a philosopher, was hinting at when he dropped the huge philosophical tome in front of us. His mission was to make us conscious of our mission—the reason our core nature is here on this earth. He knew we young people had been unconscious during our childhood, and he wanted us to become insightful.

Preview of Essential Developmental Tasks

- *Recognize where your young man or woman is right now* in the life journey. This is the final stage of adolescence (at least we hope so!), which lasts into the mid-twenties. If as you read this your young person is already launched successfully into the social systems best suited for his or her core nature—further schooling, work, relationships—then your support of him or her right now is mainly financial and "being available as needed"; if the late adolescent is not launched successfully, then interventions may be needed.

- *Try to see the world through this young person's eyes.* While your son or daughter is moving into adulthood over these years, more is still needed of you and your family team. Beyond financial and other alliances you have agreed on with this young person, you are needed for the continued assistance of helping focus the late adolescent on a sense of mission in the world. Because you are still crucial to the child's discovery of his or her own core nature's purpose in work, schooling, education, and society, you will still be "engaged": you can help the young person not only by remembering how life was for you at this age but also by trying to look at life as it is now, for this particular child.

- *Let go as you must.* Your young man or woman will move at times fitfully and at times gracefully into the larger society; your challenge will be to hold fast when this young spirit needs you to, and to let go all other times. There is a beautiful sentiment from the Pulitzer Prize–winning poet Mary Oliver. She speaks of three important tasks in the relationships in our lives: to pay attention, to attach (hold close), then to let go when it is time to do so. How simple this sounds! How difficult it is. Your twenty-three-year-old may be driving a falling-apart car, may be in an on-again, off-again relationship, may be a slob, may have strange body piercings, may even barely talk to you for months at a time, but if this young woman or man is clearly focused on some decent mission in life, you have probably completed your work for now, and can let go.

Information Essential to Nurturing the Core Nature of Your Late Adolescent

In this chapter, let's focus together on the "age of mission" that is hard-wired into the developing brains and bodies of the young women and men in your home and neighborhood during late adolescence. We'll cover how this natural development reveals itself particularly in your nineteen- to twenty-five-year-old, but of course, each late adolescent and each young adult has his or her own rhythm and timing of maturation. One of your kids might be very mature at nineteen, another a late bloomer who doesn't really finding himself till twenty-nine.

1. Diversity is the "new normal" when it comes to this age group. In other words, your child is *not* merely a statistic in a social trend: this adolescent's nearly matured brain is now able to "show off" the results of genetics and of you and your community's efforts to nurture it; thus this young person is ready to innovate and live in his or her own way. The frontal lobe is generally better connected now to the lower limbic system than it was at fifteen; at fifteen, the young woman or man was fielding countless hormonal, neural, and social pressures that distracted it from fully thinking out a life existence. Now, many of those are better integrated, and the young person's whole cerebral cortex can concentrate on "Who am I?" more clearly.

One of the most inspiring couples I've worked with was a wife and husband (he was completely blind) who raised five children with the motto, "We raised them to be who they already were." All five of these young people have become wonderfully eccentric contributing members of their towns, cities, and countries (two live overseas). Both the wife and husband told me in their own ways, "With each kid, we said, 'You'll find your way if you concentrate on your passions.' Each one of our kids has had good times and bad, but they sure don't sit around wondering if they have a place in life. They go out and find it."

2. The young people in your life still seek family time. Though they may well have individuated, they still need "shots in the arm" of us. They need help, at times; they also need a more "adult" relationship with us than they had. It is good to heed the opinions of these young people themselves. When polled by *Time* magazine in 2005, most late adolescents reported communicating with their family in the previous week; nearly half communicated with their parents via phone or e-mail, and 39 percent said their parents still have a strong influence on them.

3. Our youth also want and need in this age group to find "substitute mothers" and "substitute fathers." They have grown away from us in many ways; they have accomplished their very natural individuation by moving into their independent selves; they have found peer groups that can aid and challenge them; they have set a course by their mid-twenties that will last them a long time—and they need a diversity of

mission-targeted social assets. This can include college mentors, like Fr. Ryan, but many youth don't go to college, and instead need vocational, activity-based, and emotional mentors. These mentors can turn the life of an "underfunctioning" late adolescent around. They can help give the young person a mission.

4. Our young people are wise and self-aware. In a recent poll, young people in their twenties were asked, "Do you consider yourself an adult?" Fully one-third said no. They can sense in themselves a lack of emotional or social maturity. Indeed, our children are maturing later than we did. In the "Burning Question" section at the end of this chapter, we will look at all the various reasons, natural and cultural, for the shift in the mean age of maturity in this generation.

5. Fits and starts are normal for this age group. As the brain completes its development, it is considered a "late adolescent brain." Many of the disconnections and challenges discussed in the previous chapter are still operative: risk taking is still experimental in this brain; emotional responses and nurturing experiences are still taking shape in this brain's reactions to stimuli. Changing of boyfriends or girlfriends, jobs, and habitats, and even sexual and moral experimentation are relatively normal. There is generally no need to worry about this young person's experimentation unless it's dangerous or grossly underfunctional. (We'll look at this topic in a moment.)

6. Your young person of this age is setting his or her own moral and ethical code in place for the life mission. You and your child's mentors are still teaching values, but the moral, social, even religious system this young person ends up with by twenty-five will most probably have some differences from yours. As this young person sets his or her own mission in life, it is often helpful and a relief for us as parents to judge moral, social, and religious ideas in our progeny not by whether they fit the rigid (or loose) code by which we tried to nurture the nature of this child, but by whether this child has now formed his or her own useful ethical code. If no ethical code is in place, we must worry and intervene, but if young people are seeking an ethical framework that fits who they are, we should be proud.

7. Things are not rosy for all of our young people. For many of them, life is dangerous, lonely, media addicted, disturbing. Some of our late adolescents are not finding their way. They have no mission; they still mooch off of us but to no purpose; they even hate us, but feel entitled to live in our homes and utilize the social services we pay for. There is in some of us even a profound discomfort with our own children, which eats at our core. As we explore these issues in this chapter, I also hope you will look back at the section "Helping Adolescents Through Crisis" in Chapter Eight. If you are right now faced with a son or daughter in a crisis or very difficult situation, you may be involved in mentoring or nurturing a core nature that has gotten derailed or that needs extra help. To start dealing directly with this situation, see the Try This box for some beginning thoughts and tips. You can put them to work immediately, and you may well have to relentlessly try these as your son or daughter resists.

Natural Differences Between Young Men and Young Women

As you enjoy your young person and prod him or her toward a mission, don't be surprised when you notice that young men and women are different in their late adolescent maturation and vision.

One of the most stunning revelations of new brain science is how much later adolescent boys complete their brain's maturation than girls. This is just one difference between our young men and women in relationships, marriage, the workplace, and even the accomplishment of mission in life.

Here are some details:

• Myelination of cells on the brain happens later in males. Myelination is the white coating on the brain cells that conducts electricity throughout different brain centers. Some males complete this myelination not just months but even years after some females. Thus, although nature's inherent variety allows for both female or male "late bloomers,"

Try This

- Be absolutely sure you have an *underfunctioning* late adolescent. If he or she is "not meeting your expectations," but you haven't looked closely at *this* adolescent's developmental nature, you might not really have an underfunctioner; you might simply have bought into a social trend idea of what he or she *should* be rather than understanding who he or she actually is. Talk to others in your family and friendship system who know your young person, so as to get other opinions on whether this youngster is finding a mission in life more slowly than others, or not finding one at all.
- Once you have established that your son or daughter is indeed underfunctioning, verbally review with your child his or her core strengths and weaknesses—and sometimes you must persevere in this even if you meet resistance. If the young person is not living at home, this review can be difficult (but still can be done via phone or e-mail); if the late adolescent is living at home, privileges can be contingent on his or her engaging in family meetings that review who he or she is and what his or her mission is.
- Keep directing your late adolescent away from entertainments and toward work—chores or money-earning employment—no matter how "lame" or "beneath me" the adolescent thinks the

statistically there are more males. This is one nature-based reason that many young men may need a "gap year" before going to college—a year in which to explore, work, develop, and mature before entering the high-pressure college environment.

- When brains of males and females in their early twenties are scanned by PET, MRI, and SPECT technologies, scientists notice that the male brains still go to a "rest state" many times per day. They have done this all through life, but now, as pressures increase on the brain—

work is. Remember, one of the most significant goals in a child's inward nature during this period is financial independence and self-reliance, but sometimes you have to coax it or force it.

- Cut back on any activities that lead to instant gratification. This could mean video games, computers, and TVs (we'll look more at this later) but also eating and other habits. One mom told me, "My son (22) hates me anyway, so I have nothing to lose by being a nag and an ogre about his food, exercise, friends. If he wants to move out because he doesn't like my rules, let him move out." This kind of tough love can be necessary at times. Be hard on this kid as needed.

- Keep trying to know his or her friends and networks. Stay as connected as your adolescent will let you, and if he or she tries to cut you out completely, resist that. If your child is living with you, meet his or her friends in the hall or the yard, strike up conversations, probe for details. The house is your house, and you are its master.

- Keep talking to your child of this age about the future. Keep exposing this young person to future possibilities. Tell your own story of life at this age. Stimulate this young person to think, "What are *my* best skills? Who am *I?* What am I here on this earth to do? How am I going to make a living and survive on my own financially?"

and throughout adulthood—this rest state will become a very important time of recharge in the male brain. In this "zoning out" state, men's brain activity nearly shuts down. In young women, interestingly, there is not a similar whole brain rest state. When scanned, college-age women's brains appear constantly engaged in blood flow. The greater ability to multitask—to do and talk about many tasks at once—that females generally possess fully clarifies itself by this last stage of adolescence and lasts throughout the lifetime.

• Have you ever wondered why car insurance companies charge lower rates for women of this age group than for men? You've probably thought it had to do with the more aggressive male testosterone. That's true, but there's another reason: it's the greater ability in the female brain to switch focus even after the brain has been fixed on one task. Brain researchers in England have shown that young women will almost immediately shift attention to deal with an unexpected event and, in tandem with their biochemistry, make a safer driving choice during that time of "switching focus." Young males will more doggedly pursue their original tasking or focus, which often involves more danger.

• Male and female emotional processing has been different throughout childhood; now, after puberty, it continues to be unrelentingly different. The female brain will tend to process more emotive, sensorial, and empathic information through the verbal centers of the cerebral cortex. The male brain will tend to move more of this information toward the brain stem, being more physically active, and turning fewer subtleties of feeling, sensation, empathy, and memory into words. This "word-use" difference can come to haunt the first few years of marriages, as women try to get men to "talk more about their feelings" and men try to get women to "get to the point!"

• By the time your adolescent son and daughter reach this age, he will have 6.5 times the gray matter in the brain that she has. She will have 9.5 times the amount of white matter that he has. Gray matter is most wired for "local processing"—single-task focus and calculation, including compartmentalization of brain functioning until the end of a specific task; white matter is most wired for "integrative processing"— assimilating disparate information from more brain centers at once.

Our social trends culture has, for a few decades, pushed the idea that males and females entering the workforce are the same. Although they certainly are more similar than our old patriarchal culture had assumed—women can do most of what men can do, and vice versa— brain research shows that during their twenties, males and females will gravitate naturally toward work that fits who they are internally. The smart workplace will not be one that decides that either the male or female nature is better, but one that figures out how to get males and females to bring together their unique natural assets to create a workplace of symbiosis between the two.

• Our late adolescents experience and process stress differently, depending on their gender. Estrogen activates more neurons in the brain during stressful experiences than does testosterone. By the time adolescents reach this age, their chemical cycles are fully developed; thus, the way they each handle stress now is most probably the way they each will do so in the future. For the young woman, the disadvantage to her greater engagement and more constant "thinking about" (and thus, perhaps, brooding over) a stressful event or conversation can be the derailing of her focus on more important tasking; the advantage can be that she experience life's emotional mysteries more fully. For the young man, the disadvantage of his more simple fight-or-flight response to stress is that he becomes a less patient listener, and specifically misses or avoids a lot of important content in relationships; the advantage can be that he solves more problems more quickly. Neither the estrogen-based nor testosterone-based approach to relationships is the "correct" one (despite the constant argument in social trends theories that a female approach to emotion is inherently better): they both just *are*.

• During this stage of late adolescence, both young women and young men can form social networks that will last a lifetime—either in terms of "personnel" or systemically. By this I mean that females will form their own networking style and system—a system that continues to expand as needed, driven especially by oxytocin, the bonding chemical, which women have more of than men—that will last through the child-rearing decades, even if the particular people in the system come and go. Males will also network (join fraternities and sports teams, form a rock band, and so on) during this time, and their small cadre of core friends and large cadre of competitive or challenging friends will probably be re-created throughout life. At the same time, males will tend not to continue to expand their network. At thirty, a young mother may look for five or ten women around whom to form a system, whereas the young father at that time may be looking for one or two trusted male friends and a sports team or work team within which to challenge and hone his abilities.

The differences between young women and young men are profound during the age of mission, and you will be able to see each of them illuminated in young people's lives. As your children fully enter the world as males and females, they will bring with them their male and female brains, hopes, dreams, and needs, and they will say to the world not only, "I am forming an important mission" but also, "I as a woman [I as a man] am finding myself, forming a mission, and preparing to care for the world as I feel it needs my care."

Identifying and Helping Young Men and Young Women Who Lack a Mission in Life

As you are nurturing the nature of your children beyond high school, they may now be in college or receiving training in a trade; they may be working to support other opportunities; they may be studying with a mentor in an art form; they may be struggling or succeeding with the quest for financial independence. They may be independent young people passionate about a cause, well adjusted, even married or preparing for marriage. They may even have already provided you with grandchildren. This last stage of childhood—the extended adolescence stage—is one of immense possibility. It is a time to worry, yes, because your children are never "not your responsibility," but there is often celebration in a family as the child "moves on" and "finds herself" and "begins to make his way."

You may, however, have a child of this age who is not flourishing, not gaining self-reliance in ways that you believe fit his or her nature, not adjusted as you would hope (and as he or she may hope), not learning to provide for himself or herself the money the child will need to survive independently without you. Identifying the needs of this young person is a crucial part of your parenting now. It is essential to identify the stagnant areas of your child's natural development, especially given how late in life many of our children are maturing.

Here are some stories that illustrate issues that may resonate with your family's situation. I hope that reading them can help you recognize that your child might need you "not to let go quite yet" in ways you might have thought you should. Many young people still need the adults in their lives to help them manage and develop their core nature toward a life mission.

Young Men Without Mission

Carl, a college student, wrote, "I am a Virginia Tech student who witnesses firsthand the wasting of young men's minds and talents. Most of my male friends are quite content to spend their time playing video games and floundering in the classroom. This complacency and lack of ambition among my male friends is a trend, in my observation, throughout the university."

Sam, a father of a twenty-three-year-old, wrote, "Most of my son's friends are like him: passive, not interested in marriage, not interested in working hard or earning enough money to be on their own, short-term thinkers. Most of the girls who were his friends in high school are going to college. My son's buddies from high school are working as cooks, mechanics, warehousemen. There's nothing wrong with that, but there's also so much lost potential in these young men. I don't understand where their ambition has gone."

Alba, a mother of two, wrote, "I have a friend who has four boys. She and her husband are both professionals, so you would think the boys would be active, going to college, really making it in life, but the three oldest (who were born close together) are floundering. They work in fast-food restaurants, get into trouble, don't do much of anything to advance themselves. It is heartbreaking. During the school years, they were all put on different drugs at certain times to help them get motivated. As a mother of a young boy myself, I am afraid for what is happening with our young men."

Regina, an engineer in North Carolina, said,

I grew up in a small town, went to a high school that was 80% minority, attended college then graduate school. I'm now just graduating from law school. I mention this because the vast majority of the guys

I grew up with didn't make it. I used to think it was where I came from (high minority population, low income), but especially as I began working, and then even more so after entering law school, I saw how lost the guys are. What does it take these days to get a guy pointed in a good direction? All around me I'm seeing these citizens of society who are not making a good living financially, barely active as members of their families, particularly as husbands and fathers. I'm just turning thirty, and I can't tell you how hard it is to meet guys who aspire to be what they can. I fear that I'll have to settle for a guy who just doesn't know what it takes to be a man.

In December 2005, I wrote an article for the *Washington Post* titled "Disappearing Act." It regarded the issue of why young males are failing in the school system, and specifically why so many are not going to college. The outpouring of e-mails and comments like the ones you've just read was substantial. In one week following the article, I had received five hundred e-mails directly to my Web site telling similar stories of young men without a mission. Within three weeks, I had received a thousand such letters. I found out later that the *Washington Post* and the other newspapers that printed the article received their own similar outpouring of e-mails.

Every year that I'm involved in trying to help boys and their families set a strong course for life, I become increasingly convinced that our sons as a whole are doing worse than our policymakers think they are. In the end, this is why each of us must—always—nurture the nature of *our* child, one family at a time. We must not wait for the culture to catch up. The late adolescent nature of many boys in particular is not as well understood in our culture as we have been led to believe by social trends that say, "Boys have privilege; boys are doing fine; the system is set up to promote male success."

If you have a son who is floundering, I hope you will add to your patience the full range of options available in the following Try This box.

Many young males may need a gap year before going to college. Your son may simply not be cognitively and developmentally ready to go to college. Pushing him to college right away may lead to a year or two of floundering, then dropping out. Once he drops out, he may

Try This

If your son is not maturing as you know he ought to, some interventions may be in order.

- Use the medical model as appropriate. Consult doctors and psychological professionals who are trained not just in human biology, but at least in some part, *male* issues and male biology.

  Look for extreme medical models if necessary. If people have been telling you there is something medically or clinically wrong with your son—ADHD, ADD, or another disorder—consider the possibility of having a brain scan. About half the time, insurance companies will cover these scans. In the Notes and References section, I've listed some publications that argue the pros and cons of these scans.

- Try to have your son fulfill neuropsychological batteries. Some of these are listed in my book *The Minds of Boys*. Seek psychologists or psychiatrists who are specifically trained in male development. This professional can also answer questions about these batteries. Maybe your son did not believe at thirteen or sixteen that he had a "brain problem," but now, at twenty-one, if he completes neuropsychological batteries (or sees a scan), he might be more motivated to help himself by taking medication or advancing other solutions.

- Check out alternative solutions to his issues. Media addiction, substance abuse, lack of basic brain-friendly nutrition, food allergies leading to depression . . . all these are possible culprits if he seems unmotivated and unable to concentrate. If the medical model does not bring a successful solution, keep looking into alternatives. Alternative medicine gurus, such as Deepak Chopra and Andrew Weil, are constantly pointing out augmentations to traditional medicine. More omega-3 fatty acids, less sugar, more protein and fewer carbohydrates, homeopathic remedies . . . if clinical medicine isn't working, don't give up! Keep exploring what fits *this* young man's nature.

- Utilize the "other" parent. If motivating this boy has been mainly the mother's job, now may well be the time to get the father involved on a daily basis. The father may need to compel the son to "get off his butt" and do specific and long-lasting projects with the father—work with the father at his workplace, go on extended camping trips without any electronics in tow, travel overseas together . . . something to "kick-start" the boy toward manhood.

- Utilize parents-beyond-parents. One unmotivated young man I worked with was twenty years old and doing very little of purpose or significance. He delivered pizzas for a while, got fired for missing work, got another job, got fired. As I worked with his family, we all kept in the back of our minds that from boyhood onward he had loved to cook. Three hundred miles away, in another city, this young man's uncle and aunt owned a restaurant. A "deal" was made in this family by which this unmotivated late adolescent went to the other city and worked with his relatives in the restaurant. Of the many things that had been tried over a six-month period to help this boy become a man, it was this move to his uncle and aunt's restaurant that kick-started him to full adulthood.

- Cut back on video games and electronic stimulants. This is not possible if your unmotivated youngster is living out of the home, but if he's at home, you have more control than you think. He has to do chores, work, earn money, fulfill moral and family obligations in order to earn electronics time. He's an adolescent child. Tying his electronics to his work helps him grow up, and it also cuts down on the brain-numbing electronics. Remember that when your son plays a video game and gets the rush of success (in the basal ganglia and caudate, two reward and concentration areas of the brain), he feels he has "accomplished something" for that day. And he has . . . electronically, virtually. But in real life, he has done nothing. Moving him away from electronic rewards to real-life rewards is a way of showing his brain that he cannot live forever on virtual success.

- Pay him for accomplishing specific jobs around the house and in the family. Connect work to pay so that he gets a clear sense of the future—that, to some extent, he is what he earns. With a hyperresponsible youth, we tend to want to say, "Just do something for the fun of it, would you? Just relax." But with the undermotivated youth, tying his "doing" to his "earning" is essential.

- Set time limits to your plans of action. For instance, if your undermotivated son is nineteen, agree with him that you and he will take one year to accomplish any important short-term tasks, and then he must go into some kind of higher education. Make sure to keep providing goals and help with goal setting in this adolescent's life.

become depressed, listless, undirected. In parts of Europe a gap year is not stigmatized, but in the United States it is. The core natures of many of our young people need us to remove this stigma. If a young person works for a living or travels or volunteers in service work (or does a combination of these things) for a gap year, he is still developing naturally.

A number of parents and young men have mentioned to me the Web site www.leapnow.com, which provides the service of helping families plan out the young person's gap year with useful and service-oriented activities.

What Young Women Face

Boys and young men, of course, are not alone in lacking ambition and mission.

Carrie, twenty-three, told me, "I have tried to find a place to fit in college and outside of college. I just can't. I work, but it's boring. I've been in counseling. I don't know what's wrong with me. I see everyone succeeding around me, and I just feel like I'm stupid."

Carrie's mother echoed her assessment:

Carrie cannot seem to concentrate on anything for very long and has no ambition, really, whether it's for school or a job. We've had her checked for bipolar, depression and ADD. Medication helps her, but the doctors say there's no real proof she has any mental disorder. I think Carrie will probably end up in the fallback position of getting married as soon as possible. She has been a really late bloomer. She's just now learning how to earn and manage money, pay bills. I think she'll be living at home for a long time. I just don't understand what's going on with her.

Gale, a physicist and a mother of three, wrote,

If you think it's only boys who suffer in the school system today, you're wrong. It can be just as bad for girls—the difference with boys is that girls adapt better, they're more compliant. But I had to fight every step of the way for my four daughters. I tried to keep them in classrooms where the teacher would give them some ambition, not just have them do paste cutouts of 25 identical clowns, or color in the lines. I had to fight to help them pursue science careers. Girls are taught to succeed in mimicking. When they get to college, they're still mimicking, especially in the sciences. How will they ever have the ambition to lead if they are just copies of what society tells them they should be? I see my college age girls just treading water, wanting to get out and get going. My girls are too independent to find themselves in the system of school and college.

A therapist in California's prison system, Trey, wrote, "The amount of sexual pressure and stress college age women experience is frightening to me. I read years ago in Margaret Mead's work that when young women in a culture turn violent, the culture is on its way down. That's what we're seeing now: a lot more young women turning against the pressures, the abuse, the neglect with violence. It used to be only about 10 percent of individuals in the criminal justice system were female. Now we're seeing more young women getting enraged and hurting others."

Whether you are raising a young man or a young woman, your child faces the possibility of significant stress during the last stage of adolescence, this betwixt-and-between stage of life from after high school graduation to the mid-twenties. Many of these young women are not truly adults yet, even though they can drink legally, serve in the military, vote, and otherwise be called adults. Many of them do not have an adult mission yet, and this lack of mission is a hidden stressor for them. These young women do not live in a sense of mission and hope. They lack an age-appropriate completed self and thus can barely find independent mission. They hold on to the promise of "social systems," trying to find a self in the social systems or trends provided—college, early marriage, piecemeal work—but feel unhappy or lost.

Try This

To help your underfunctioning daughter, you might look at these possibilities.

- Fulfill the same medical, clinical, and alternative protocols we listed in the Try This box regarding undermotivated young men, but make sure the health professional is trained in *female* biology. Remember that many M.D.s and Ph.D.s did not receive training in female hormonal biology, female brain development, or women's issues when they were receiving their medical or psychological training. Interview the health professional closely to make sure this person can put into action the pharmacological, neural, psychological, and even alternative strategies that fit your young woman's nature.
- Help your daughter find stress management classes and support groups. Generally I have found that young women who

are in significant distress regarding self-development are constantly putting themselves under stress—not only the stress they feel in their vocational or college classes but also the constant internal stress of self-denigration and feelings of inadequacy and failure. They may say, "I thrive on stress. I love it." Indeed, for some young people, that is an accurate assessment of their core nature and leads to success; but for the troubled late adolescent girl, those kinds of statements are often a mask of chronic stress symptoms.

• Help her nurture two to three primary relationships with mentors or peers who will encourage rather than discourage. These people need to encourage your child verbally and through celebrations of her specific talents and ways of being. This is indeed a time for targeted "good job on that" reinforcement. These mentors and peers may also have the role of saying, "Are you sure you want to take on this other thing? Won't it distract you from what you're really about?" or "Are you sure you want to take on this relationship with this person? Is he healthy for you?" Years of trusting two or three powerful people in her life will help this young woman come to fruition.

• Help her learn to build realistic and self-satisfying relationships. Because of oxytocin and other chemicals, late adolescent girls tend to operate from what I call a *malleable self.* I spend a great deal of time on this in my book *The Wonder of Girls,* should you wish to pursue the topic further. This natural malleability often leads late adolescent females to hyperbond with one or more men in order to feel adequate and successful as a self. If your daughter is involved with someone who is helping her develop parts of herself that need developing (and even if the young man is just treating her well enough for her to be growing her inner assets in his presence), you have no place, really, to interfere. She is on her own journey. But if she constantly bonds with inappropriate men, gets rejected, and suffers depression from the rejection, she may well be in a cycle of malleability—an unconscious pattern of chronic stress in relationships—that can prevent her from maturing. If you note this pattern by the time she is nineteen or older, you may well want to consult a professional and see if together a plan of intervention can be developed.

I've divided information and suggestions regarding helping our young people into separate categories for males and females because the needs of our youth are dependent to some extent on their gender. By the time they are twenty or twenty-two or twenty-five they are not children or young adults as much as young men and young women. To be fully whole and to take into their own future families the assets of their core natures, they must define themselves not only as individuals or people but also as men and women.

At the same time, there are some things we can try that can help any youth, male or female. These kinds of assistance can be tailored by the young person to fit his or her core nature.

• Encourage travel. If you can, pay for your young person to take two or three months to travel and simply live life as it comes. Especially encourage travel to ancestral places: the country or countries from whence his or her bloodline comes. Encourage this young person to go back to Ireland and visit relatives there, go back to Africa and see where his or her ancestors were taken into slavery, go back to Auschwitz in Poland and see where his or her grandparents were killed. Help this young person go back into his or her genetic field in order to go forward into a strong future.

- Encourage education and work wherever they come. Throw out assumptions that there is only one kind of work (highly competitive, highly lucrative) that is right for a young person. Keep searching with this young person for the work and education that fits *this* core nature.

- Encourage financial independence. A mother of a twenty-three-year-old college graduate told me, "John [her husband] and I could see that Dusty was making the wrong decision about the car he bought, and we did try to warn him, but we knew it was important that he feel financially independent. When he refused our help, we backed off. We noticed that he did indeed buy a car that needed $2,000 extra in repairs, but on the other hand, he became more of an adult through the experience—being completely 'his own boss' in how he earned and spent money, the $2,000. It helped grow him up."

Financial independence can indeed be a major developmental milestone. In whatever ways your young person needs, encourage financial self-reliance, even if it means a little more suffering for the youth (and for you as you watch the process) in the short term.

- Help your young person seek apprenticeships and mentoring relationships. No matter what the work or school, help your child find "masters" to whom he or she can "apprentice." Especially if the young person gets overstimulated by large group settings, see what "art" is in him or her and what "artist" might become the leader of this struggling core nature. Throughout human history, our youth learned how to find appropriate missions in life through the visions and under the tutelage of masters.

- Whether the young person is a young woman or a young man, and indeed, even if he or she is very motivated and very well adjusted, it is essential and quite beautiful to engage with him or her in conversations regarding, "Who are you? What do you hope for?" Every young person is asking these deep questions of himself or herself; every young man or woman wants in his or her lifetime to answer them, even if it takes more years to accomplish that than we parents might wish.

Burning Question: Why Are Young People Maturing So Much Later Than We Did?

It will often take far more years than we would have thought, even a generation ago, for our young people to mature. Because many people can see so many late-maturing women and men, I am frequently asked, "Is our actual human nature changing?" Often the hidden question is "Is it a good thing or a bad thing that so many of our kids are waiting so long to 'launch themselves' into full adulthood?"

The answer is a fascinating yes and no to both the first and second questions. As always, the answer depends on the individual nature of *your* child, but there are also some fascinating new trends in both social functioning and human nature.

- Thirty years ago, the median age of marriage for women was twenty-one. She had her first child at twenty-two. Today, the median age for both is twenty-five. This indicates liberation of women from early marriage and into the workplace, from an economic point of view. It also indicates the extension of social maturity timelines, some of which can be attributed to a general increase in human life span.

- If you have a "late bloomer," some of his or her late maturity in personal responsibility may be linked to developmental issues in school and family systems. A new study shows that more than 50 percent of students at four-year colleges and more than 75 percent at two-year colleges lack the skills to perform complex literacy tasks, from understanding the written work to using math skills in the real world. Many of our youth are having to spend time in their early twenties catching up on what they didn't learn as kids.

- There are also a greater number of chronically stressed children and adolescents who grow to their early twenties and are clinically depressed (including the depression correlating with substance abuse). No one knows how many of these young people there are, but if you have a child you think could be launching late because of depression, the battle to be fought may well be a biochemical one that requires medication and other interventions. Ambition, mission, purpose may not be possible until this battle is fought.

• Many of our children are "taking a breather" after the chronic stress of childhood—they've lived through parental divorces, overscheduling, and school failures, and need to pause for breath. They need to recharge and are extending adolescence in order to do that. They are living at home longer and asking for more emotional and psychological help from us in developing into fully independent adults.

• Many of our children lack significant rites of passage (which naturally cause maturity to happen in the child), and are thus somewhat aimless in their sense of mission, community spirit, path to worth, and road of self-sacrifice. They remain narcissistically adolescent for a longer period of time than their ancestors because they were not led through the adolescent phase in a spiritually and psychologically vigorous way. Further, the social trends culture keeps them hooked on consumerism, mindless entertainments, and an existence relatively purposeless except for the "purpose" of spending parents' or self-earned money on youth-entertainment consumer products.

• Many of our youth—especially the males—no longer join the military and thus no longer are forced to grow up through this system. They're unsure how to grow up in our social trends culture.

• Many of our youth are, quite simply, media addicted. They spend so much time living inside the mission statements of virtual humans that they convince themselves that they themselves either already have one ("I'll get rich by the time I'm thirty, you'll see") or don't need one: the people whose lives they voyeuristically enjoy are lively enough and important enough, in their minds, to keep them occupied with passive stimulation during a given day. A new study by the Nielsen Media Research company discovered that even college students watch an average of three hours and forty-one minutes of TV per day.

If you have a late bloomer or a child who is "failing to launch," you might indeed need to let this young person have extra time to regroup from the chronic stress of childhood; you might need to get medical or other help for this young person; you might need to send this young person off to travel or compel him or her into work; you might need to apprentice this youngster to one or more father or mother figures. All of the possibilities we've noted in this chapter can be helpful.

Most helpful, I think, is to make sure this young person has a family team close by that will take a year or two to help him or her discover not just some escape from stress, not just a minimal way of surviving, but indeed a sense of life mission by which this person can thrive and take on the burdens and joys of the generations.

The Mission in Life

Each young person is a gift in this world, and no matter how much positive or negative stress that young person experiences, each young man or woman wants to succeed.

I hope you will never let go of helping this young adult focus on a sense of mission. As you watch your child—that baby who is now an adult—carry his or her core nature struggling or flourishing into the world, I hope you will look into his or her eyes with the same vigor and mission you had at this child's birth—and nurture the nature. As your adolescent now (we hope!) makes most of his or her decisions independently, I hope you'll feel a state of growth in your family that can be felt only as children walk out the door saying, "I am prepared to do what I must in life and find the tools to do it, and I will live in genuine hope and happiness."

Wisdom of Practice

I WANT TO TELL YOU ABOUT MY CONFUSING, WONDERFUL DAUGHTER. She's now twenty-five, but wow, it has been a journey. We learned from her that you just never know what parts of these kids will express themselves when. You just have to keep being there, watching, adapting, holding firm, letting go.

Clara started out loving to draw cartoons. From very young, she would draw little cartoon books. We got her into all those classes, and then one day she just switched to piano. She had to play piano every day. She even lost control of some of her school work, and we had to help her get back on track. She had a wonderful piano teacher who said, "Everything in moderation!"

When Clara was in her early teens, she was listening to one of my Bob Dylan tapes one day (we had cassettes then, no CDs), and she decided to learn everything about him. She got totally enamored of folk music and thought about starting a band. We thought, "Wow, this kid is all over the map."

In high school, she was in band and became very rebellious, too. We had to back off a little, adjust to her. I was more strict than her dad, but he supported me. By the time she finished high school, she had decent (not great) grades, but just *knew* she had to go to Juilliard. She wanted to be a classical or jazz musician.

Well, she ended up going to University of Chicago, and guess what she studied (and just graduated in)—economics! We would never have thought that would be her passion, not when she was so into art and music.

But you know what, as my husband and I look back on it, it does make sense. She was always into how money worked, how fair our household was, the division of labor. She watched the news at a young age. She and my husband—an architect—used to talk about how much things cost. There were a lot of clues, actually, when we thought about it. Then when we learned from brain research that actually economics and music happen in similar parts of the brain, we suddenly understood our daughter.

To end my story, I told her at Christmas break about how I had been thinking about all this, and she was so sweet; she said, "Mom, you did great. You let me be myself every step of the way. If it weren't for you guys, I wouldn't have found my passions." I cried right then. That was one of the greatest moments of my life!

EPILOGUE

It would be a poor result of all our anguish and our wrestling, if we won nothing but our old selves at the end of it.

—GEORGE ELIOT, *ADAM BEDE*

Those of us who want to nurture the individual and inborn core nature of our children are blessed by the possibility of leaving a legacy of our healthy, individually developed child. Every step of this parenting journey, we have been called to action and patience by our child who has grown in his or her own way and at his or her own pace.

As you end this book and ponder your children's adult futures, I hope you have been able to add science-based philosophy and nature-based theory to your toolbox as a parent. I think over the next decade you will see yet a lot more science emerge for the sake of good parenting.

The world of parenting has changed a great deal in our recent generations. Thirty years ago some people thought science had little to offer parents beyond new appliances and medical innovations. Thirty years ago some people thought that technology would be the panacea of family life, creating the "best" new foods, products, learning and development tools, and social options for children and families.

Now we know that science has a great deal to offer parents, far more than just technologies and pills.

Now we know that technology is not only potentially life-saving but also potentially toxic.

Perhaps most subtle among all these changes, thirty years ago most of us were not able to identify the chronic stress in which our society is trying to raise our children. Now we can. We can see the numbers of children on medication, failing in school, running away, committing crimes, and crying out in loneliness for the basic attention of all the family members they need in order to express their core natures.

My own journey as a science-based philosopher and family therapist has been one of constantly modifying my hard-held views to accommodate the new things I learn about children. In the end, most stimulating for me and for my children has been the relentless desire to look deeply into their eyes and learn from them what they need.

I hope this book helps you look deeply into the eyes of your own children. I hope, too, that this book provides you with templates for book discussions and for social reform. Please feel free to cut and paste portions of it into e-mails, onto refrigerator doors, and into other resources for your personal use. Appendix A, for instance, is written specifically so you can do that. We must fight the chronic stress of childhood together, and we must use all the resources available to us.

I believe there is truly no feeling like knowing that you have nurtured the nature of your own offspring, your own nature. Knowing it is a kind of fulfillment that grows from the long-term and immortalizing success of helping shape the being to whom our own nature gives life, and holds forever dear.

APPENDIX A
PRINCIPLES OF NATURE-BASED FAMILIES

1. Each child is born with a biopsychological template that requires life-stage-appropriate nurturance by family and society in order for genetic vulnerabilities to be managed and genetic assets to be expressed.

2. Nature drives gene expression by way of the nurture principles of attunement, support, and challenge. Nature and nurture are thus not contradictory but perfectly complementary.

3. The most lasting success model for development of children is one of nature-friendly adaptations—one in which each child is supported in adapting to challenges—rather than a social hierarchy model in which success is defined only by the "top dog."

4. Children in all cultures gain biological and social advantage (flourish best) when no parental or social influence or activity (including work and marriage) is separated from the purpose of raising healthy children.

5. Nature-based families recognize that human beings are by nature polyfilial rather than monofilial. Though a single parent loves his or her children deeply, many parents and mentors are still needed to ensure the full development of a child's core nature.

6. In nature-based families, symbiotic marriage (the blending of parental gifts and assets) is considered essential and is encouraged and protected in the long term. This includes symmetrical

and complementary (not necessarily similar) parenting by mothers and fathers.

7. Nurturing the nature of a child requires sequential and developmental attention to evolving natural needs. With each new year of life, the child's adaptations to nature need new adaptations by family and society.

8. Gender typology (not gender stereotype) is a crucial part of nurturing the nature of each boy and girl. Boys and girls, women and men are inherently different—we need all their different gifts in our families and our world.

9. Integrative psychology (which acknowledges that humans are diverse and that each family thus must look into the eyes of each of its children for specific signals of need and attention) is more valuable than uniform psychology (which seeks the one "magic bullet" technique that can fit all kids).

10. Character and moral development, as well as spiritual reflection and moments of joy, are crucial for fully developing the nature of each child.

APPENDIX B
TRACKING YOUR CHILD'S CORE PERSONALITY THROUGH GENETICS: HOW TO DRAW AND UNDERSTAND A GENOGRAM

It is fun to look into the eyes of your child and discover his or her personality through his or her genetic legacies.

Gathering Information to Create a Genogram

Before beginning this genogram exercise, wonder in your journal or aloud among your family, "Who in our family lines does my child resemble, and in what ways? Does Bruce resemble Aunt Carol in the way he talks, or in mannerisms? Does Alice resemble Grandpa Joe, and in what ways?" This is a good time to make phone calls, search memories, and write letters and e-mails to family members in order to look back at the maternal and paternal family lines and to write down observations about this child in the context of those individuals who are the child's genetic inheritance.

Ask also: "What of my own genetics seems active in this child?" Honestly reflect on your own core nature. Determine how like or unlike you the child is becoming. It helps to write down your thoughts, intuitions, observations, and memories. Focus on such key words as *temperament, intuitiveness, a talker, clean, sloppy, very emotional, a thinker . . .* try to come up with more categories like these to stimulate comparisons among aspects of you, your relatives, and your children.

Remember, your child is a "gene expressor." He or she is expressing genes inherited from others. If you want to get more deeply into family genealogies, you can go onto the Internet. There are many ways to access your ancestry. For the sake of this exercise—the understanding of your child's core nature—make sure to focus on your ancestors' personalities, temperaments, talent sets, and ways of living, not just their country of origin.

A last note before you begin: this genogram activity and Chapter Two of this book are only a beginning point for understanding your child's core nature. There are many tools you can use, including the Myers-Briggs Type Indicator, tests based on Jungian archetypes, and the Big Five (all readily available on the Internet using Google or other search engines).

Creating the Genogram

To begin a genogram, place a piece of poster board on your dining room table. The left half of the board will display Dad's family, and the right half of the page will display Mom's family. Mom and Dad's marriage will meet in the middle about two-thirds of the way from the top.

In the upper left-hand corner, begin with Dad's great-grandparents. A square indicates a male, and a circle indicates a female. A line connecting the two indicates a marriage. Perpendicular lines with squares

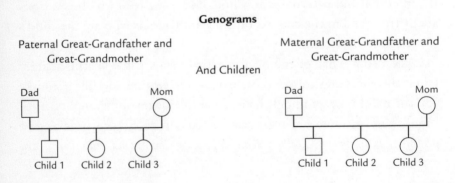

Genograms

Paternal Great-Grandfather and Great-Grandmother

And Children

Maternal Great-Grandfather and Great-Grandmother

Dad   Mom   Dad   Mom

Child 1   Child 2   Child 3   Child 1   Child 2   Child 3

The male is noted by a square, the female by a circle. The male is placed to the left of the female in the father/mother dyad. Marriage is shown by a line connecting the two.

Children are noted oldest to youngest, left to right. The index person of the genogram (or person from whose perspective it is being drawn) is set off from the others and marked with double lines. Birth dates are often recorded to the upper left or right. If the first two digits of the year can't be mistaken, the last two digits of the year are often all that's needed.

Other important notations are shown below:

| identical twins | fraternal twins | adopted child | foster child | stillbirth | miscarriage | abortion | pregnancy |

Liaisons or a couple living together are displayed similar to marriage but with a dotted line.

Marriage dates are recorded above the line connecting husband and wife.

m. 90

A **separation** of a couple is marked with one slashed line. The date is also usually recorded.

m. 90, s. 94

A **divorce** of a couple is marked with two slashed lines. The date is also usually recorded.

m. 90, s. 94, d. 96

The **death** of a person is indicated by an "X" through the shape. The birth and death dates are also usually recorded.

45–98

A **remarriage** (or former marriage) is shown to the side with a smaller shape. The focus couple is the one in the middle with the larger shapes.
Note: If there has been more than one remarriage, the marriages are usually placed from left to right, with the most recent marriage coming last.

m. 1990, d. 96   m. 99

Source: Kathleen M. Galvin and Carma L. Bylund, "Understanding, Interpreting and Creating Genograms," copyright © 2000 Northwestern University.

http://faculty-web.at.northwestern.edu/commstud/galvin/genograms. Used with permission.

and circles attached indicate children from that marriage. The marriages of Dad's paternal and maternal grandparents are illustrated in the first figure. The second figure illustrates additional symbols for various relationships and people.

Using the first figure as an example, draw Dad's paternal and maternal grandparents' marriages and children. Use a connecting line to indicate the marriage between the grandparents. Draw the children from the grandparent's marriage.

Following the same pattern, draw Dad's parents' families, their marriage and children. One of these children, of course, is Dad.

Now move to the right half of the board. Following the same process, draw Mom's parental and maternal great-grandparents, grandparents, and parents, and their marriages and children. Your (Mom and Dad) circle and square should be on the same line; draw a line connecting them to indicate your marriage. Draw perpendicular lines to indicate your children.

APPENDIX C
MORE HELP WITH FOOD, SHELTER, AND CLOTHING: A DISCUSSION STARTER FOR PARENT GROUPS

Focus for a moment now on specific areas—food, shelter, and clothing—where excess might be occurring in your family.

Food

First, of course, is to ascertain that your child is eating enough food each day. From that base, expand your perspective on the healthy use of food to consider these questions:

- *Does my child eat a junk-food meal more than three times per week?* If so, your child is in danger of obesity and many other health problems.
- *Does my child eat only carbohydrates and sugar (sugar cereals) in the morning before needing to do thinking work in school?* If so, your child's brain is not primed to do math or reading or other cognitive tasks; instead it is primed to need to run around in the morning during school, the very behavior that puts his or her core nature out of sync with classroom needs.
- *Does my child eat enough omega-3 fatty acids?* These are present in fish products. Our children's brains need them! They are brain food.
- *Does my child have food allergies I don't know about?* Many children are allergic to nuts, a dangerous condition that is recognized easily—when the child goes into shock. Other allergies—for instance to yeast,

wheat, and dairy—can go unrecognized. Depression, lack of perform-ance, and health problems have all been linked to these allergies.

• *Does our family eat a number of meals together per week?* The core na-ture of children shines through during family meals. New research shows that family meals probably tap into ancient and developmental brain patterns for family connection through sharing food together.

Shelter

First, of course, you must determine that your child has a roof over his or her head. Then you can think about shelter in terms of what "shel-ters within the shelter" you are providing. A number of influences now come into our homes that our young children attach their nature to in ways that we must control for the sake of the children's core-nature de-velopment. Ask yourself these questions:

• *Does my child watch too much television?* At the age of five, a half hour of television per day and an animated kid's movie on the weekend are probably enough. More may well impede the core-nature develop-ment of this child.

• *Does my child spend too much time on the computer?* At four, five, or six, the child's naturally developing brain does not need computer time. It needs outdoor time, time touching actual physical objects, and time spent with human beings and animals. A half hour a day of screen time is more than enough. Computer games are unnecessary at this age. And screen time is screen time. In other words, if the child has spent an hour in front of a computer screen or TV on a given day, "screen time" may have been fulfilled for that day.

• *Does my child play video games?* Video games have become a part of the "shelter" of our families. They can be fun and stimulating, and they can teach valuable lessons in heroism and self-motivation. At the same time, if your child of six is playing video games on a Gameboy in the car, on the computer, and at his friend's house on the XBox, his or her core-nature development is probably in jeopardy. Be very careful about the "sheltering storm" that has become video game culture. We mustn't overreact—but we must impose limits.

Clothing

First, of course, is to determine whether your child has enough material goods to remain healthy against the cold. Beyond basic protection, clothing becomes cultural costuming, and may exceed limits. Consider these questions:

• *Are my child's physical expectations realistic in terms of his or her own physiological core nature?* When children strive to "clothe" themselves in physical stereotypes pressed on them by the social trends culture, they are unprotected selves. Their inherent nature—genetically inherited and therefore of immediate value to their core-nature development—becomes in their minds potentially inferior to the new social trend.

• *Are my child's expectations of social dress and material procurement linked to his or her own earnership?* A certain amount of human costuming is essential for children's growth and is not dangerous. We as parents are glad to provide our children with the clothes they need. We need also to make sure that our children "earn" the privilege of clothes they need and want by doing chores, being civil, and caring for their family.

• *Is my child as interested in core nature as in costuming?* If your child is constantly aware of what people are wearing, that is not in itself dangerous—as long as your child also cares about other important things in life. If your child becomes overly aware of clothes or other material costuming and thus is constantly afraid of his or her "image inferiority," then your family is moving into a partially dangerous situation. You may need to curtail magazines, TV shows, and other external stimulants and reestablish mentors, rituals, and exposure to core-nature development.

• *Is my child's sense of costuming too dependent on celebrity culture?* Our celebrities often serve as valuable models for children and can become children's core nature-mentors, helping children bring out of themselves potentialities that their parents might miss. At the same time, celebrities can become too much of an influence on a child's costuming. When they do, the child will turn away from his or her own nature. This becomes dangerous to long-term meaning and purpose.

NOTES AND REFERENCES

INTRODUCTION: REDISCOVERING OUR CHILDREN

NATURE-BASED THEORY

I first used the term *nature-based theory* in 1996 when I published *The Wonder of Boys*. I developed this term as a philosophical aid in exploring children's development through actual hard sciences (such as neurobiology). Because I am a philosopher, not a scientist, it was crucial for me to read and study many sources of neural science. This need led me to take a multicultural view of the new sciences. My childhood experiences in Asia and adult experiences in Europe and the Middle East were a further stimulus in this direction. I enjoy discovering sources of scientific material not only from the United States but from all over the world; some of these appear in the pages of this book.

Paul Thompson's work is featured in Nicholas Wade, "Scans Show Different Growth for Intelligent Brains." *New York Times,* Mar. 30, 2006.

PART ONE
PROTECTING THE NATURE OF *YOUR* CHILD

I ESCAPING THE SOCIAL TRENDS PARENTING SYSTEM

WHAT IS CHRONIC STRESS IN THE AMERICAN FAMILY?

Stress research from the University of Maryland Medical School appears on www.helpguide.org/mental/stress_signs.htm.

See also Michael Craig Miller, "The Dangers of Chronic Distress." *Newsweek,* Oct. 3, 2003. The Michigan Healthy Start Survey, 2005. The Regents of the University of Michigan, Ann Arbor, MI 48109.

The Carnegie-Mellon studies appear in a very important book on childhood stress, *Ghosts from the Nursery* (New York: Atlantic Monthly Press, 1997), by Robin Karr-Morse and Meredith S. Wiley.

David Elkind. *The Hurried Child.* (3rd ed.) Cambridge, Mass.: Perseus, 2001.

Jane M. Healy. *Failure to Connect.* New York: Simon & Schuster, 1998.

T. W. Myers. "Kinesthetic Dystonia." *Journal of Bodywork and Movement Therapies,* 1998, 2(2), 101–114.

Studies and experts on college and stress are from Hara Estroff Marano, "A Nation of Wimps." *Psychology Today,* Nov.-Dec. 2004. Available at www.psychologytoday.com/ articles/pto-20041112-000010.html.

Depression statistics provided in Katrina Woznicki, "Drugs Are Up and Talk Is Down for Depressed Teens." *Medpage Today,* Nov. 16, 2005. Available at www.medpage today.com/Psychiatry/Depression/tb/2164.

Peter Breggin, author of *Talking Back to Ritalin,* is interviewed in the *Frontline* report "Medicating Kids," 2001. Available at www.pbs.org/wgbh/pages/frontline/shows/ medicating/interviews/breggin.html.

Statistics on increase of psychotropic medication to preschoolers are provided by Julie Magno Zito of the University of Maryland. She originally published this information in the Feb. 2000 issue of the *Journal of the American Medical Association.* The Web site www.pbs.org/wgbh/pages/frontline/shows/medicating/drugs/dontknow.html discusses her findings.

Karr-Morse and Wiley, *Ghosts from the Nursery,* 1997.

Eating disorder statistics provided by the National Institute of Mental Health; see www.annecollins.com/eating-disorders/statistics.htm.

Jeffrey Kluger. "The Cruelest Cut." *Time,* May 16, 2005.

Siobhan McDonough. "Prison Population Swells to 2.1 Million in Mid-2004." Associated Press, Apr. 25, 2005. Available at http://starbulletin.com/2005/04/25/news/ story7.html.

Statistics regarding substance abuse and binge drinking are from www.alcohol freechildren.org.

Statistics about children's inadequate sleep are from www.sleepfoundation.org/ hottopics/index.php?secid+11&id+82.

Dr. Philip Thomas is quoted in Danica Kirka, "Childhood Obesity to Rise Significantly." Associated Press, Mar. 6, 2006. Available at http://seattletimes.nwsource.com /html/health/2002846931_obesity06.html.

See also these articles and resources:

Peg Tyre. "Fighting Anorexia: No One to Blame." *Newsweek,* Dec. 5, 2005.

National Adolescent Health Information Center. "A Health Profile of Adolescent and Young Adult Males: 2005 Brief." Available at http://nahic.ucsf.edu/ downloads/MaleBrief.pdf.

Linda A. Johnson. "Behavior Drug Spending Up: More Kids Taking Pills for ADHD." Associated Press, May 17, 2004. Available at www.spokesmanreview.com/all stories-news-story.asp?date=051704&ID=s1520617.

Lindsey Tanner. "More Kids Are Getting Anti-Psychotic Drugs." Associated Press, Mar. 17, 2006. Available at www.biopsychiatry.com/antipsychotics/index.html.

National Center for Health Statistics. News release. Mar. 31, 2004.

Howard Schubiner, Arthur L. Robin, and Joel Young. "Attention Deficit/ Hyperactivity Disorder in Adolescent Males." *Adolescent Medicine,* 2003, 14(3), 663–675.

MTA Cooperative Group. "National Institute of Mental Health Multimodal Treatment Study of ADHD Follow-up: Changes in Effectiveness and Growth After the End of Treatment." *Pediatrics,* 2004, 113(4), 762–769.

Michael D'Antonio. "The Fragile Sex." *Los Angeles Times Magazine,* Dec. 4, 1994.

Barbara L. Wenger, H. Stephen Kaye, and Mitchell P. LaPlante. *Disabilities Among Children.* (Disability Statistical Abstract Number 15). University of California, San Francisco: Disability Statistics Rehabilitation Research and Training Center, 1995.

THE SOCIAL TRENDS PARENTING SYSTEM

Wendy Melillo. "Advocacy Group Targets Baby Einstein." Available at www.adweek.com/aw/national/article_display.jsp?vnu_content_id=1002425832. May 1, 2006.

2 UNDERSTANDING THE CORE NATURE OF YOUR CHILD

Deborah Sichel and Jeanne Watson Driscoll. *Women's Moods.* New York: Morrow, 1999.

Michael Gurian. *The Wonder of Girls.* New York: Atria, 2001.

Michael Gurian and Kathy Stevens. *The Minds of Boys.* San Francisco: Jossey-Bass, 2005.

THE MYTH OF THE BLANK SLATE CHILD

The books of Steven Pinker are fascinating in this area. Also see Eric Jaffe, "Empirical Science for the Spotless Mind." *APS Observer,* 2005, *18*(8). Available at www.psychologicalscience.org/observer/getArticle.cfm?id=1814. This article includes some of Steven Pinker's assessment of the blank slate myth, as well as a number of ways of debunking it.

EIGHT NEW SCIENCES THAT CAN HELP YOU UNDERSTAND YOUR CHILD'S CORE NATURE

An easy-to-read article on genetics, including haplotypes, is "Genome Mappers Now Hunt for Shortcut." Associated Press, Oct. 30, 2002.

See also Christine Gorman, "Resetting the Brain." *Time,* Mar. 21, 2005.

Lawrence Wilkinson and David Haig are quoted in Carl Zimmer, "Silent Struggle: A New Theory of Pregnancy." *New York Times,* Mar. 20, 2006.

A study of twins by J. Philippe Rushton of the University of Western Ontario is reviewed in "Nice Pair of Genes." *APS Observer,* 2005, *18*(4), 11. Available at www.psychologicalscience.org/observer/getArticle.cfm?id=1751.

The National Institute of Mental Health's 2005 study regarding chromosome seven is featured in Emily Bazelon, "A Question of Resilience." *New York Times Magazine,* Apr. 30, 2006.

Paul D. Tieger and Barbara Barron-Tieger. *Nurture by Nature.* New York: Little, Brown, 1997. These authors also have a Web site, www.personalitytype.com.

Jeffrey Kluger. "Secrets of the Shy." *Time,* Apr. 4, 2005, pp. 50–52.

Glen O. Gabbard. "A Neurobiologically Informed Perspective on Psychotherapy." *British Journal of Psychiatry,* 2000, *177*, 117–122.

Also see the following:

Judith R. Harris. *The Nurture Assumption.* New York: Free Press, 1998.

Richard Willing. "DNA Rewrites History for African-Americans." *USA Today,* Feb. 2, 2006.

Daniel G. Amen's work can be found on www.amenclinics.com, as well as in numerous very helpful books, including his *Change Your Brain, Change Your Life* (New

York: Random House, 1999). I have also quoted him from his forthcoming book, *Sex on the Brain.*

Gary W. Evans and others. "The Role of Chaos in Poverty and Children's Socioemotional Adjustment." *Psychological Science,* 2005, *16*(7), 560–565.

For more on gender and the brain, see Michael Gurian, Patricia Henley, and Terry Trueman, *Boys and Girls Learn Differently!* (San Francisco: Jossey-Bass, 2001); Linda Karges-Bone, *More Than Pink and Blue* (Carthage, Ill.: Teaching & Learning Company, 1998); and the many books and articles referenced in the notes for Parts Two and Three. Every day, some new detail regarding brain-based gender differences is discovered.

The work of Arlene Taylor in the area of "brain styles" is fascinating. Certified therapist Susie Leonard Weller (www.susieweller.com) has called my attention to this work, and I thank her. As she notes, originating theory and information about the Herrmann Brain Dominance Instrument can be found on www.hbdi.com. Ned Herrmann pioneered brain style assessments in the 1970s. These Web sites and their tools can not only help with understanding your child's brain style but also suggest some interesting genetically based gender comparisons.

Allan N. Schore (ed.). *Infant Mental Health Journal,* 2001, *22*(1–2). This entire issue is fascinating; it provides in-depth analysis, from many specialists' viewpoints, of both how hardwiring works in the baby's brain and how attachment affects hardwiring.

Robert G. Maunder and Jonathan J. Hunter. "Attachment and Psychosomatic Medicine: Developmental Contributions to Stress and Disease." *Psychosomatic Medicine,* 2001, *63,* 556–567.

Katy Butler. "Alice in Neuroland." *Psychotherapy Networker,* Sept.-Oct. 2005. Available at www.psychotherapynetworker.org/index.php?category=magazine&sub_cat= articles&type=articles&id=Alice%20in%20Neuroland.

Sichel and Driscoll, *Women's Moods,* 2000.

Louann Brizendine. *The Female Brain.* New York: Morgan Road Books, 2006.

Jed Diamond. *The Irritable Male Syndrome.* Emmaus, Pa.: Rodale Books, 2004.

Gurian, *The Wonder of Girls,* 2001.

Paul Thompson is a researcher at UCLA. His scans can be found in various places on the Internet, should you wish to Google his name and "brain scans."

Daniel G. Amen. *Which Brain Do You Want?* DVD available through www.amen clinics.com.

A fascinating study is Tracey Shors, "Effects of Stress on Memory in Males and Females." *Dialogues in Clinical Neuroscience,* 2002, *4*(2), 139–147.

Francis S. Collins. *The Language of God.* New York: Free Press, 2006.

Andrew Newberg. *Why God Won't Go Away.* New York: Random House, 2001.

CREATING A PROFILE OF YOUR CHILD'S CORE NATURE

Kathy Stevens and Pat Crum were instrumental in helping me create the core-nature assessment tools discussed in the chapter.

There are a number of ways of looking at your child's core personality, including the Myers-Briggs, Jungian, and genogram approaches. (Tools based on these approaches are easy to find on the Internet using Google.) Here are some others.

Lanna Nakone has written a fascinating book called *Every Child Has a Thinking Style* (New York: Perigee Trade, 2006). You might enjoy adding her "mental styles" approach to your assessment of your child's core nature. Her categories include "maintainer," "harmonizer," "innovator," and "prioritizer."

If you go onto the Internet and Google "big five personality," you'll see a number of Web offerings for this fascinating approach to core nature.

See Claudia Kalb, "In Our Blood." *Newsweek,* Feb. 6, 2006. This article is one of the most comprehensive popular media reviews of the new possibilities of DNA testing.

For another popular science-based article on the effect of genetics on one's personality, see Jeffrey Kluger, "Why Some People Are Most Likely to Succeed." *Time,* Nov. 14, 2005. Even ambition, drive, and goal setting have genetic components.

We must always remember that our efforts to identify key traits in our child's core nature are not meant to limit the child to those traits—instead, they should help us focus on the complex and beautiful song this particular child is trying to sing in the world. To hear that song rise out of the distractions of everyday life is our goal and our great joy—it is also the key to helping this child succeed. As we search to know our child's unique song, we must be constantly vigilant against limiting him or her (in effect creating "personality stereotypes" for this child) by overemphasizing only one tool, one personality type, one way of reading the child's core nature. Any kind of stereotyping or limiting on our part becomes family "trend making" and thus becomes inadvertent participation in the kind of social trends parenting system we are fighting against.

For a cogent analysis of eugenics possibilities, see Margo Weiss, "Eugenics." *Family Therapy Magazine,* Jan.-Feb. 2006.

There is vigorous debate in the professional community regarding to what degree brain scans are useful. Here are some articles and books that give both points of view:

Daniel G. Amen. *Making a Good Brain Great.* New York: Harmony, 2005.

Jay Giedd. "Neuroimaging of Pediatric Neuropsychiatric Disorders: Is a Picture Really Worth a Thousand Words?" *Archives of General Psychiatry,* 2001, *58*(5), 443-444.

F. X. Castellanos and others. "Developmental Trajectories of Brain Volume Abnormalities in Children and Adolescents with Attention-Deficit/Hyperactivity Disorder." *Journal of the American Medical Association,* 2002, *288*(14), 1740-1748.

Jay Belsky. "Quantity Counts." *Developmental and Behavioral Pediatrics,* June 2002, pp. 167-170.

The study and application of brain science to natural male-female differences require care and constant adaptation by researcher and parent. Although the basics of gender science do not change over the decades, there can be variation in the interpretation and research of details. For instance, two studies of a particular area of the brain (for example, the cingulate gyrus or the corpus callosum) might show different results. It is important to go into this field with openness to changes in information as the years pass.

At the same time, I have found from personal experience that the most important element of gender biology and of your everyday application of it does not change: that the brains of boys and girls and women and men are wired to be different and need both similar and different care. Some references for your perusal include the following:

Steven E. Rhoads. *Taking Sex Differences Seriously.* San Francisco: Encounter Books, 2004.

Reuwen Achiron, Shlomo Lipitz, and Anat Achiron. "Sex-Related Differences in the Development of the Human Fetal Corpus Callosum: In Utero Ultrasonographic Study." *Prenatal Diagnosis,* 2001, *21,* 116-120.

Maria Elena Cordero, Carlos Valenzuela, Rafael Torres, and Angel Rodriguez. "Sexual Dimorphism in Number and Proportion of Neurons in the Human Median Raphe Nucleus." *Developmental Brain Research,* 2000, *124,* 43–52.

Amanda Onion. "Sex in the Brain: Research Showing Men and Women Differ in More Than One Area." *ABC News,* Sept. 21, 2004.

Deborah Blum. *Sex on the Brain.* New York: Viking Penguin, 1997.

Simon Baron-Cohen. *The Essential Difference.* New York: Basic Books, 2003.

Marian Diamond. *Male and Female Brains.* Lecture at the annual meeting of the Women's Forum West, San Francisco, 2003. Summary available at http://newhorizons .org/neuro/diamond_male_female.htm.

Anne Moir and David Jessel. *Brain Sex: The Real Difference Between Men and Women.* New York: Dell, 1989.

Hara Estroff Marano. "The Opposite Sex: The New Sex Scorecard." *Psychology Today,* July-Aug. 2003, pp. 38–44.

Ruben Gur. *Weekend House Call* (CNN Saturday Morning News), Dec. 6, 2003. Transcripts available at www.fdch.com.

Leonard Sax. *Why Gender Matters.* New York: Doubleday, 2005.

See also www.gurianinstitute.com and click Research. We update the research list often.

Twin studies appear in "Nice Pair of Genes," *APS Observer,* 2005. J. Philippe Rushton is quoted here.

Sichel and Driscoll, *Women's Moods,* 2000.

Gurian, *The Wonder of Girls,* 2001.

Diamond, *The Irritable Male Syndrome,* 2004.

Angela L. Duckworth and Martin E. P. Seligman explore hardwired and "soft-wired" strengths (nature and nurture) in "Self-Discipline Outdoes IQ in Predicting Academic Performance of Adolescents." *Psychological Science,* 2005, *16*(22), 939.

WISDOM OF PRACTICE

Many thanks to Judith Kleinfeld, professor of psychology at the University of Alaska-Fairbanks, for allowing me to include and slightly alter her story of her daughter's development.

PART TWO
NURTURING THE NATURE OF YOUR CHILD

3 NURTURING THE NATURE OF YOUR INFANT

Matthew Melmed is quoted from Robin Karr-Morse and Meredith S. Wiley, *Ghosts from the Nursery.* New York: Atlantic Monthly Press, 1997, p. 281.

INFORMATION ESSENTIAL TO NURTURING THE CORE NATURE OF YOUR INFANT

Pat Wingert and Martha Brant. "Reading Your Baby's Mind." *Newsweek,* Aug. 15, 2005, pp. 33–39. Leslie Cohen is quoted in this article.

American Academy of Pediatrics. *Caring for Your Baby and Young Child.* New York: Bantam Books.

Dr. Lawrence's comments on breast milk appear in Heather Lalley, "An Important Bond." *Spokesman Review,* Dec. 6, 2006, p. D3.

Wendy Melillo. "Advocacy Group Targets Baby Einstein." Available at www .adweek.com/aw/national/article_display.jsp?vnu_content_id=1002425832. May 1, 2006.

The Campaign for a Commercial-Free Childhood. www.commercialfree childhood.org.

The Kaiser Family Foundation. www.kff.org.

A number of these resources can take you even more deeply into what the baby's brain is and needs:

Dimitri A. Christakis, Frederick J. Zimmerman, David L. DiGiuseppe, and Carolyn A. McCarty. "Early Television Exposure and Subsequent Attentional Problems in Children." *Pediatrics,* 2004, *113*(4), 708–713.

Allan N. Schore. "Effects of a Secure Attachment Relationship on Right Brain Development, Affect Regulation, and Infant Mental Health." *Infant Mental Health Journal,* 2001, *22*(1–2), 7–66.

Eleanor Reynolds. *Bonding: A Family Affair.* Monterey, Calif.: Excelligence Learning, 2002.

Paula Wiggins. "Infant Brain Development: Making the Research Work for Early Childhood Programs." *Texas Child Care,* Spring 2000, pp. 2–8.

Phyllis Porter. "Early Brain Development: What Parents and Caregivers Need to Know!" *Educarer,* January 10, 2006. Available at www.educarer.com/brain.htm.

Everett Waters, Kiyomi Kondo-Ikemura, German Posada, and John E. Richters. "Learning to Love: Mechanisms and Milestones." In M. Gunner and Alan Sroufe (eds.), *Minnesota Symposium on Child Psychology,* Vol. 23: *Self Processes and Development,* pp. 217–255. (This paper is available online at www.johnbowlby.com.)

Robert Karen. *Becoming Attached.* New York: Warner Books, 1994.

Allan N. Schore. *Affect Regulation and the Origin of the Self: The Neurobiology of Emotional Development.* Hillsdale, N.J.: Erlbaum, 1994.

Rita Carter. *Mapping the Mind.* Berkeley: University of California Press, 1998.

Dale Purves and others (eds.). *Neuroscience.* Sunderland, Mass.: Sinauer Associates, 2001.

Richard F. Catalano and others. "The Importance of Bonding to School for Healthy Development: Findings from the Social Development Research Group." *Journal of School Health,* 2004, *74*(7), 252–261.

"Babies and Autism." *Newsweek,* Feb. 28, 2005.

NATURAL DIFFERENCES BETWEEN INFANT BOYS AND GIRLS

Phoebe Dewing, Tao Shi, Steve Horvath, and Eric Villain. "Sexually Dimorphic Gene Expression in Mouse Brain Precedes Gonadal Differentiation." *Molecular Brain Research,* 2003, *118*(1–2), 82–90.

Reuwen Achiron, Shlomo Lipitz, and Anat Achiron. "Sex-Related Differences in the Development of the Human Fetal Corpus Callosum: In Utero Ultrasonographic Study." *Prenatal Diagnosis,* 2001, *21,* 116–120.

Maria Elena Cordero, Carlos Valenzuela, Rafael Torres, and Angel Rodrigues. "Sexual Dimorphism in Number and Proportion of Neurons in the Human Median Raphe Nucleus." *Developmental Brain Research,* 2000, *124,* 43–52.

Amanda Onion. "Sex in the Brain: Research Showing Men and Women Differ in More Than One Area." *ABC News,* Sept. 21, 2004.

T. Berry Brazelton. "A Window on the Newborn's World: More Than Two Decades of Experience with the Neonatal Behavioral Assessment Scale." In S. J. Meisels and E. S. Fenichel (eds.), *New Visions for the Developmental Assessment of Infants and Young Children.* Washington, D.C.: Zero to Three, 1996. (Zero to Three: National Center for Infants, Toddlers and Families, 734 15th Street NW, 10th floor, Washington, DC 20005)

Leonard Sax. *Why Gender Matters.* New York: Doubleday, 2005.

ESSENTIAL MOTHERS, ESSENTIAL FATHERS

Susan Hrdy. *Mother Nature.* New York: Ballantine, 2000.

Helen Fisher. *Anatomy of Love.* New York: Ballantine, 1992.

Shelley E. Taylor. *The Tending Instinct.* New York: Times Books, 2002.

Kyle Pruett. *Fatherneed.* New York: The Free Press, 2000.

The study on compensatory relationships in Asian families is discussed in Judith Harris, *The Nurture Assumption.* New York: Touchstone, 1998, p. 49.

Also see the following:

Jeff Donn. "Mentors Fill In for Dads Away at War." Associated Press, June 19, 2005. Available at www.findarticles.com/p/articles/mi_qn4188/is_20050619/ai_n14673031.

Marvin Thomas. *Personal Village.* Seattle: Hara Publishing Group, 2003.

THE IMPORTANCE OF THE MOTHER-INFANT BOND

Carl Jung is quoted in Robert Bly, James Hillman, and Michael Meade (eds.), *Rag and Bone Shop of the Heart.* New York: HarperCollins, 1992, p. 385.

Interview with Shelley E. Taylor. *UCLA College of Arts and Sciences Newsletter,* July 12, 2002, p. 1. In this interview, Dr. Taylor said, "The genome is like an architect's first plan . . . this plan is revised during the building process. . . . A mother's tending can completely eliminate the potential effects of a gene; a risk for disease can fail to materialize with nurturing. . . . Who we are—our character, even our physical health—depends on the people who tend to us." Dr. Taylor's research and philosophy help parents move away from the false dualism that the social trends parenting system seems, at least to me, to carry into such topics as the mother-infant bond. This nature-versus-nurture dualism can seem to justify the idea that yes, sure, moms are important to their infants, but . . . an infant can get by without the intense bonding with mother—he or she will simply grow into a person (whether through genetics or culture) who doesn't need that bond as much as we might think. I believe that Dr. Taylor's research shows that the core nature of the child desperately needs the mother-infant bond if it is to remain a strong genome package (with successful gene expression) within the challenges of life, nature, and society.

A very strong study, one that echoes Taylor and influenced this section of Chapter Three as strongly as it did Chapter Two, is Robert G. Maunder and Jonathan J. Hunter, "Attachment and Psychosomatic Medicine: Developmental Contributions to Stress and Disease." *Psychosomatic Medicine,* 2001, *63,* 556–567.

The work of Seth D. Pollak on the role of oxytocin and vasopressin in the forming of mother-child bonds is reported in Nicholas Wade, "Exploring a Hormone for Caring." *New York Times,* Nov. 22, 2005. See also Dario Maestripieri, "Biological Bases of Maternal Attachment." *Current Directions in Psychological Science,* 2001, *10*(3), 79–83.

Schore, "Effects of a Secure Attachment Relationship on Right Brain Development, Affect Regulation, and Infant Mental Health," 2001.

Michael Gurian. *What Could He Be Thinking?* New York: St. Martin's, 2003.

Kristen Rowe-Finkbeiner and Joan Blades are cited in Jamie Tobias Neely, "Time to Challenge the Motherhood Penalty." May 14, 2006, p. D8.

The poll of mothers' preferences appears in Sharon Jayson, "Study Finds Moms Feeling a Little Undervalued." *USA Today,* May 8, 2005.

See the special issue on fathers and infants, *Infant Mental Health Journal,* Fall 1999.

Adoption has its own biological expression in infant bonds. See Marinus H. van Ijzendoorn and Femmie Juffer, "Adoption Is a Successful Natural Intervention Enhancing Adopted Children's IQ and School Performance." *Current Directions in Psychological Science,* 2005, *14*(6), 281–337.

Karr-Morse and Wiley, *Ghosts from the Nursery,* 2001.

The following are additional resources discussing the need for mothers and the importance of the mother-infant bond:

Kawanza L. Griffin. "Love Helps Kids Beat Poverty, Study Reports." *Milwaukee Journal Sentinel,* May 31, 2004. Griffin is reporting on a study in England and Wales (with cooperation from University of Wisconsin-Madison) published in *Child Development.*

Also see corroboration in Leon Sloman, Leslie Atkinson, Karen Milligan, and Giovanni Liotti, "Attachment, Social Rank, and Affect Regulation." *Family Process,* 2002, *41,* 313. This article has a very extensive bibliography.

Sharon Vandivere, Kristin Anderson Moore, and Martha Zaslow. "Children's Family Environment: Findings from the National Survey of America's Families." *Snapshots of America's Families II,* 1999. Available at www.urban.org/pdf/family-environ.pdf.

"Trauma, Brain and Relationship." Interview with Bruce Perry. www.trauma resources.org.

Cori Young. "The Science of Mother Love." *Mothering,* Apr. 2005. Available at www.mothering.com/articles/new_baby/bonding/mother-love.html. This article is packed with information on oxytocin and the "chemistry of mother-love."

For very strong professional articles that discuss the importance of different parenting styles between women and men, see Jonathan P. Schwartz, Sally E. Thigpen, and Jennifer K. Montgomery, "Examination of Parenting Styles of Processing Emotions and Differentiation of Self." *Family Journal,* 2006, *14,* 41–48.

Also see Daniel Eckstein and Renea Marie Ford, "The Role of Temperament in Understanding Couples' Personality Preferences." *Family Journal,* 1999, *7,* 298–301.

BURNING QUESTION: CAN VACCINATIONS HARM MY INFANT?

My thanks to the following clinicians for their personal correspondence on this issue:

Daniel G. Amen, M.D.

Harold Koplewicz, M.D. Dr. Koplewicz provided me with the research by Eric Frombonne, M.D.

Howard Schubiner, M.D.

See Sarah K. Parker, Benjamin Schwartz, James Todd, and Larry K. Pickering, "Thimerosal-Containing Vaccines and Autistic Spectrum Disorder." *Pediatrics,* 2004, *114*(3), 793–804.

PARENTING AS A SPIRITUAL DISCIPLINE

A very important international organization that supports parents is Parents as Teachers. This organization helps educate parents on how to be the best teachers of their children. The Web address is www.parentsasteachers.org.

4 NURTURING THE NATURE OF YOUR TWO- TO THREE-YEAR-OLD

Walt Whitman's poem is "A Child Goes Forth." It was quoted in a wonderful book by Richard Louv, *Last Child in the Woods* (Chapel Hill, N.C.: Algonquin Books, 2005). This book explores how our social trends culture is robbing our children of all important contact with nature.

INFORMATION ESSENTIAL TO NURTURING THE CORE NATURE OF YOUR TODDLER

Laura Hubbs-Tait, Jack R. Nation, Nancy F. Krebs, and David C. Bellinger. "Neurotoxicants, Micronutrients, and Social Environments." *Psychological Science in the Public Interest,* 2005, *6*(3), 57. Available at www.psychologicalscience.org/pdf/pspi/pspi6_3_1.pdf.

Colleen F. Moore. "An Unhealthy Start in Life—What Matters Most?" *Psychological Science in the Public Interest,* 2005, *6*(3), i–ii. Available at www.psychologicalscience.org/pdf/pspi/pspi6_3editorial.pdf.

Pamela Wyngate. "Fishing for Good Nutrition." *Northwest Health,* Summer 2005.

Jamie Stengle. "Obesity Can Start in Toddler-Hood, Doctors Now Say." Associated Press, Apr. 19, 2005. Available at www.ocregister.com/ocr/2005/04/19/sections/news/focus_health/article_486092.php.

The research on peptides and food allergies is fascinating. Some of the early work was done with schizophrenic patients, but it has expanded to autism and depression as well as physical symptomatology. Relevant articles include the following:

F. C. Dohan. "Schizophrenia: Possible Relationship to Cereal Grains and Celiac Disease." In S. Sankar (ed.), *Schizophrenia: Current Concepts and Research.* Hicksville, N.Y.: PJD, 1969.

A. M. Knivsberg and others. "A Randomized, Controlled Study of Dietary Intervention in Autistic Syndromes." *Nutritional Neuroscience,* 2002, *5*(4), 251–261.

Marco R. della Cava. "Out-of-Line Preschoolers Increasingly Face Expulsion." *USA Today,* Sept. 21, 2005. Available at www.usatoday.com/news/nation/2005-09-20-expelled-preschoolers_x.htm.

Heather Lalley. "Study Finds Pets, Dirt Okay for Kids." *Spokesman Review,* Apr. 11, 2006.

NATURAL DIFFERENCES BETWEEN TODDLER GIRLS AND BOYS

Jean Christophe Labarthe. "Are Boys Better Than Girls at Building a Tower or a Bridge at Two Years of Age?" *Archives of Diseases of Childhood,* 1997, *77,* 140–144. Available at www.fetalneonatal.com/cgi/content/abstract/77/2/140.

Amanda Ripley. "Who Says a Woman Can't Be Einstein?" *Time,* Mar. 7, 2005.

Elizabeth Sowell and others. "Development of Cortical and Subcortical Brain Structures in Childhood and Adolescence: A Structural Magnetic Resonance Imaging Study." *Developmental Medicine and Child Neurology,* 2002, *44,* 4–16.

Richard Schmitz. "Understanding Male and Female Differences: The Adult Brain." *Family Therapy Magazine*, 2004, *3*(4), 18–22.

Hara Estroff Marano. "The Opposite Sex: The New Sex Scorecard." *Psychology Today*, July-Aug. 2003, pp. 38–44.

Chris Boyatzis, E. Chazan, and C. Z. Ting. "Preschool Children's Decoding of Facial Emotions." *Genetic Psychology*, 1993, *154*, 375–382.

Also see the following:

Steven E. Rhoads. *Taking Sex Differences Seriously*. San Francisco: Encounter Books, 2004.

Ruben Gur and others. "Sex Differences in Brain Gray and White Matter in Healthy Young Adults." *Journal of Neuroscience*, 1999, *19*(10), 4065–4072.

Mark Jude Tramo, M.D., Ph.D., director, Harvard University Institute for Music and Brain Science.

THE IMPORTANCE OF PLAY, ORDER, AND DISCIPLINE

A very fine general book on discipline (including time-outs and other discipline skills) is Jane Nelsen, Cheryl Erwin, and Roslyn Duffy, *Positive Discipline for Preschoolers: For Their Early Years—Raising Children Who Are Responsible, Respectful, and Resourceful.* (2nd rev. ed.) New York: Random House, 1998.

On issues of healthy food and possible obesity, see the following:

Stengle, "Obesity Can Start in Toddler-Hood, Doctors Now Say," Apr. 19, 2005.

Claudia Kalb and Karen Springen. "A Head Start to Fitness." *Newsweek*, Apr. 25, 2005.

"Children Who Eat Fries Raise Breast Cancer Risk." Reuters, Aug. 18, 2005. Available at www.msnbc.msn.com/id/8995031.

Samantha Critchell. "Food Fight." Associated Press, June 27, 2005.

Lisa Fairbanks-Rossi. "Teach Your Children to Eat Right." *Inhealth Northwest,* Fall 2004.

"Obesity Trims U.S. Life Spans." *Washington Post,* Mar. 17, 2005. This article reviews clinical studies.

Eric Schlosser. *Fast Food Nation*. Boston: Houghton-Mifflin, 2001.

Eric Jensen. "Water and Learning: Optimal Hydration." Science-Class.Net. Available at http:/science-class.net/water_learning.htm.

Robert Arnot. *The Biology of Success*. New York: Little, Brown, 2001.

Judith Wurtman. *Managing Your Mind and Mood Through Food*. New York: Harper-Collins, 1986.

Alok Jha. "Why Do the Japanese Live So Long?" *Guardian*, June 10, 2004. www.guardian.co.uk.

On visual media, see the following:

Julie Davidow. "TV—any TV—harms toddlers." *Seattle Post Intelligencer,* July 5, 2005. This article reports on the work of Dimitri Christakis and others at the University of Washington.

Dimitri A. Christakis, Frederick J. Zimmerman, David L. DiGiuseppe, and Carolyn A. McCarty. "Early Television Exposure and Subsequent Attentional Problems in Children." *Pediatrics*, 2004, *113*(4), 708–713.

Jane M. Healy. "Understanding TV's Effects on the Developing Brain." *AAP News*, May 1998.

Jennifer L. St. Sauver. "Study Confirms ADHD Is More Common in Boys." *Mayo Clinic Proceedings,* 2004, *79,* 1124–1131.

Jane M. Healy. *Failure to Connect.* New York: Simon & Schuster, 1998.

Barbara J. Brock. *No TV, No Big Deal.* Cheney: Eastern Washington University Press, 2005.

Barbara J. Brock. "TV Free Families." National survey conducted Feb.-Mar. 2000. Cheney: Eastern Washington University.

Barbara A. Dennison, Theresa J. Russo, Patrick A. Burdick, and Paul L. Jenkins. "An Intervention to Reduce Television Viewing by Preschool Children." *Archives of Pediatrics and Adolescent Medicine,* 2004, *158*(2), 170–176.

National Center for Health Statistics. "Fact Sheet." www.cdc.gov/nchs/pressroom/04facts/obesity.htm. Oct. 6, 2004.

Jerome Kagan is quoted in Hara Estroff Marano, "A Nation of Wimps," *Psychology Today,* Nov.-Dec. 2004. Available at www.psychologytoday.com/articles/pto-20041112-000010.html.

Dr. Warneken's fascinating experiment with toddlers was reported by Lauran Neergaard in "Toddlers Eager to Assist Clumsy Scientist." Associated Press, Mar. 3, 2006. Available at http://seattletimes.nwsource.com/html/nationworld/2002840717_baby03.html.

I highly recommend Randy White and Vicki Stoecklin's *Children's Outdoor Play and Learning Environments: Returning to Nature.* Kansas City: White Hutchinson Leisure & Learning Group, 2004.

5 NURTURING THE NATURE OF YOUR FOUR- TO SIX-YEAR-OLD

Epigraph paraphrased from Angeline Stoll Lillard, *Montessori.* New York: Oxford University Press, 2005, p. 129.

INFORMATION ESSENTIAL TO NURTURING THE CORE NATURE OF YOUR FOUR- TO SIX-YEAR-OLD

Diane Yapko. "Key Aspects of Asperger's Syndrome." *Family Therapy Magazine,* Nov.-Dec. 2004.

Useful Web sites include:www.faaas.org, www.autismresearchinstitute.com, and www.autism-society.org.

For information about diet and possible brain disorders, such as ADD/ADHD, autism, and Asperger's, a good link is http://borntoexplore.org/omega.htm. Also, if you Google "omega-3 fatty acids ADD ADHD," you'll find additional links.

Because the brain is a natural organism, its "muscles" can always be aided in flexing and working. Programs in "brain gymnastics" and "educational kinesiology" are interesting and worth exploring on the Net and with your local professional. I have heard from parents and other readers that good results can occur when children have worked with nutritional strategies set up by the Pfeiffer treatment center (www.hriptc.org). Any resource that helps parents understand the cognitive and physical ramifications of food allergies is worth a close look.

Marilynn Marchione. "Soda Causes Obesity, Researchers Assert." Associated Press, Mar. 5, 2006. Available at www.signonsandiego.com/uniontrib/20060305/news_1n5soda.html.

Bruce Taylor Seeman. "Science Stumped on Food Allergy Trend in Kids." Newhouse News Service, Nov. 29, 2005. Available at www.newhousenews.com/archive/seeman112905.html.

Steve Karnowski. "Study: Sweets Fatten Student Bodies." Associated Press, Dec. 6, 2005.

The study by the Children's Television Council is cited in David Bauder, "Study Finds Children's TV Studded with Violent Acts." Associated Press, Mar. 4, 2006.

Alicia Sadler. "Age of Innocence?" *APS Observer*, 2005, 8(6). Available at www.psychologicalscience.org/observer/getArticle.cfm?id=1787. Ed Donnerstein, dean of the college of social and behavioral sciences at the University of Arizona, has completed a three-year study in which he found that many of the TV shows designated as safe for four- to six-year-olds are in fact not safe. Donnerstein is cited in this article.

Jeffrey Zaslow. "Kids Fail to Connect with Wider World." *Wall Street Journal*, Oct. 10, 2005.

Victor Godinez. "Plugged In: Half of U.S. Homes Are Connected to Cyberspace." *Dallas Morning News*, Nov. 11, 2005.

"Report: Kids Don't Need So Much Technology Ed." *Spokesman Review*, Oct. 1, 2004. "Tech Tonic," the report from the Alliance for Childhood (www.allianceforchildhood.net/projects/computers), confirms research by Jane M. Healy and others in the late 1990s showing that technology education in early childhood is not needed for technological success later in life. An even more detailed story is

Lowell W. Monke, "The Overdominance of Computers." *Educational Leadership*, Dec. 2005.

NATURAL DIFFERENCES BETWEEN BOYS AND GIRLS AGE FOUR TO SIX

Details in this section are the tip of the iceberg in terms of male-female differences in this very critical "starting school age." For more help and references, see Michael Gurian and Kathy Stevens, *The Minds of Boys* (San Francisco: Jossey-Bass, 2005), and Michael Gurian, Patricia Henley, and Terry Trueman, *Boys and Girls Learn Differently!* (San Francisco: Jossey-Bass, 2001). These books specifically integrate brain-based gender information into the school setting.

HANDLING SIBLING RIVALRY

Kathy Stevens, training director of the Gurian Institute and formerly a professional in the nonprofit world for twenty-five years, told me that the Kidpower program does a good job of helping kids learn strategies for dealing with aggression. Kathy has seen this program in action. You can learn more at www.kidpower.org.

BeechAcres, a parenting assistance corporation in Cincinnati, provides parent coaching over the phone and on the Net. I've worked with this organization over the last six years; they are very impressive. You can check out their services at www.beechacres.com.

The importance of siblings in a child's development was recently explored by Jeffrey Kluger in "The New Science of Siblings." *Time*, July 10, 2006.

HELPING YOUR SELF-EDUCATING CHILD ASK, "WHO AM I?"

Chiang Tsu's story is rendered in *Awakening the Buddha Within* (New York: Broadway Books, 1997), by Lama Surya Das.

REDEFINING FOOD, SHELTER, AND CLOTHING

Angela Kennedy. "Enough Is Enough." *Counseling Today,* Dec. 2005. Also see Jean Illsley Clarke, Connie Dawson, and David Bredehoft, *How Much Is Enough?* New York: Marlowe & Company, 2003. These experienced therapists define overindulgence of children as involving giving them too much of what looks good; giving them age-inappropriate things or experiences; giving them things to meet adult needs, not theirs; giving family resources to one child that are not appropriate to need.

Virginia de Leon. "Money Can't Buy Meaning." *Spokesman Review,* July 9, 2006.

Search on "affluenza" on Google or another search engine. A number of useful links will come up. My conception of material anxiety shares a number of qualities with affluenza.

Thomas Lickona has done a great deal of work in this area. His books and other helpful pamphlets and products can be found at the Center for the Fourth and Fifth Rs: www.cortland.edu/character.

Also see Appendix C.

BURNING QUESTION: HOW DO I FIND THE BEST SCHOOL FOR MY FOUR- TO SIX-YEAR-OLD?

My team and I hope you will find these articles and books useful for the education of specific populations of children.

Pedro A. Noguera. "The Trouble with Black Boys: The Role and Influence of Environmental Factors on the Academic Performance of African American Males" (pt. 3). *In Motion Magazine,* May 13, 2002. Available at www.inmotionmagazine.com/er/pntroub3.html.

Alan Bowd. *Identification and Assessment of Gifted and Talented Youth Particularly in Northern, Rural and Isolated Communities.* Thunder Bay, Ont.: Centre of Excellence for Children and Adolescents with Special Needs, Lakehead University Task Force on Learning and Communication, 2003. (Centre of Excellence for Children and Adolescents with Special Needs, 954 Oliver Road, Thunder Bay, Ontario P7B 5E1. Phone: 807-343-8196)

For a resource on helping improve math and science skills, see the February 2004 issue of *Educational Leadership.* The entire issue is devoted to the topic of improving achievement in math and science. The many perspectives and tools in this publication are very helpful.

Michael W. Smith and Jeffrey D. Wilhelm. *"Reading Don't Fix No Chevys":* *Literacy in the Lives of Young Men.* Portsmouth, N.H.: Heinemann, 2002.

An inspiring and very usable book for any parent or teacher of a child with special needs is Mel Levine, *A Mind at a Time* (New York: Simon & Schuster, 2002).

The comments of Google's founders appear in Adi Ignatius, "In Search of the Real Google." *Time,* Feb. 20, 2006.

Also see the following:

U.S. Department of Education. National Center for Education Statistics. http://nces.ed.gov.

Leah Ariniello. "Music Training and the Brain." Washington, D.C.: Society for Neuroscience, 2000. Available at https://dev.sfn.org/content/Publications/Brain Briefings/music_training_and_brain.htm.

Daniel G. Amen. "Music and the Brain." Available at http://amenclinics .com/ bp/care/music.php.

Zenalda Serrano. "Families Need Quality Play Time." *Spokesman Review,* Sept. 13, 2004.

U.S. Department of Education. "SPECTRA+ Crafts Curricula by Infusing Core Subjects with the Arts." *Education Innovator,* 2004, 2(26), 1. Available at www.ed.gov/ news/newsletters/innovator/2004/0712.html#1.

Bonnie Varner of Spokane, Washington, provided us with the name of a cutting-edge program used successfully in a number of places, including the Kalispell Indian Reservation, to help low-performing readers. It is called Readright and can be accessed at www.readright.com.

A wonderful addition to any coffee table is a "hidden word search" book. On every page is a box within which are about a hundred letters that hide words. Children find and circle the hidden words. These books vary in their degree of difficulty, so there is bound to be a level suitable for your child.

6 NURTURING THE NATURE OF YOUR SEVEN- TO TEN-YEAR-OLD

INFORMATION ESSENTIAL TO NURTURING THE CORE NATURE OF YOUR SEVEN- TO TEN-YEAR-OLD

Work regarding short alleles and long alleles can be reviewed in Nathan A. Fox and others, "Evidence for a Gene-Environment Interaction in Predicting Behavioral Inhibition in Middle Childhood." *Psychological Science,* 2005, 16(12), 921.

Emily Bazelon. "A Question of Resilience." *New York Times Magazine,* Apr. 30, 2006.

Christine Gorman. "Why We Sleep." *Time,* Dec. 20, 2004.

The National Sleep Foundation (www.sleepfoundation.org) has discovered that 60 percent of children ten and under have sleep problems.

Isadore Rosenfeld. "Heart Health Should Start Early." *Parade,* Sept. 25, 2005.

"Scientists Use DNA to Advise Diet." Associated Press, Oct. 14, 2005.

Also see Cathy Booth-Thomas, "The Cafeteria Crunch." *Time,* Dec. 13, 2004. This story tracks statistics from all over the country regarding the increase in childhood obesity.

NATURAL DIFFERENCES BETWEEN SCHOOL-AGE GIRLS AND BOYS

Samantha Critchell. "Meaningful Praise Makes a Difference." Associated Press, Apr. 17, 2006.

The scientific material on brain injuries and the right parietal lobe has been shared with me by Daniel G. Amen, M.D., and can also be found in his handout "From ADD to Alzheimer's," from a workshop presented by the Amen Clinics. www.amen clinics.com.

Simon Baron-Cohen, *The Essential Difference.* New York: Basic Books, 2003.

J. Gail Armstrong-Hall has written a very informative chapbook called *Understanding Children's Success and Frustrations in School: Recognize Your Child's Spatial Talents.* Sterling Heights, Mich.: Cader, 2002. See p. 17 regarding differences between boys and girls and their ways of learning science concepts.

FOCUSING ON THE ART OF RELATIONSHIP TO PROTECT YOUR CHILD'S CORE NATURE

Karen Mapp and Anne Henderson. "A New Wave of Evidence." *Education Update*, Mar. 2005, p. 3.

Meg Cox has written widely on how to help families develop rituals and traditions that will protect children's growing natures. One of them is *The Book of New Family Traditions* (Philadelphia: Running Press, 2003).

Here are resources on anger management and kids that you might find useful:

Jerry Wilde. *Hot Stuff to Help Kids Chill Out*. Richmond, Ind.: LGR, 1997. (Phone: 800-369-5611)

Jerry Wilde. *More Hot Stuff to Help Kids Chill Out*. Richmond, Ind.: LGR, 2001.

Eliane Whitehouse and Warwick Pudney. *A Volcano in My Tummy*. Gabriola Island, B.C.: New Society, 1996. www.newsociety.com.

Research from the University of Michigan is cited in James H. Humphrey. *Helping Children Manage Stress*. Washington, D.C.: Child & Family Press, 1998.

Hilary Stout. "Family Style: Research Suggests Regular Dinner with Parental Units Improves Child's Health, Grades, Behavior." *Wall Street Journal*, Nov. 22, 2004. Also see Nancy Gibbs, "The Magic of the Family Meal." *Time*, June 12, 2006. A wonderful way to gauge whether your family is working well is to track how many family dinners and family game nights you have. If you have none, your family is probably under some unnecessary stress.

PROTECTING A CHILD'S CORE NATURE BY CREATING SYMBIOTIC MARRIAGE OR SYMBIOTIC DIVORCE

Edward Teyber. *Helping Children Cope with Divorce*. (Rev. and updated ed.) San Francisco: Jossey-Bass, 2001.

The study by Ruth Stein and her colleagues was discussed in Ronald Kotulak, "Study Finds Social Ills Unhealthy for Children." *Chicago Tribune*, May 2, 2006.

Judith Wallerstein, Julia M. Lewis, and Sandra Blakeslee. *The Unexpected Legacy of Divorce*. New York: Hyperion, 2000.

Judith Solomon is featured in "Infants and Joint Custody," an excerpt from Wallerstein, Lewis, and Blakeslee, *The Unexpected Legacy of Divorce*, 2000. Available at www.attachmentparenting.org/artinfantjointpfv.shtml.

Elizabeth Marquardt. *Between Two Worlds*. New York: Crown, 2005.

Peg Tyre interviews Marquardt in "The Secret Pain of Divorce." *Newsweek*, Oct. 24, 2005.

Robert E. Emery, Randy K. Otto, and William T. O'Donohue. "A Critical Assessment of Child Custody Evaluations." *Psychological Science in the Public Interest*, 2005, *6*(1), 1. Available at www.psychologicalscience.org/pdf/pspi/pspi6_1_1.pdf.

Teyber, *Helping Children Cope with Divorce*, 2001.

The May-June 2006 issue of *Family Therapy Magazine* is devoted to the effects of divorce. See especially Constance R. Ahrons, "Long-Term Effects of Divorce on Children."

Among nature-based resources on marital repair is a study by Richard E. Lucas of Michigan State University and the German Institute of Economic Research: "Time Does Not Heal All Wounds: A Longitudinal Study of Reaction and Adaptation to Divorce." *Psychological Science*, 2005, *16*(12), 945. This powerful study shows that couples who divorce are not generally happier for having divorced. One wound may be salved by the divorce—the wound of unfulfilled emotional and romantic ideals—but many others open.

Also see Linda J. Waite and others. "Does Divorce Make People Happy?" New York: Institute for American Values, 2002. This research report is available at www.american values.org/html/does_divorce_make_people_happy.html.

Robert E. Emery. *The Truth About Children and Divorce.* New York: Viking Penguin, 2004. This is a very fine resource for moving into symbiotic divorce.

Patrick F. Fagan, Robert E. Rector, Kirk A. Johnson, and America Peterson. "The Positive Effects of Marriage: A Book of Charts." This can be accessed through the Heritage Foundation. An overview of the book is available at www.heritage.org/Research/Features/Marriage/index.cfm. (Phone: 202-546-4400)

Scott Haltzman and Theresa Foy DiGeronimo. *The Secrets of Happily Married Men: Eight Ways to Win Your Wife's Heart Forever.* San Francisco: Jossey-Bass, 2005. www.secrets ofhappilymarriedmen.com.

BURNING QUESTION: HOW MUCH MEDIA IS TOO MUCH?

Dr. Barbara J. Brock of Eastern Washington University has devoted much of her professional career to studying the effects of TV and other media on kids. Her book *Living Outside the Box* (Cheney: Eastern Washington University Press, 2006) is going to become a classic, I believe. It is packed with statistics, information, and anecdotes re-garding media use; it also tracks the positive effects of "turning off" TVs and other media in the home.

Liz Szabo. "Exercise Shown as a Way to Counteract ADHD." *USA Today,* Mar. 27, 2006. This article refers to a number of studies, including the seminal study reported in *Pediatrics* by Dmitri Christakis and his colleagues, in which the researchers revealed that every extra hour of TV watched by children under age three increases the odds of the child's having attention problems at age seven by 10 percent per daily hour of viewing.

Thomas G. Moeller. "How 'Unequivocal' Is the Evidence Regarding Television Violence and Children's Aggression?" *APS Observer,* 2005, *18*(10). Available at www .psychologicalscience.org/observer/getArticle.cfm?id=1852.

I recommend the Lindamood-Bell system for helping children with ADD (and other kids too) with reading and other instructional comprehension. I mention it here, in the notes for this media section, because a number of readers have talked about its success in tandem with cutting back on TV, podcast, and Internet time.

The Kaiser Family Foundation research is cited in Jezz Zeleny, "TV Sex Scenes Doubled Since '98." *Chicago Tribune,* Nov. 10, 2005.

Michelle M. Weil and Larry D. Rosen have written a book titled *TechnoStress: Coping with Technology at Work at Home at Play.* Hoboken, N.J.: Wiley, 1997. It helps set up manage-able limits. (This book is available through Amazon only through independent sellers.)

The Kaiser Family Foundation and the National Institute on Media and the Family are two highly respected sources for up-to-date material on the effects of media on kids. As the years go by, you can keep up with new research through their Web sites (www.kff.org and www.mediafamily.org).

My thanks to Mary Jacobs for the "Nutcracker" story.

PART THREE
NURTURING THE NATURE OF YOUR ADOLESCENT

7 NURTURING THE NATURE OF YOUR ELEVEN- TO FOURTEEN-YEAR-OLD

INFORMATION ESSENTIAL TO NURTURING THE CORE NATURE OF YOUR PUBESCENT CHILD

Daniel G. Amen. *Sex on the Brain* (forthcoming, pp. 28, 65).

Jay Giedd is interviewed in the *Frontline* report "Inside the Teenage Brain," 2002. Available at www.pbs.org/wgbh/pages/frontline/shows/teenbrain/interviews/giedd.html.

The following are two good scientific articles on how the brain handles adaptations internally:

"The Multitasking Generation." *Time*, Mar. 27, 2006. This article looks at the medial parietal lobes and Brodmann's area 10, two key areas in the pubescent brain that grow and can become overstressed. Podcasting, cyberconnections, cell phones, and other technologies whose use becomes rampant in this age group can increase relationality for the young teen, but also overstress the growing brain.

Claudia Wallis and Sonja Steptoe. "Help! I've Lost My Focus." *Time*, Jan. 16, 2006.

Mary Carskadon, sleep researcher, is interviewed in the *Frontline* report "Inside the Teenage Brain," 2002. Available at www.pbs.org/wgbh/pages/frontline/shows/teenbrain/interviews/carskadon.html.

Judy A. Owens and Jodi A. Mindell. *Take Charge of Your Child's Sleep.* New York: Marlowe & Company, 2005.

Claudia Wallis. "What Makes Teens Tick." *Time*, May 10, 2004.

NATURAL DIFFERENCES BETWEEN EARLY ADOLESCENT BOYS AND GIRLS

Daniel G. Amen. *Sex on the Brain* (forthcoming).

Neil S. Kaye. www.courtpsychiatrist.com/audio.html.

A wise resource on the use of male-female brain difference material with youth sex education is Kathy Flores Bell of Youth Sexuality Programs/Carondelet Health Network. Contact her at kbell@carondelet.org.

Also see the following:

Liz DeCarlo. "How to Talk to Your Kids About Sex." *U.S. Catholic*, Oct. 2005.

Jane DiVita Woody. *How Can We Talk About That?* San Francisco: Jossey-Bass, 2002.

We tend to think of ADD/ADHD as a "boy" disorder, and it is indeed predominantly experienced by boys; however, given how differently boys' and girls' brains are wired, there is a new dialogue about the possibility that more girls than we realize have the disorder, but their cognitive functions are able to adapt around it better than boys. Girls may experience other problems—for instance, an increase in depression. The Practical Parenting Network, through its magazine *Connections,* has been looking at this issue and has a brief review of the literature in its Winter 2005–2006 issue. If you are a parent of a daughter who is having any trouble, check out this topic via the Internet.

Family Practice News and the National Institute of Mental Health are good sources for information, as are psychologists who specialize in girls' issues.

HELPING YOUR PUBESCENT CHILD THROUGH EARLY ADOLESCENT ADAPTATIONS OF CORE NATURE

Giedd *Frontline* interview, 2002.

Sol Gordon is cited on the Peel Public Health Web site, "Raising Sexually Healthy Children." www.region.peel.on.ca/health/commhlth/parov1yr/rshcintr.htm. This Web site is a valuable source of information and suggestions.

For possible rites of passages in both girls' and boys' lives, see www.icajourneys .org. This organization provides a number of options. Another very strong program is COA-MATT, developed by the Washington Ethical Society (www.ethicalsociety.org). To create your own rite of passage for a boy, see my *A Fine Young Man* (New York: Tarcher/Putnam, 1998).

Also see the following:

A set of detailed and helpful reports appear in "Being 13." *Time,* Aug. 8, 2005.

Kevin Helliker. "Exploring the Bicycle-Brain Connection: How Exercise Boosts Cognitive Function." *Wall Street Journal.* This article reviews a number of significant studies, including one in the *Journal of Exercise Physiology* that looked at 884,715 fifth through ninth graders and confirmed the importance of exercise to adolescent brain functioning.

"Changes in Brain May Explain Teen Troubles." Reuters, Sept. 8, 2005. Available at www.msnbc.msn.com/id/9258184. Studies out of England and Ireland show the difficulty that twelve- to fourteen-year-olds have reading social cues.

David Noonan. "A Little Bit Louder, Please." *Newsweek,* June 6, 2005. This is a very fine science-based article showing how much hearing loss we are experiencing in the United States, and looking at some of the reasons for it—including the technological—among our teens.

If you have a child for whom you suspect video games to be actually helpful, you might be interested in Mike Snider's "Videogames Actually Can Be Good for You." *USA Today,* Sept. 27, 2005. Under some specific circumstances, video games can help concentration.

Many thanks to psychiatrist Scott Haltzman for pointing out these two studies regarding soccer header brain injuries. If you have an avid soccer player in the pubescent years, you might want to look at them:

National Health Council of the Netherlands. "Brain Damage in Boxers and Soccer Players." Executive summary available at www.gr.nl/adviezen.php?ID=845& highlight=brain%20injury.

A. D. Witol and F. M. Webbe. "Soccer Heading Frequency Predicts Neuropsychological Deficits." *Archives of Clinical Neuropsychology,* 2003, *18*(4), 397–417.

John Crace. "Children Are Less Able Than They Used to Be." *Guardian,* Jan. 24, 2006. Available at http://education.guardian.co.uk/schools/story/0,,1693061,00.html.

JOINING TOGETHER TO LINK FATHERS AND MEN TO EARLY ADOLESCENTS

Alexis de Tocqueville is quoted in Robert Bly, James Hillman, and Michael Meade (eds.), *The Rag and Bone Shop of the Heart*. New York: HarperCollins, 1992.

Bly, Hillman, and Meade, *The Rag and Bone Shop of the Heart*, 1992, pp. 119, 120.

Bettina Arndt. "Without Dad Little Girls Grow Up Too Fast." *Sydney Morning Herald*, Mar. 9, 2002.

Kyle D. Pruett, *Fatherneed*. New York: Free Press, 2000.

Steven E. Rhoads, *Taking Sex Differences Seriously*. San Francisco: Encounter Books, 2004.

Michael Gurian. *What Could He Be Thinking?* New York: St. Martin's, 2003.

The following offer valuable information about the need for fathers:

National Fatherhood Initiative. See members.aol.com/aherah/fatherlessness 2.html.

David Blankenhorn. *Fatherless America: Confronting Our Most Urgent Social Problem*. New York: Basic Books, 1995.

www.rainbows.org/statistics.html.

www.nebraskaschildren.org/about_us/programs/fathergood/statistics.

Also see the following:

www.osdoj.gov/reentry/responsible.html

Alfred A. Messer. "Boys' Father Hunger." *Medical Aspects of Human Sexuality*, 1989, 23(1), 44–50.

N. Vaden-Kiernan, N. S. Ialongo, J. Pearson, and S. Kellam. "Household Family Structure and Children's Aggressive Behavior." *Journal of Abnormal Child Psychology*, 1995, 23, 553–568.

Teacher and public school administrator Cynthia Martone has written an important book, *Loving Through Bars: Children with Parents in Prison*. Santa Monica, Calif.: Santa Monica Press, 2005. There are 2.3 million children with a parent in prison. Most of the parents in prison are fathers.

BURNING QUESTION: HOW DO I PROTECT MY EARLY ADOLESCENT'S SELF-ESTEEM?

Jennifer Crocker and Katherine Knight. "Contingencies of Self-Worth." *Current Directions in Psychological Science*, 2005, 14(4), 200–203.

Daniel T. Willingham. "How Praise Can Motivate—or Stifle." *American Educator*, Winter 2005–2006. Available at www.aft.org/pubs-reports/american_educator/issues/winter05-06/cogsci.htm.

Bullying is a hot-button issue in the self-esteem debate because it is so real and so painful. If your child is being bullied—whether physically or through cyberspace—you know how it hurts. Some very fine resources include Michele Borba's work. If you go to www.micheleborba.com, you'll find a number of books and resources. Other helpful Web sites include the following:

www.operationrespect.org.

www.naspcenter.org/factsheets/bullying_fs.html.

"Addressing the Problem of Juvenile Bullying." (Fact sheet). www.ncjrs.org/pdffiles1/ojjdp/fs200127.pdf.

"The Bully Roundup" (an interactive board game) at www.bam.gov/sub_your flie/yourlife_bullyroundup.html.

A fascinating scholarly study is J. P. Piek and others, "The Relationship Between Bullying and Self-Worth in Children with Movement Coordination Problems." *British Journal of Educational Psychology,* 2005, *75,* 453–463.

Positive groupings are great ways to help protect your early adolescent's sense of self-worth. The Boy Scouts, the Girl Scouts, Boys and Girls Clubs, Big Brothers and Big Sisters of America . . . these and many local, regional, and national mentoring groups are responding to our adolescents' natural needs. Scott Daniels of the Boy Scouts of America sent me a number of reports on the success the Boy Scouts have had. You can access these on the Boy Scouts Web site, bsa.org. Each of the groups has Web sites and success information. It is fun and very powerful to get involved with these groups.

The self-esteem dialogue in our culture is a complex one. My analysis of it in the chapter is an attempt to move it toward a nature-based approach. As you can tell from what I've written, I believe that a strong science-based argument can be made for moving the dialogue away from a focus on "increasing self-esteem" at a given moment (which I see as a social trends quantitative approach) to seeing self-esteem as part of a lifelong journey. Let me add a bit more analysis to this.

As noted earlier and discussed in the chapter, Crocker and Knight conducted a study published in *Current Directions in Psychological Science* in 2005. They studied adolescents and discovered that self-esteem has less effect than people think. As they point out, "High self-esteem does little to cause positive outcomes in life, and low self-esteem is not to blame for most social and personal problems."

Apparently contradicting Crocker and Knight, M. Brent Donnellan and colleagues (*Psychological Science,* 2005, *16*[4], 328–335) discovered that children and adults with low self-esteem tend to externalize their moods and emotions more than those with high self-esteem—that is, they tend to act with more relational and physical aggression in their families and society. In the words of these researchers, "Individuals with low self-esteem were more likely to engage in antisocial behaviors as reported by their parents and teachers." This research seems to say just the opposite of Crocker and Knight. How can this be?

I believe that if self-esteem continues to be seen as it is in our present social trends dialogue, we'll never get beyond the seeming contradiction. Thus I hope you will sift carefully through self-esteem research to find the truth that works for your child in the long term.

A further study by Crocker (a 2001 study of thirteen hundred students) is reported in Sue Shellenbarger, "Good Intentions, Bad Results." *Wall Street Journal.* She found that "looking for your self-worth in others fosters more intense and volatile emotions in general—higher highs and lower lows." The areas of the brain that respond to emotional stress are triggered more by looking outward than looking inward.

J. David Creswell and others. "Affirmation of Personal Values Buffers Neuroendocrine and Psychological Stress Responses." *Psychological Science,* 2005, *16*(11), 846–851.

8 NURTURING THE NATURE OF YOUR FIFTEEN- TO EIGHTEEN-YEAR-OLD

Mark's story illustrates a growing phenomenon: girls who are out of control in their social impulses and risk not getting enough of the right interventions. The following are two very helpful books:

Rachel Simmons. *Odd Girl Out.* Orlando, Fla.: Harcourt, 2002.

Rosalind Wiseman. *Queen Bees and Wannabes.* New York: Crown, 2002.

INFORMATION ESSENTIAL TO NURTURING THE CORE NATURE OF YOUR MIDDLE ADOLESCENT

Pat Crum was instrumental in helping research the facts presented in this section. The following are two helpful articles on teens doing well:

Data from the National Survey on Drug Use and Health are reported in Leslie Brody, "Tame Teens." *The Record,* May 23, 2005.

Barbara Kantrowitz and Karen Springen. "A Peaceful Adolescence." *Newsweek,* Apr. 25, 2005.

Deborah Yurgelun-Todd explains her research and results in an interview for the *Frontline* report "Inside the Teenage Brain," 2002. Available at www.pbs.org/wgbh/pages/frontline/shows/teenbrain/interviews/todd.html.

Doug Cowan. "The ADHD Diet for Your Attention Deficit Disorder." The ADHD Information Library. www.newideas.net/adddiet.htm, 2004.

"Unlocking the Secrets of the Brain." *Anderson Cooper 360* (CNN), May 20, 2004.

Aldo Leopold is quoted in the *UU World,* Spring 2006, p. 1.

Barbara Kantrowitz and Karen Springen. "A Peaceful Adolescence." *Newsweek,* Apr. 25, 2005.

NATURAL DIFFERENCES BETWEEN MIDDLE ADOLESCENT GIRLS AND BOYS

Yurgelun-Todd *Frontline* interview, 2002.

J. Gail Armstrong-Hall. *Understanding Children's Successes and Frustrations in School.* Sterling Heights, Mich.: Cader, 2002. This book is packed with information about differences between boys' and girls' brains and ways of thinking.

Information about the cingulate gyrus is from a personal communication with Daniel G. Amen.

The Amen Clinics have developed a DVD titled *Which Brain Do You Want?* which is used in the school systems to show students graphically what happens to their brains when they engage in alcohol or substance abuse and other high-risk behavior. This DVD shows actual SPECT scans of brains of teens who have not abused substances and those who have. Learn more at www.mindworkspress.com.

Richard Morin. "Testosterone and Trust." *Washington Post,* Dec. 4, 2005.

Shankar Vedantam. "Hormone That Induces Trust Could Be Both Cure and Curse." *Spokesman Review,* June 2, 2005.

Shelley E. Taylor. *The Tending Instinct.* New York: Times Books, 2002.

Kathleen M. Galotti. *Cognitive Psychology in and out of the Laboratory.* (3rd ed.) Belmont, Calif.: Thomson/Wadsworth, 2003. See the chapter on gender differences in cognition.

Also see the following:

Kimberly Renk, Laura Liljequist, Jennifer E. Simpson, and Vicky Phares. "Gender and Age Differences in the Topics of Parent-Adolescent Conflict." *Family Journal,* 2005, *13*(2), 139–149.

Suniya S. Luthar and Shawn J. Latendresse. "Children of the Affluent: Challenges to Well Being." *Current Directions in Psychological Science,* 2005, *14*(1), 49.

ADAPTING YOUR FAMILY TO ACCOMMODATE YOUR MIDDLE ADOLESCENT'S INDIVIDUATION OF CORE NATURE

Anusha Mohan. "You've Got Hate Mail—Now What?" Knight-Ridder, Jan. 23, 2006.

David Goodman. "'MySpace' Teen Back from Middle East." Associated Press, June 10, 2006. Available at www.washingtonpost.com/wp-dyn/content/article/2006/06/09/AR2006060900516.html?sub=AR.

Teens don't sleep enough. Too many gadgets (especially before bedtime) and too much Internet time can exacerbate the problem. The Web site of the National Sleep Foundation can give you more information. www.sleepfoundation.org.

Corporate Alliance to End Partner Violence. www.girlsallowed.org.

Teen girls are becoming more physically aggressive. Two popular articles that lay out the problem are Jeffrey Kluger, "Taming Wild Girls." *Time,* May 1, 2006, and Julie Scelfo, "Bad Girls Go Wild." *Newsweek,* June 13, 2005. This increased violence among girls is not just a social trend that will pass on its own.

Denise Gellene. "Study Links Anxiety to Teen Cell Phone Use." *Los Angeles Times,* May 24, 2006. A study presented at the annual meeting of the American Psychiatric Association in Toronto (2006) confirms what many parents have suspected—a lot of cell phone use among teens is affecting mood.

Martha Irvine. "iPod Trend Brings Spike in Noise-Induced Hearing Loss." Associated Press, Sept. 13, 2005. Available at www.boston.com/news/nation/articles/2005/09/13/ipod_trend_brings_spike_in_noise_induced_hearing_loss.

See www.dangerousdecibels.org. Teen hearing issues, especially in the age of iPods, need our close attention.

Virginia de Leon. "Group Offers Gay Youth Chance to Find Acceptance." *Spokesman Review,* July 12, 2004. Available at http://209.157.64.200/focus/f-news/1170169/posts.

For more on the biology of homosexuality, see the Jan. 1994 issue of the *Harvard Medical Letter.*

Also see Dean Hamer and Peter Copland, *The Science of Desire: The Search for the Gay Gene and the Biology of Behavior.* New York: Simon & Schuster, 1994.

Rita Carter. *Mapping the Mind.* Berkeley: University of California Press, 1998.

John Cloud. "The Battle Over Gay Teens." *Time,* Oct. 10, 2005.

HELPING ADOLESCENTS THROUGH CRISIS

Brian Swimme and Thomas Berry. *The Universe Story.* San Francisco: HarperSanFrancisco, 1992.

Tracey Shors. "Effects of Stress on Memory in Males and Females." *Dialogues in Clinical Neuroscience,* 2002, 4(2), 139–147.

Sora Song. "The Price of Pressure." *Time,* July 19, 2004. Thirty years of stress research published in early July 2005 in the *Psychological Bulletin* shows that modern stresses trigger adolescent and adult stress responses in more complex ways than we once thought.

Laura Sessions Stepp. "Religious Benefits." *Spokesman Review,* Apr. 3, 2004.

Edythe Mencher. "Our Children Need God." *Reform Judaism,* Summer 2006.

M. F. Maples and others. "Suicide by Teenagers in Middle School." *Journal of Counseling and Development,* Fall 2005.

See www.qprinstitute.com to learn about a state-of-the-art program for helping suicidal teens (and others). QPR (question, persuade, refer) was created by psychologist Paul Quinnett.

BURNING QUESTION: WHAT IS THE BEST WAY TO HANDLE PEER GROUPS?

One of the social trends myths that afflicts teen life is that "being popular" will lead to all good things. Joseph Allen of the University of Virginia completed a study funded by the National Institute of Mental Health (see the May-June 2005 issue of *Child Development*). He found that popular teens can indeed be well adjusted, but also that they may use more drugs and engage in more vandalism and shoplifting.

Sheryl Mead and Cheryl MacNeil. "Peer Support: A Systemic Approach." *Family Therapy Magazine,* May-June 2005.

9 NURTURING THE NATURE OF YOUR ADOLESCENT OF NINETEEN AND OLDER

Mary Oliver's poem is called "In Blackwater Woods." It appears in her *New and Selected Poems: Volume 1* (Boston: Beacon Press, 1992, pp. 177–178). It is also available at www.breakoutofthebox.com/blackwaterwoods.htm.

INFORMATION ESSENTIAL TO NURTURING THE CORE NATURE OF YOUR LATE ADOLESCENT

Lev Grossman. "Grow Up? Not So Fast." *Time,* Jan. 24, 2005.

NATURAL DIFFERENCES BETWEEN YOUNG MEN AND YOUNG WOMEN

Daniel G. Amen. *Sex on the Brain: 12 Lessons to Enhance Your Love Life.* New York: Harmony, 2007.

Rosie McIntosh. "Brainpower Gives Women Drivers the Edge." *Herald,* Nov. 7, 2005.

William D. S. Killgore, Mika Oki, and Deborah Yurgelun-Todd. "Sex-Specific Developmental Changes in Amygdala Responses to Affective Faces." *NeuroReport,* 2001, 12(2), 427–433. Available at http://ldc.upenn.edu/myl/llog/KillgoreAmygdala.pdf#search=%22NeuroReport%20Sex-Specific%20Developmental%20Changes%20Amygdala%20Responses%20Affective%20Faces%22.

Deborah A. Prentice and Dale T. Miller. "Essentializing Differences Between Women and Men." *Psychological Science,* 2006, 17(2), 129.

Also see Megan R. Gunnar, *Quality of Care and the Buffering of Stress Physiology: Its Potential in Protecting the Developing Human Brain.* Minneapolis: University of Minnesota Institute of Child Development, 1996.

Ruben Gur. *Weekend House Call* (CNN Saturday Morning News), Dec. 6, 2003. Transcripts available at www.fdch.com.

IDENTIFYING AND HELPING YOUNG MEN AND YOUNG WOMEN WHO LACK A MISSION IN LIFE

Mel Levine's *Ready or Not, Here Life Comes* (New York: Simon & Schuster, 2005) provides very useful advice for parents trying to help late adolescents "launch" into the real world.

For useful screening techniques for young adult depression, see the National Mental Health Association's depression-screening.org Web site.

Center for Labor Market Studies. *The Growing Gender Gap in College Enrollment and Degree Attainment in the U.S. and Their Potential Economic and Social Consequences.* Boston: Northeastern University, May 2003.

Paul D. Slocumb. *Hear Our Cry.* Highland, Tex.: aha! Process, 2004.

Cliff Hocker. "More Brothers in Prison Than in College?" Oct. 11, 2002. Available at www.globalblacknews.com/Jail.html.

To help you make your own decision regarding the use of brain scans, see the following:

Daniel G. Amen. *Making a Good Brain Great.* New York: Harmony, 2005.

Jay Giedd. "Neuroimaging of Pediatric Neuropsychiatric Disorders: Is a Picture Really Worth a Thousand Words?" *Archives of General Psychiatry,* 2001, *58*(5), 443–444.

F. X. Castellanos and others, "Developmental Trajectories of Brain Volume Abnormalities in Children and Adolescents with Attention-Deficit/Hyperactivity Disorder." *Journal of the American Medical Association,* 2002, *288*(14), 1740–1748.

Jay Belsky. "Quantity Counts." *Developmental and Behavioral Pediatrics,* June 2002, pp. 167–170.

Ruby K. Payne. *A Framework for Understanding Poverty.* (3rd rev. ed.) Highland, Tex.: aha! Process, 2003.

Patricia W. Bass. "Law School Enrollment and Employment for Women and People of Color." Available at www.mcca.com/site/data/corporate/BP/Watch/nalp899 .htm.

I continue to highly recommend *Women's Moods,* by Deborah Sichel and Jeanne Watson Driscoll. It is a wonderful nature-based resource on girls and women. Also see my *Wonder of Girls* (New York: Atria, 2001). *The New Feminine Brain* (New York: Free Press, 2005), by Mona Lisa Schulz, is also a nature-based book. It argues that the female brain has actually changed over the last few hundred years to accommodate changing stresses of life.

BURNING QUESTION: WHY ARE YOUNG PEOPLE MATURING SO MUCH LATER THAN WE DID?

Grossman, "Grow Up? Not So Fast," 2005.

Jed Diamond. *The Irritable Male Syndrome.* Emmaus, Pa.: Rodale Books, 2004.

Grossman, "Grow Up? Not So Fast," 2005.

Here are some resources that can inspire and provide practical techniques for mentoring youth into healthy adulthood:

Nan Henderson, Bonnie Benard, and Nancy Sharp-Light (eds.). *Mentoring for Resiliency: Setting Up Programs for Moving Youth from "Stressed to Success."* Ojai, Calif.: Resiliency in Action, 2000. This book is available through the publisher at www .resiliency.com.

Jack Welch, with Suzy Welch. *Winning.* New York: HarperCollins, 2005. This book is actually about how to become a leader.

Robert I. Lerman and Hillard Pouncy. "Why America Should Develop a Youth Apprenticeship System." Progressive Policy Institute Policy Report. Mar. 1, 1990. Available at www.ppionline.org/ppi_ci.cfm?contentid=2003&knlgAreaID=107&subsecid =175.

EPILOGUE

Michael Crichton. *State of Fear.* New York: Avon, 2004, p. 627.

APPENDIX C

Hilary Stout. "Family Style: Research Suggests Regular Dinner with Parental Units Improves Child's Health, Grades, Behavior." *Wall Street Journal,* Nov. 22, 2004. Also see Nancy Gibbs, "The Magic of the Family Meal." *Time,* June 12, 2006.

BIBLIOGRAPHY

Amen, Daniel G. (1999). *Change Your Brain, Change Your Life*. New York: Random House.

Amen, Daniel G. (2001). *Healing ADD*. New York: Putnam.

Amen, Daniel G. (2002). *Healing the Hardware of Your Soul*. New York: Free Press.

American Academy of Pediatrics. (1991). *Caring for Your Baby and Young Child*. New York: Bantam.

Arnot, Robert. (2001). *The Biology of Success*. New York: Little, Brown.

Baron-Cohen, Simon. (2003). *The Essential Difference: The Truth About the Male and Female Brain*. New York: Basic Books.

Bear, Mark, Barry Connors, and Michael Paradiso. (1996). *Neuroscience: Exploring the Brain*. Baltimore: Williams and Wilkins.

Blum, Deborah. (1997). *Sex on the Brain: The Biological Differences Between Men and Women*. New York: Viking Penguin.

Bly, Robert. (1990). *Iron John*. Reading, Mass.: Addison-Wesley.

Bolen, Jean Shinoda. (1984). *Goddesses in Everywoman*. New York: HarperCollins.

Bolen, Jean Shinoda. (1989). *Gods in Everyman*. New York: HarperCollins.

Borba, Michele. (2003). *No More Misbehavin': 38 Difficult Behaviors and How to Stop Them*. San Francisco: Jossey-Bass.

Borba, Michele. (2004). *Don't Give Me That Attitude! 24 Rude, Selfish, Insensitive Things Kids Do and How to Stop Them*. San Francisco: Jossey-Bass.

Braver, Sanford L., with Diane O'Connell. (1998). *Divorced Dads*. New York: Tarcher/Putnam.

Cameron, Julia. (1992). *The Artist's Way*. Los Angeles: Tarcher.

Campbell, Joseph. (1968). *The Hero with a Thousand Faces*. Princeton, N.J.: Princeton University Press.

Campbell, Joseph. (1988). *Myths We Live By*. New York: Bantam.

Campbell, Susan. (1980). *The Couples Journey*. San Luis Obispo, Calif.: Impact.

Carter, Rita. (1998). *Mapping the Mind*. Berkeley: University of California Press.

Cox, Meg. (2003). *The Book of New Family Traditions*. Philadelphia: Running Press.

Damon, William. (1988). *The Moral Child*. New York: Free Press.

Doe, Mimi. (2004). *Nurturing Your Teenager's Soul*. New York: Penguin Books.

Eisenberg, Arlene, Heidi E. Murkoff, and Sandee E. Hathaway. (2002). *What to Expect When You're Expecting.* (3rd rev. ed.) New York: Workman.

Elkind, David. (2001). *The Hurried Child.* (3rd ed.) Cambridge, Mass.: Perseus.

Ellison, Katherine. (2005). *The Mommy Brain: How Motherhood Makes Us Smarter.* New York: Basic Books.

Estes, Clarissa Pinkola. (1992). *Women Who Run with the Wolves.* New York: Ballantine.

Feinstein, David, and Stanley Krippner. (1988). *Personal Mythology.* Los Angeles: Tarcher.

Fisher, Helen. (1992). *Anatomy of Love.* New York: Fawcett.

Flinders, Carol. (2002). *The Values of Belonging.* San Francisco: HarperSanFrancisco.

Garbarino, James. (1999). *Lost Boys.* New York: Free Press.

Gilmore, David. (1990). *Manhood in the Making.* New Haven, Conn.: Yale University Press.

Goleman, Daniel. (1995). *Emotional Intelligence.* New York: Bantam.

Gurian, Jay P., and Julia Gurian. (1983). *The Dependency Tendency: Returning to Each Other in Modern America.* Lanham, Md.: Rowman & Littlefield.

Gurian, Michael. (1996). *The Wonder of Boys: What Parents, Mentors and Educators Can Do to Shape Boys into Exceptional Men.* New York: Tarcher/Putnam.

Gurian, Michael. (1998). *A Fine Young Man.* New York: Tarcher/ Putnam.

Gurian, Michael. (1999). *Plugged In: From Boys to Men—All About Adolescence and You.* Los Angeles: Price, Stern, Sloan.

Gurian, Michael. (1999). *Plugged In: Understanding Guys—A Guide for Teenage Girls.* Los Angeles: Price, Stern, Sloan.

Gurian, Michael. (2002). *The Wonder of Girls: Understanding the Hidden Nature of Our Daughters.* New York: Pocket Books.

Gurian, Michael, with Patricia Henley and Terry Trueman. (2001). *Boys and Girls Learn Differently! A Guide for Teachers and Parents.* San Francisco: Jossey-Bass.

Gurian, Michael, and Kathy Stevens. (2005). *The Minds of Boys: Saving Our Sons from Falling Behind in School and Life.* San Francisco: Jossey-Bass.

Hallowell, Edward, and John Ratey. (1994). *Driven to Distraction.* New York: Touchstone.

Haltzman, Scott, and Theresa Foy DiGeronimo. (2005). *The Secrets of Happily Married Men: Eight Ways to Win Your Wife's Heart Forever.* San Francisco: Jossey-Bass.

Harris, Judith R. (1998). *The Nurture Assumption.* New York: Free Press.

Healy, Jane M. (1998). *Failure to Connect.* New York: Simon & Schuster.

Hirsh-Pasek, Kathy, Roberta Michnick Golinkoff, and Diane Eyer. (2003). *Einstein Never Used Flashcards.* New York: Rodale.

Houston, Jean. (1987). *The Search for the Beloved.* Los Angeles: Tarcher.

Jensen, Eric. (2005). *Teaching with the Brain in Mind.* (2nd rev. and updated ed.) Alexandria, Va.: Association for Supervision and Curriculum Development.

Johnson, Steven. (2004). *Mind Wide Open.* New York: Scribner.

Jung, Carl. (1986). *Man and His Symbols.* New York: Doubleday. (Originally published 1964.)

Kandel, Eric, James Schwartz, and Thomas Jessell. (1995). *Essentials of Neural Science and Behavior.* Norwalk, Conn.: Appleton & Lange.

Karen, Robert. (1994). *Becoming Attached.* New York: Warner Books.

Karges-Bone, Linda. (1998). *More Than Pink and Blue: How Gender Can Shape Your Curriculum.* Carthage, Ill.: Teaching & Learning Company.

Karr-Morse, Robin, and Meredith S. Wiley. (1997). *Ghosts from the Nursery.* New York: Atlantic Monthly Press.

Kelemen, Lawrence. (2001). *To Kindle a Soul.* Southfield, Mich.: Targum Press.

Kornhaber, Arthur. (2004). *The Grandparent Solution: How Parents Can Build a Family Team for Practical, Emotional, and Financial Success.* San Francisco: Jossey-Bass.

Kurcinka, Mary. (2006). *Sleepless in America.* New York: HarperCollins.

Ladner, Joyce, and Theresa Foy DiGeronimo. (2003). *Launching Our Black Children for Success: A Guide for Parents of Kids from Three to Eighteen.* San Francisco: Jossey-Bass.

Larson, Jeffry H. (2000). *Should We Stay Together? A Scientifically Proven Method for Evaluating Your Relationship and Improving Its Chances for Long-Term Success.* San Francisco: Jossey-Bass.

Levine, Mel. (2002). *A Mind at a Time.* New York: Simon & Schuster.

Lickona, Thomas, and Matthew Davidson. (2005). *Smart & Good High Schools.* Cortland, N.Y.: Center for the Fourth & Fifth Rs.

Lillard, Angeline Stoll. (2005). *Montessori: The Science Behind the Genius.* New York: Oxford University Press.

Louv, Richard. (2005). *Last Child in the Woods: Saving Our Children from Nature-Deficit Disorder.* Chapel Hill, N.C.: Algonquin.

Mastrich, Jim. (2002). *Really Winning.* New York: St. Martin's Press.

Moir, Anne, and David Jessel. (1992). *Brain Sex: The Real Difference Between Men and Women.* New York: Delta. (Originally published 1989.)

Moir, Anne, and Bill Moir. (1999). *Why Men Don't Iron.* New York: Citadel.

Moore, Robert, and Douglass Gillette. (1990). *King, Warrior, Magician, Lover.* San Francisco: HarperSanFrancisco.

Moore, Thomas. (1992). *Care of the Soul.* New York: HarperCollins.

Murphy, Shane. (1999). *The Cheers and the Tears: A Healthy Alternative to the Dark Side of Youth Sports Today.* San Francisco: Jossey-Bass.

Nylund, David. (2000). *Treating Huckleberry Finn: A New Narrative Approach to Working with Kids Diagnosed ADD/ADHD.* San Francisco: Jossey-Bass.

Payne, Ruby K. (2003). *A Framework for Understanding Poverty.* (3rd rev. ed.) Highlands, Tex.: aha! Process.

Pease, Barbara, and Allan Pease. *Why Men Don't Listen and Women Can't Read Maps.* New York: Broadway Books.

Pipher, Mary. (1993). *Reviving Ophelia.* New York: Random House.

Pipher, Mary. (1996). *The Shelter of Each Other.* New York: Grosset & Dunlap.

Pruett, Kyle D. (2000). *Fatherneed.* New York: Free Press.

Restak, Richard. (2003). *The New Brain.* New York: Rodale.

Rhoads, Steven E. (2004). *Taking Sex Differences Seriously.* San Francisco: Encounter Books.

Sachs, Brad E. (2005). *The Good Enough Teen.* New York: Harper Paperbacks.

Santrock, John. (2006). *Lifespan Development.* New York: McGraw-Hill.

Sichel, Deborah, and Jeanne Watson Driscoll. *Women's Moods: What Every Woman Must Know About Hormones, the Brain, and Emotional Health.* New York: Morrow, 1999.

Siegel, Daniel. (1999). *The Developing Mind.* New York: Guilford Press.

Siegel, Daniel J., and Mary Hartzell. (2003). *Parenting from the Inside Out.* Los Angeles: Tarcher.

Simmons, Rachel. (2002). *Odd Girl Out: The Hidden Culture of Aggression in Girls.* Orlando, Fla.: Harcourt.

Slocumb, Paul D. (2004). *Hear Our Cry: Boys in Crisis.* Highlands, Tex.: aha! Process.

Sousa, David A. (2001). *How the Brain Learns*. (2nd ed.) Thousand Oaks, Calif.: Corwin Press.

Sprenger, Marilee. (2002). *Becoming a "Wiz" at Brain-Based Teaching*. Thousand Oaks, Calif.: Corwin Press.

Stabiner, Karen. (2005). *My Girl*. New York: Little, Brown.

Stein, David. (1999). *Ritalin Is Not the Answer: A Drug-Free, Practical Program for Children Diagnosed with ADD or ADHD*. San Francisco: Jossey-Bass.

Stephenson, Bret. (2004). *Slaying the Dragon: The Contemporary Struggle of Adolescent Boys*. Available at www.adolescentmind.com.

Sykes, Bryan. (2003). *Adam's Curse*. New York: Norton.

Taylor, Shelley E. (2002). *The Tending Instinct*. New York: Times Books.

Tieger, Paul D., and Barbara Barron-Tieger. (1997). *Nurture by Nature*. New York: Little, Brown.

Wallerstein, Judith S., Julia M. Lewis, and Sandra Blakeslee. (2000). *The Unexpected Legacy of Divorce*. New York: Hyperion.

Warner, Judith. (2005). *Perfect Madness*. New York: Riverhead.

Williams, Kate. (1995). *A Parent's Guide for Suicidal and Depressed Teens*. Center City, Minn.: Hazelden.

Wiseman, Rosalind. (2002). *Queen Bees and Wannabes*. New York: Crown.

Wiseman, Rosalind. (2006). *Queen Bee Moms and Kingpin Dads*. New York: Crown.

Wolfe, Patricia. (2001). *Brain Matters: Translating Research into Classroom Practice*. Alexandria, Va.: Association for Supervision and Curriculum Development.

Woody, Jane DiVita. (2001). *How Can We Talk About That? Overcoming Personal Hangups So We Can Teach Kids About Sex and Morality*. San Francisco: Jossey-Bass.

THE GURIAN INSTITUTE

If you would like to help your community better meet the developmental needs of both boys and girls, please contact the Gurian Institute. The Institute works with parents, schools, business corporations, the juvenile and adult corrections systems, medical and mental health professionals, and others who serve children and adults.

Gurian Institute staff and trainers provide training and regional conferences, working throughout the United States, as well as in Canada and abroad. The Institute provides resources and services through four divisions:

Families (www.understandingfamilies.com)

Education (www.thegitd.com)

Corporate (www.gendertrainings.com)

Human Services (www.betterhumanservices.com).

Each separate Web site can be accessed through www.gurianinstitute.com.

The Institute is committed to providing both science-based information and practical and relevant applications for everyday life. We help build self-sufficiency in communities. We believe that alone, each parent and each professional is a visionary; at the same time, by working together, we become the protective and successful social force our children and families most need.

To learn more, please visit www.gurianinstitute.com.

ABOUT THE AUTHOR

Michael Gurian is a social philosopher, family therapist, and the New York Times best-selling author of twenty books published in twenty-one languages. The Gurian Institute, which he cofounded, conducts research internationally, launches pilot programs, and trains professionals and parents. Michael has been called "the people's philosopher" for his ability to bring together people's ordinary lives and scientific ideas.

As a social philosopher, he has pioneered efforts to bring neurobiology and brain research into homes, schools, workplaces, and public policy. A number of his groundbreaking books in human development, including *The Minds of Boys, The Wonder of Boys, Boys and Girls Learn Differently!, What Could He Be Thinking?* and *The Wonder of Girls,* have sparked national debate.

Michael has served as a consultant to families, corporations, therapists, physicians, school districts, community agencies, churches, criminal justice personnel, and other professionals, traveling to approximately twenty cities a year to deliver keynotes at conferences. His training videos for parents and volunteers are used by Big Brother and Big Sister agencies in the United States and Canada. As an educator, Michael has fulfilled speaking engagements at Harvard University, Johns Hopkins University, Stanford University, University of Colorado-Colorado Springs, University of Missouri-Kansas City, and UCLA. Michael previously taught at Gonzaga University and Ankara

University. His philosophy reflects the diverse cultures (European, Asian, Middle Eastern, and American) in which he has lived, worked, and studied.

Michael's work has been featured in various media, including the *New York Times*, the *Washington Post, USA Today, Newsweek, Time*, the *Wall Street Journal, Parenting, Good Housekeeping, Redbook, Today, Good Morning America*, CNN, PBS, and National Public Radio.

Michael lives in Spokane, Washington, with his wife, Gail, and their daughters, Gabrielle and Davita.

He can be reached at www.gurianinstitute.com.

INDEX

A

Able-ness, 220
Adaptability, 205–206
Adaptation, 214, 226; age of, 214, 218
Adolescent brain, science of, 60
Adolescent individuation, 240–241
Adrenaline, 208
Affluenza, 324
Africa, 122
Aggressive behavior, 181, 196, 245
Albert Einstein College of Medicine, 185
Alcohol abuse, 31. *See also* Substance
    abuse
Alexander, P., 203
Alleles, 172
Allender, D., 54
Allergies, 120, 285
Altruism, 130
Amen Clinics, 56–57, 113, 176
Amen, D. G., 56, 113, 176, 207, 208, 244
American Medical Association, 91
American Psychological Association, 258
Amygdala, 122, 133, 207, 209, 242, 246
Anatomy of Love (Fisher), 95
Ancestry, 304
Anger, 174, 181
Anorexia, 194, 195, 254–256
Antidepressants, 30, 142
Antipsychotic drugs, 30
Antisocial Personality Disorder, 30
Anxiety, 130

Apprenticeships, 292
Asian households, 101
Asperger's, 143
Asthma, 120
Attachment and bonding, 88–90, 118, 120;
    science, 58–59
Attachment and emotional style assess-
    ment, 71–74
Attention Deficit Disorder (ADD), 25, 57,
    195, 199, 213, 285, 328–329
Attention Deficit Hyperactivity Disorder
    (ADHD), 25, 57, 194, 195, 199, 213, 285,
    328–329
Authority thinking, 99
Autism, 112, 143

B

Baby Einstein videos, 22, 91
Baron-Cohen, S., 177
Barron-Tieger, B., 54
Basal ganglia, 207, 286–287
Batman Begins, 257
Bed-wetting, 143–144
Belenky, G., 173
Bering Sea, 81
Berry, T., 256
*Between Two Worlds: The Inner Lives of
    Children of Divorce* (Marquardt), 186
Big Five, 304
Biology, hormonal, 59–60
Blades, J., 108

345